A MONETARY HISTORY OF FRANCE IN THE TWENTIETH CENTURY

A Monetary History of France in the Twentieth Century

Jean-Pierre Patat
and Michel Lutfalla

Translated by Patrick Martindale and
David Cobham

St. Martin's Press New York

First published in the United States of America in 1990

Printed in Hong Kong

Library of Congress Cataloging-in-Publication Data

Patat, Jean Pierre.
[Histoire monétaire de la France au XXe siècle.] English:
A monetary history of France in the twentieth century/Jean Pierre Patat and Michel Lutfalla; translated by David Cobham and Patrick Martindale.
p. cm.
Translation of: Histoire monétaire de la France au XXe siècle.
Bibliography: p.
Includes index.
ISBN 0–312–03257–9
1. Monetary policy–France–History. I. Lutfalla, Michel.
II. Title.
HG975.P3813 1990 89–6284
332.4′944–dc20 CIP

Contents

List of Figures

List of Tables

Foreword

This monetary history of France is in the authors' phrase a 'history of the monetary conjuncture'. The bulk of the book consists of 13 chapters each covering different subperiods, from the gold standard period of 1897–1914 through to the 'expansion with inflation' of 1968–73. Each chapter gives an account of the economic situation and economic policy in general, as a background to more detailed analysis of monetary and financial developments. Chapter 14 draws some general conclusions, particularly with respect to the broad contrasts between the periods before and after the Second World War, and provides a brief account of the period since 1974. This is then followed by a substantial statistical appendix, upon which the preceding chapters have all drawn.

There were several reasons for translating the book into English. One was simply the conviction that English-speaking economists ought to know more about the monetary systems of the other major countries of the world, particularly, perhaps, at a time when European monetary union and even central bank integration are under discussion. Most UK monetary economists know at least something of the US system, and a few US economists are familiar with the UK system, but beyond this the 'veil' that a monetary system constitutes is often impenetrable.

This is not altogether surprising, for even apart from the language difficulty it is hard for an economist whose thinking has long been in terms of a particular institutional context to familiarise himself or herself with another context which involves not merely different institutions but also different policy preoccupations. Nevertheless, such a process of familiarisation can be extremely valuable, for it inevitably raises questions that had not been considered before: why have the determinants of the demand for government bonds been such a preoccupation of UK monetary policy but of so little interest to the French? why do direct credit controls seem to have 'worked' in France so long after they were abandoned in the UK? how and why do the operations and effects of the French Fonds de Stabilisation des Changes and the British Exchange Equalisation Account differ? Moreover, it is hard to see how any serious discussion of, say, European Community central bank integration could be undertaken without a thorough knowledge of the variety of institutional arrangements in the countries concerned.

However, the more important reasons relate to the nature of the book itself: it contains an excellent statistical appendix presenting monthly and quarterly data on the broad money stock in France (M2) from 1910 and (in monthly terms from 1947 only) on its main counterparts, many of these series being entirely new estimates; and the text of the book provides a comprehensive guide to the key factors in what its authors call the 'monetary conjuncture' in each subperiod. Indeed the authors are too modest in describing their work as an 'annotated statistical dossier', for the successive chapters of the text give an impressively balanced account of the range of factors affecting both policy and economic and monetary developments in each subperiod.

It should be noted that the years covered by the book (essentially 1897–1973 with a less detailed account of the following decade) involved a considerably more varied experience for France than for the UK or even the USA in terms of developments in the real economy, monetary trends, and changes in the monetary and financial system, not to mention the period of occupation during the Second World War. It is therefore even more than usually important that the statistical data should be understood in their true context. Here the text of the book is invaluable for an understanding of when and how other things have been unequal, and such an awareness should surely prevent the glib use of the statistical data on their own without the appropriate qualifications.

* * *

For Anglo-Saxon readers with little prior knowledge of the history and nature of the French monetary and financial system, some brief introduction may be helpful, first of all on Patat and Lutfalla's general approach to monetary growth, or the 'creation of money' as it is commonly called in French. Their immediate starting point is the counterparts of the money stock, that is, the assets in the balance sheet of the banking system which stand against its liabilities, the money stock; in this Patat and Lutfalla follow the traditional practice of monetary economists not only in France but also in most of Western Europe (see for example Goodhart, 1973, on the UK, and Hansen, 1973, on the 'European budget constraint'). However, they also discuss the 'factors affecting bank liquidity', that is, movements in the fiduciary circulation, in official foreign exchange reserves and in the central bank's claims on the Treasury, which affect the commercial banks' reserves at the central bank and therefore, perhaps, their willingness to lend and their ability to 'create money'. Furthermore, they look at the public's demand not only for monetary but also for non-monetary assets, in particular Treasury bills, savings bank (*caisse d'épargne*) deposits and bonds.

Analytically this means that their approach has much in common with the 'new view' expounded in Tobin (1963), although they make no direct reference to Tobin's work. In practice it means that they place emphasis on an analysis of the 'financing of the economy' in which the 'sources of financing' are counterposed to 'financial investments'. 'Sources of financing' here refers to the origins or causes of *processes* of financing rather than the sources of financial flows themselves: thus it consists of the budget deficit, new lending by banks and non-bank financial institutions, and the external counterpart. 'Financial investments' include acquisitions of bonds, Treasury bills and savings bank deposits as well as notes and coin and bank deposits. In broad terms the growth of the money stock is equal to the sources of financing *minus* the total of non-monetary financing. However, it is important to note that this framework of analysis does not prejudge questions about the *determination* of the money stock, nor does it prejudge questions about the direction of causality between money and money income. On the latter Patat and Lutfalla distinguish (in chapter 14) between the pre-Second World War period, for which they regard the growth of the money stock as largely 'passive' because of the role of the external counterpart, and the postwar period for which they consider monetary growth as more 'active'. The Anglo-Saxon reader may find it useful to read the first few pages of the statistical appendix in this connection, before embarking upon the detailed monetary analysis of chapter 1.

Next, a few brief points on the French monetary and financial system may be in order. First, the State has long played a larger role in this system in France than in the Anglo-Saxon countries, at least. Indeed the French Treasury has itself fulfilled some of the functions of a bank, taking in deposits from certain 'correspondent' institutions and even from individuals, while the French post office has operated since 1918 a money transmission service, the *comptes chèques postaux* (postal chequing accounts), roughly comparable in nature to, but much larger in size than, the National Giro in the UK; a large part of these deposits are also available to the Treasury. Secondly, the savings banks in France (*caisses d'épargne*) have been of much greater importance than, for example, the trustee savings banks in the UK.

Traditionally they were organised on a local or regional basis but with a single central institution, the Caisse des Dépôts et Consignations (CDC), which channelled the resources collected by the individual savings banks mainly towards the funding of the budget deficit (via purchases of Treasury bills or deposits at the Treasury) and towards types of lending to the private sector regarded by the government as particularly desirable (via the refinancing or discounting of commercial bank loans to the private sector, or via the provision of funds to specialised state lending agencies). It is only in the last few years that the savings banks have begun to assume (like the building societies in the UK) the characteristics of commercial banks. Thirdly, it should be noted that over the pre-Second World War period in particular France experienced significant fluctuations both in the public's confidence in the franc (and therefore its willingness to hold monetary assets of any kind) and in the public's confidence in the banking system (and hence its willingness to hold bank deposits rather than notes).

Finally it may be useful to emphasise here some of the preoccupations of French monetary policy and monetary economics. First, the problem of financing the budget deficit, which in the UK, for example, has had its main influence on the Bank of England's tactics in the gilt-edged market, in France has led to rather different concerns: in very broad terms it can be argued that in the pre-Second World War period budget deficits frequently resulted in excessive monetary expansion; in the 1950s the authorities developed the Treasury's own 'financial circuit', in the 1960s they tried to eliminate budget deficits altogether, and only in the early 1980s did the existence of large 'structural' deficits lead to a large-scale development of the government bond market.

The Treasury circuit was essentially the collection of institutions and mechanisms by which a large proportion of the spending involved in a budget deficit would return to the Treasury in one way or another, through purchases of Treasury bills by the banks or the Caisse des Dépôts et Consignations, through individual deposits with the Treasury or through the increase in the balances held in postal chequing accounts: such financing of budget deficits was monetary rather than non-monetary, but less visible to the uninformed public and at least in some circumstances less susceptible to multiplication than direct borrowing from the banking system (chapter 9). Similarly the 'debudgetisation' of the 1960s, which reduced the obvious effects of the government's activities on the money supply by reducing the budget deficit, in fact involved a transfer of both expenditure and borrowing out of the 'State budget' into 'the economy' in the sense used in the term 'claims on the economy' – that is, the private sector *plus* the nationalised industries and certain 'hived-off' state agencies – rather than a genuine reduction of expenditure and borrowing.

Secondly, economic policy has traditionally been concerned more generally with the need to 'encourage stable savings', that is, to encourage the public to use their savings to purchase long-term non-monetary financial assets (for instance, bonds, shares or savings bank deposits) rather than monetary assets (bank deposits or notes). The reluctance of the public, whose strong preference for liquidity in the face of uncertainty had been repeatedly demonstrated, to respond to these encouragements led in the postwar period to an emphasis on 'transformation', that is, the transformation by the banks of short-term or sight deposits into medium and long-term loans to industry: the official thinking was that if the public would not provide funds for industry directly it would have to be done in this way (chapter 12). Subsequently French industry became so heavily dependent on bank lending that the economy came to be characterised as an *économie d'endettement* (literally an 'indebtedness economy'), that is, an 'overdraft economy' in the sense of Hicks (1974) (chapter 14). Only from the mid-1980s have wholesale reforms of the financial and monetary system been introduced which are likely to reverse this process and bring the French system closer to those of the US and the UK.

* * *

The Anglo-Saxon reader who wishes to study the French monetary and financial system in more detail could start with Melitz's (1985) brief account, and go on to Raymond (1983). Both of these focus on the period from the 1960s and 1970s to the early of mid-1980s, as do Cobham and Serre (1986, 1987), which try to spell out some of the contrasts between the French and UK systems. These publications are in English; more comprehensive coverage, with more historical perspective, can be found in Penaud (1982) and Patat (1982), both of which are in French, and of course in the various references given here by Patat and Lutfalla. A good background survey in English of French political history over the period is McMillan (1985), while Caron (1979) provides an overview in English of the economic history of France.

David Cobham

REFERENCES

Caron, F. (1979), *An Economic History of Modern France* (London: Methuen).

Cobham, D. and Serre, J-M. (1986), 'Monetary targeting: a survey of French and UK experience', *Royal Bank of Scotland Review*, no. 149, March.

Cobham, D. and Serre, J-M. (1987), 'The variability of monetary growth in France and the UK, 1970–84', in C. Goodhart, D. Currie and D. Llewellyn (eds), *The Operation and Regulation of Financial Markets* (London: MacMillan).

Goodhart, C. A. E. (1973), 'Analysis of the determination of the stock of money', in J. M. Parkin and A. R. Nobay (eds), *Essays in Modern Economics* (Harlow: Longman).

Hansen, B. (1973), 'On the effects of fiscal and monetary policy: a taxonomic discussion', *American Economic Review*, vol. 63, no. 4, pp. 546–71.

Hicks, J. R. (1974), *The Crisis in Keynesian Economics* (Oxford: Blackwell).

McMillan, J. F. (1985), *Dreyfus to De Gaulle: Politics and Society in France 1898–1969* (London: Edward Arnold).

Melitz, J. (1985), 'The French financial system: mechanisms and questions of reform', in J. Melitz and C. Wyplosz (eds), *The French Economy: Theory* and Policy (Boulder: Westview).

Patat, J-P. (1982), *Monnaie, institutions financières et politique monétaire* (Paris: Economica).

Penaud, R. (1982), *Les institutions financières françaises*, 2nd edn (Paris: La Revue Banque).

Raymond, R. (1983), 'The formulation and implementation of monetary policy in France', in P. Meek (ed.), *Central Bank Views on Monetary Targeting* (New York: Federal Reserve Bank of New York).

Tobin, J. (1963), 'Commercial banks as creators of "money"', in D. Carson (ed.), *Banking and Monetary Studies* (Homewood: Irwin).

Translators' Note

In preparing this English-language edition we have adopted a number of procedures which are standard in Anglo-Saxon economics publications. Thus all references are given in the text or the notes in the form 'Aftalion (1948)', for example, with the title and publisher of Aftalion's book given only in the bibliography at the end of the book. Similarly we have numbered the figures and tables (lists of which follow the contents page); this means that the tables do not need always to be placed in the text at the exact point at which they are referred to.

We have kept the titles of various institutions in French, and have not introduced translators' notes on these or other points by way of footnotes or supplementary endnotes. However, we have provided a more than usually comprehensive index which gives translations of French words and titles used in the text and also provides occasional notes of explanation.

We have used billion in the American sense which is now nearly universal, that is, 'a thousand million' (*milliard*), and we have used the symbol 'FFr' for French francs, both 'old' and 'new': the 'new' franc introduced in 1959 was worth 100 'old' francs but the relevant unit is always obvious from the context (the statistical appendix gives data up to and including 1958 on the old basis, and data from 1959 in separate tables on the new). We have translated 'Angleterre' as 'Britain' in cases where this is clearly correct.

Finally it is worth noting that Jean-Pierre Patat and Michel Lutfalla's book is written in a style that is much more literary and rhetorical than would be found in a comparable work in English; we have toned this down a little in places for the benefit of the dour Anglo-Saxon reader, but we have not attempted to rewrite the book as an Anglo-Saxon economist might have written it, for the style is an intrinsic part of the work and not a detachable or exchangeable characteristic.

Patrick Martindale
David Cobham

Preface

This book by Jean-Pierre Patat and Michel Lutfalla represents a Proustian approach to economics. Such an idea may appear surprising, but it is so only in contrast to the severe and rigorous style of the book, which is the result of its accumulation of statistical material.

At a time when money is dissolving before our very eyes in the melting-pot of the new instruments that have appeared in the short- and long-term capital markets, there springs to mind the memory that we used to have of a money stock as well organised as bourgeois life in Combray, and there stirs a curiosity to pursue the search for it into the inmost depths of our subconscious (which itself shapes our monetary culture and reflexes) through the subterranean passages of our earlier lives.

Today as throughout the ages, money, like memories, remains difficult to grasp precisely, and so one must bow before the talent of these authors who, imbued with modern monetary analysis, have gone against the tide of history.

What remains clear, on the other hand, is that the need for money is a consistent feature of behaviour in developed societies and will without doubt remain so for a long time yet.

Why then is there this need for money? It is undoubtedly linked to the market economy and the role of money as a medium of exchange. The essence of money is thus to form cash balances for transactions.

Is it also really a reserve for savings? That is another question. The authors have clearly indicated that from this point of view the world of tomorrow may perhaps be structurally different from the one which they have observed over a long period. In fact, new instruments are being developed which are better suited than money in circulation to the function of saving. Even until recently the means of payment (M1) contained a relatively stable share of savings which households had casually abandoned there. Only a short time ago – and the authors recall this judiciously – this scenario began to change. For the public better education and more rapid information have gone hand in hand with the desire to obtain a positive real return. It may certainly be considered, as is indicated at the end of the conclusion, that real interest rates have today risen to an exceptional degree and that they will not be maintained indefinitely at these high levels. In compensation, the slow erosion (which is also mentioned) of intermediation by the banks, and the reduction of the protection provided to certain institutions which in tomorrow's world will have to abandon their special positions, are equally factors making for an aggressive competition between banks or quasi-banks, which will compel the financial professionals to offer the saver the best investment possible. The maximisation by every household and every business of the profit which their monetary and financial assets can procure (in short, the extension of 'cash management' techniques) must tend to confine those assets which are the most liquid and carry the lowest return to the settlement of transactions, and to purge them of any element of intentional savings.

In reality the term 'money' conceals a range of more or less broad concepts, and its definition is a matter of convention. The essential thing is to modify these conventions only advisedly, when lasting structural changes are brought about in the demand for money. Insofar as this develops within a stable framework, variations in the money stock and in its relationship to prices and economic growth remain significant in that they reflect the reactions of economic agents to the conjuncture, and often signal new phases of it.

This is why, even if we are at a turning point between two epochs, general lessons emerge from the observation of the past. Why did Proust attach so much interest to the reminiscences of bygone days? Because the past is a mirror which reflects our soul and our acquired behaviour. It is the same with economics. What has been will be no longer, but it is the same human nature – the subtlety of which emerges as the observer stands back to examine the past – that tomorrow will have to face up to new circumstances.

By providing their readers with long series of statistics, the authors are inspiring in them the temptation to extract simple laws from the statistics. Money would have been the same throughout the generations and some correlations would be able to link it in a constant manner with certain economic data.

Paradoxically, but rightly, at the same time as they have been reconstructing the unity of monetary phenomena, the authors have given a warning against such an over-simplification. For each period they have recalled the dominant characteristics of the environment in which the monetary mechanisms played their part. They have recalled the shocks which have struck society and the mechanism of production: wars, changes in the relative price of oil, the shift from agriculture towards industry, scientific and technical progress. The acceleration of history, particularly for France after 1945, comes through strongly in this book.

It is right and proper that these transformations should be recalled, for they demand that precautions should be taken in the interpretation of apparently homogeneous data. For this reason the same 'gold and foreign exchange' counterpart of the money stock cannot be regarded at the present time in the same way as for a period when the national currency was internally convertible into gold. Certainly in both cases, in the absence of local production, gold could be acquired only by the accumulation of external surpluses; but its function has changed. When it was accessible to holders of banknotes by simple exchange, it was sterilised in its role as a security with regard to the public. In a regime of inconvertibility gold and foreign exchange reserves fluctuate; they vary according to the more or less interventionist nature of exchange rate policy and the international constraints to which it must submit. What is more, the gross value of reserves does not measure exactly the resources available to the central bank, such is the development of international credit mechanisms.

All the same, the major differences affecting the economic structures and the relative position of France are opportunely emphasised, to suggest that the same policies could not have the same effects in all circumstances. Should one approve the authors' views when they indicate that the over-valuation of the franc between the two wars was catastrophic, whilst its frequent periods of weakness after 1945 – however regrettable they might be – helped to speed up the engine of growth? It is certainly easier to agree with them that the highly open nature of the French economy today makes the benefits to be expected from a devaluation more than problematic.

These judgements are not conclusions which emerge from simply reading the statistical series which are presented. They ought rather to be considered, once again, as necessary warnings. The figures have no significance if they are not taken in conjunction with the changing background to which they are applicable. This book is not an overall analysis of the economic facts over nearly a century: it extracts one of them, but constantly invites the reader not to forget the others. In its necessarily concise form, such a judgement acts to provoke a salutary reaction from the researcher, to whom it falls to refine his ideas himself.

One of the great merits of history is thus that it places dogmas in their proper context. Is this to say that monetarism is dead? Two observations make plain the virtues in it which give it still the position of the statue of the Commander in the offices of many Governors. First, if the need for money is a permanent datum in developed societies, it is natural to find a long-term relationship between the money stock and the level of inflation. In this respect, the study which follows brings out the astonishing stability of the liquidity ratio of the economy over long periods. Secondly, central banks work in the short to medium term, that is to say that in general, from day to day, the structures are relatively fixed. In this case too much money in nominal terms cannot fail to induce an inflation which brings real cash balances back to their desired level, whether the rise in prices is triggered by internal mechanisms or by external depreciation. Periods of transition, during which the picture becomes blurred, make exceptions and create particular difficulties. We are approaching one, but it should not make us forget that some constants remain.

Robert Raymond
Director General of Research of the Banque de France
Director of the Centre for Advanced Research in Banking

Experience, however, shows that neither a state nor a bank ever had the unrestricted power of issuing paper money without abusing that power.

David Ricardo

Experience, however, shows that neither a state nor a bank ever have had the unrestricted power of issuing paper money without abusing that power.

David Ricardo

Introduction

There are already in existence several good economic histories of France. To mention only recent works, there is the series published under the direction of F. Braudel and E. Labrousse (1970–82) – where the contribution of J. Bouvier to the subject in which we are interested is essential; the great work of A. Sauvy (1984) on the period between the wars – to which we have had frequent recourse; and as regards more strictly monetary history the recent surveys by M. Saint-Marc (1983) and H. Koch (1983).

With the exception of the latter, which covers a part of our subject but for a more limited period, none of these excellent books corresponds exactly to our subject.

We shall be concerned here with a history of the monetary conjuncture. Such a history presupposes the availability of monetary statistics with a frequency of less than a year, which exist only from 1945. Failing the construction of such series, works dealing with the period before the Liberation and earlier than our own have essentially used either annual points – in general those at the ends of years, the artificial nature of which, as a result of the window-dressing of balance sheets, is well known – or information which is of higher frequency but only partial, for example notes in circulation or the deposits in the four major banks alone. It is not therefore surprising that the estimates in this volume are sometimes rather different from those of earlier writers.

Thus our ambition has been at the same time both wider and narrower than that of our predecessors:

- wider, because we have tried to offer the reader, by making use of the statistical methods described in the appendix, statistical series for the money stock and for the counterparts at monthly and/or quarterly intervals (at least, wherever possible: it will be seen that for the period before 1911 the information is insufficient);
- more limited, since we have not described the totality of the social facts for the periods studied, but have confined ourselves to the comparison of these series with other political and economic information for these periods.

Our statistical model has been the great work of M. Friedman and A. Schwartz (1963) for the United States. The subsequent exposition will make clear why it could not be our theoretical inspiration as well. There are too many phases of French monetary history for which 'monetarism' has proved inadequate. Other people have said this before for some of these phases, for example A. Aftalion in his *Monnaie, prix et change* (1948), whose conclusions will be found again here.

We have limited this history to the twentieth century, making the starting-point of this century not 1914, as with many historians, but 1897. We shall justify this at the beginning of Part I.

We have grouped our history in 14 chapters on a chronological basis:

1. 1897–1914: The classical system
2. 1914–18: The first world war
3. 1919–26: The failure of monetary deflation
4. 1926–31: The strong franc
5. 1931–36: To deflate or to devalue
6. 1936–39: The relapse
7. 1939–44: The Second World War
8. 1944–45: The Liberation
9. 1946–51: Reconstruction at the expense of the currency
10. 1952–55: The return to stability
11. 1956–58: The renewal of inflation
12. 1959–67: The 'grande époque' of the Fifth Republic
13. 1968–73: Expansion with inflation
14. Concluding remarks.

As well as these periods, two major divisions appear clearly: before and after 1939.

Until the Second World War the French economy remained relatively little 'monetarised'; of course the creation of money experienced strong pressures for expansion (often linked to speculation on the franc) such as the 1914–18 war, the years 1920–23, and the year 1926; or contraction (1930–35). In 1938 the income velocity (national income/M2) was at practically the same level as in 1928, 2.22 against 2.25; in other words the liquidity ratio of the economy, M2/national income, did not vary.

This weak monetarisation is attested to by the volume of investments on the capital market, which apart from exceptions (the 1914–18 war, the years 1925–28, 1936 and finally 1938 and 1939) was always greater than the growth of M2.

This was the period when the creation of money followed the lending provided by the banking system to the Treasury and the credits of the banks, the latter always short term, such that there was a particularly erratic development even from month to month: savings did not anticipate, but were somehow adapted *ex ante* to, investment.

With the Second World War there began an uninterrupted tendency to monetary expansion, often particularly accelerated. France gradually became an 'overdraft economy': the capital market collapsed and the financing of the economy became increasingly monetary in nature; this development was particularly marked between 1965 and 1974. The French economy achieved one of the most brilliant performances of the western world in terms of growth, but its inflation was also one of the highest and the franc experienced substantial depreciation.

* * *

This work constitutes an annotated statistical dossier, capable of providing material for the historian or the economist concerned for references.

The idea of the work came from Jean-Pierre Patat who also put together the whole of the monetary statistical series. He took charge of writing up the developments from 1939, the first six chapters being due to Michel Lutfalla. The responsibility for remaining imperfections and errors is, of course, shared between the two authors.

The seasonal adjustments and the majority of the figures are the work of Mlle Colette Grifoul. The typing of successive versions was carried out, with efficiency and patience, by Mmes Florence Cordel and Marilyn Gaonarc'h. We are most grateful to them.

Part I
1897–1944

1 1897–1914: The Classical System

WHY START FROM 1897?

This book is a monetary history of France in the twentieth century. However, in economics as in history, centuries rarely start on the 1st of January of year one. For many specialists the nineteenth century ended in 1914. The *Belle Epoque* was only an extension of it.

We have chosen to take the year 1897 as the starting point for this book, not from a taste for paradox, but because at least four reasons seemed to us to justify this choice:

(i) the first is that later developments, notably those of the 1920s, can be understood only when we start by taking account of the earlier system, in this instance the classical system of the gold standard, 'a rigid monetary structure with instruments of payment organised into a hierarchy' (R. Marjolin);

(ii) the second is that the time divisions of historians are sometimes arbitrary. The *Belle Epoque* is not uniquely the extension of the nineteenth century. In our field it is modern in some respects:

- the banking system had reached maturity after the 'revolution' of the years 1848–75 (according to the concept of J. Bouvier);
- there was a new phase of the industrial revolution with electricity, chemistry and the origin of the motor-car, which are all characteristic of the twentieth century.

As for the date of 1897 itself, it is justified for the following two reasons:

(iii) it is the starting point of a long phase of rapid growth, first of prices (Simiand's or Kondratiev's 'phase A of increase', which was not the discovery of these economists but was commonly so described at the time), then – if not from 1897, at least from 1905 – of activity. This phase lasted until 1919, intensified by the war. One of the classic aspects of this phase is a long acceleration of the growth of the monetary aggregates and a rise in interest rates;

(iv) the year 1897 is symbolic from two points of view as far as French monetary history is concerned:

- a major monetary enquiry was carried out in this year, following

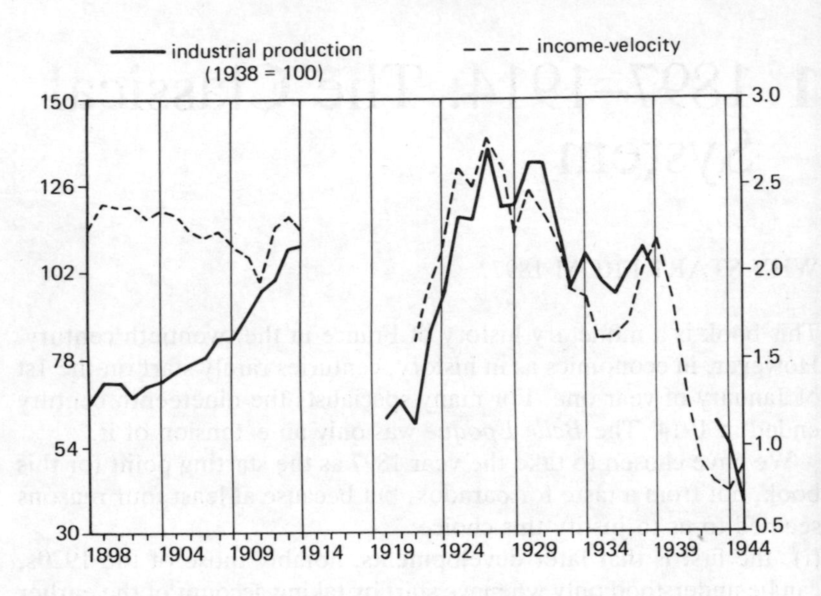

FIGURE 0.1 *Industrial production and income-velocity 1897–1944*

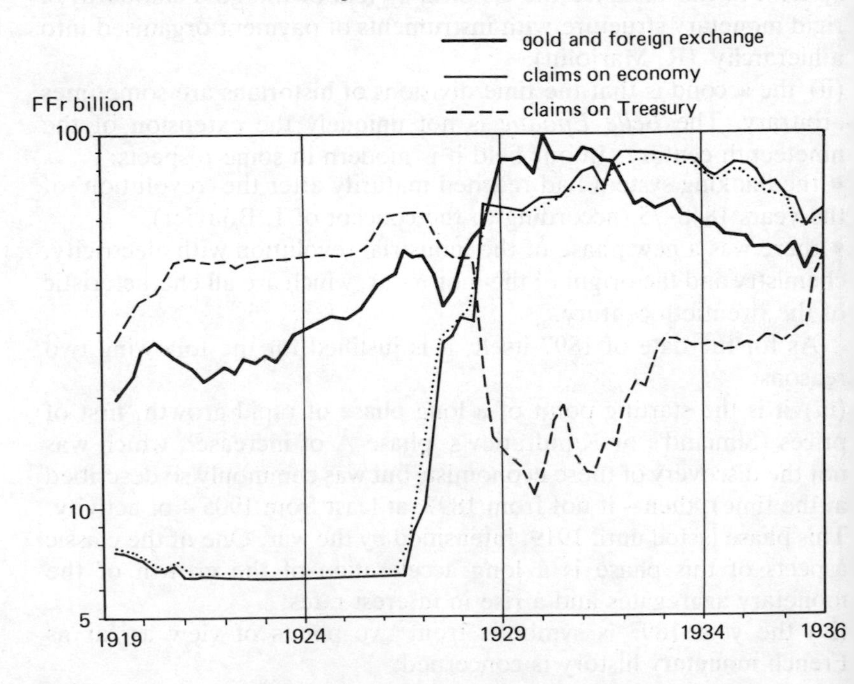

FIGURE 0.2 *Counterparts of M2 1919–36*

TABLE 1.1 *Major Annual Statistics 1897–1914*

	1897	*1898*	*1899*	*1900*	*1901*	*1902*	*1903*	*1904*	*1905*
GDP (% change)	(54) – 1.8 1929 = 100	5.6	5.3	1.7	–3.3	0	3.4	4.9	–1.6
Industrial production (% change)	(66) 3.6 1913 = 100	2.8	3.9	–4.8	–0.3	–2.1	6.8	–5.5	11.5
Balance of payments (FFr million)									
Trade including precious metals	–322	–759	–267	–613	–397	–231	–527	–321	–399
Invisibles	913	1109	1115	1197	1203	1292	1297	1472	1543
Net exports of capital	545	930	810	1000	1280	1080	1295	1440	1620
FFr/$	5.18	5.18	5.18	5.18	5.18	5.18	5.18	5.18	5.18
Prices (% change)									
Wholesale	1.2	2.4	9.3	6.4	–5	–1.2	2.4	–2.4	3.6
Retail, Paris	–2.7	1.4	1.4	0	0.5	–1.1	–0.5	–1.4	–0.5
Balance of the State budget (FFr million)	4.6	92.4	67.4	–9.6	–182.5	–173.5	58.5	89	48.4
M2 (% change)	3.7	–0.2	3.7	4.9	2.3	4.3	1.4	9.8	8.7

	1906	*1907*	*1908*	*1909*	*1910*	*1911*	*1912*	*1913*	*1914*
GDP (% change)	1.6	1.6	1.5	1.5	0	4.5	8.6	0	
Industrial production (% change)	2.0	4.2	–1.9	6.8	–2.4	9.5	15.2	–2.3 (100)	
Balance of payments (FFr million)									
Trade including precious metals	–300	–738	–1296	–404	–632	–1779	–1254	–1729	
Invisibles	1670	1716	1807	1973	2164	2179	2181	2420	
Net exports of capital	1790	1220	1490	1460	1830	1030	1340	1115	
FFr/$	5.18	5.18	5.18	5.18	5.18	5.18	5.18	5.18	
Prices (% change)									
Wholesale	7.0	4.3	–7.3	0	6.7	5.3	4	–2.0	2.0
Retail, Paris	1.6	1.4	2.3	–0.2	1.3	9.4	–1.2	1.2	2.6
Balance of the State budget (FFr million)	–39.5	88.1	–54.1	–45.2	–48.0	141.1	114.7	24.8	–5517
M2 (% change)	3.4	–1.2	3.9	8.8	9.4	3.0	7.2	3.2	11.7

SOURCES GDP – Carré, Dubois et Malinvaud (1972); industrial production – Crouzet (1970); balance of payments – White (1933); FFr/$ – Statistique Générale de la France (1932); wholesale prices – Statistique Générale de la France (1932): up to 1901, annual value of imports of 45 products determined by the Commission des valeurs en douane, from 1902 market prices of 45 products; retail prices – index of cost of living in Paris calculated by Singer-Kerel (1961); balance of national budget – Jèze (1934); M2 – authors' calculations.

those of 1878, 1885 and 1891; two others took place before the First World War, in 1903 and 1906;
- a new law was passed defining the relations between the State and the Banque de France, and a new Governor, G. Pallain, was appointed (who was to hold this office for 23 years).

The Banque de France then developed, first by opening branches, and secondly by accentuating its commercial character: it competed with the credit establishments on their own ground. In this way, taking one year with another, it was responsible for about a fifth of what we should now call claims on the economy.

Furthermore, gold now triumphed completely over silver. On the eve of war, the Banque de France held one seventh of the world's reserves of gold.

THE BELLE EPOQUE

Viewed from a distance and compared with either the Great Depression of the last quarter of the nineteenth century or the interwar years, the *Belle Epoque* indeed appears as a brilliant period in French history: it was the period of the apogee of the Third Republic – a 'radical republic'[1] – which no longer feared the monarchists. The regime of the Assembly did not prevent a certain ministerial stability, particularly between 1899 and 1905 when two presidents of the Council beat the records for length of term: Waldeck-Rousseau (1899–1902) and even more Combes (1902–05)[2]; the longevity of Delcasse at the Quai d'Orsay is well known.[3]

THE RENEWED RISE IN WORLD PRICES

The *Belle Epoque* was such above all because it was a period when world prices resumed their rise, after the Great Depression. This resumption was associated with an acceleration of economic growth, still tentative between 1897 or 1905 but thereafter decisive. Without entering into the discussion as to whether the turning point for economic activity was 1897 and 1905,[4] it may be noted, using the index of industrial production calculated by F. Crouzet, that between 1871 and 1896 in 17 of the 25 years, that is two thirds, the index increased less quickly than its long-term trend for the period 1815–1913, whilst there are only nine instances of this, that is, only one half, between 1897 and 1913.[5]

The political situation and the trend to improvement in the economic conjuncture resulted in a long period of balance in the public finances. After a series of deficits, 1897 marked the return to surplus; deficits reappeared only at times of cyclical crisis (1900–02 and 1908–10).[6]

THE TRIUMPH OF GOLD

The *Belle Epoque* is finally that of the triumph in France of the classical system of the gold standard. Bimetallism, even in the shaky form of recent years, was no more than a memory. The availability of South African gold, which had been exploited from the beginning of the 1890s, ensured that there was no longer any problem in expanding the monetary base. Gold coin was in circulation: its share in this base remained stable throughout the period. The system was completed by the maturing of the networks of banks. Furthermore, the franc was strong: France was 'an old rentier country'. On average she exported between a third and a half of her savings.[7] The revenues from these savings invested abroad made possible both a trade deficit and the export of capital. France was essentially an open economy: these exports compensated for the *relatively* slow growth of internal demand.

As with any period of a long rise in prices and of more intense activity, the *Belle Epoque* was a phase of increasing nominal interest rates.

However, the *Belle Epoque* was not without difficult episodes:

- political and social problems were numerous and often serious, with the Dreyfus Affair, religious disputes, and the multiplication of social conflicts, notably in 1907–08. 1907 was also the year of the uprising in the wine-growing Midi;
- the 'classical' economy was cyclical. The period was marked by three economic crises: 1900, 1907 and 1913. However, they were on the whole less profound in France than in other countries, notably Germany and the United States.[8] France did not have the same dynamism, particularly demographically, as these two countries, but she suffered the consequences of their fluctuations. More generally, in view of her openness, she was sensitive to external developments. Thus the 1900 crisis was the result of the completion of the great Russian railway projects, largely financed by France (and which in return meant orders for France). The 1907 crisis was primarily American and German, that of 1913 German.

FRANCE THE UNIVERSAL RENTIER

Foreign investment is risky, as people have recently had cause to remember. France lent massively to Russia but also to the Balkan countries and to Latin America. Savers were encouraged in this direction by the banks. More generally, the development of the banks and their role in the foreign investment of surplus savings was frequently criticised in France. Thus a series of articles appeared between 1905 and 1910 signed Lysis, the collected version of which, *Contre l'oligarchie financière en France*, enjoyed a great success[9]: the great French banks 'not only did not support initiative but they thwarted it by the power of their organisation . . . they diverted their customers away from all the new businesses'; they did not participate in the activity of the regions 'from which they drain the money sent to Paris and make France the universal usurer'. In these conditions the projects and bills which punctuated French parliamentary life are hardly surprising: thus in 1911, a commission for banking reform, on the initiative of Caillaux, was supposed to 'research into ways of granting more extensive credit facilities to medium- and small-scale commerce, and to small- and medium-scale industry'; but it produced no result.

THE MONETARY STRUCTURE AT THE START OF THE PERIOD

'An economy with a rigid monetary structure and with a hierarchy of payment instruments.'[10] As A. Dauphin-Meunier wrote, 'In the first place, in Western Europe (. . .) money is not homogeneous. It consists of a series of superimposed layers, gold and silver, banknotes, deposits. Banknotes are guaranteed by gold and silver, deposits by gold, silver and banknotes. More or less rigid rules, varying with time and space, fix the conditions of this guarantee'.[11] Among the precious metals which formed the base of the system (the fundamental money), one, gold, was dominant. The bimetallism instituted by the Latin Union of 1865 was more and more 'shaky'. During this period, under the driving force of G. Pallain, the Banque de France sold its silver écus,[12] and reinforced its holdings of gold until, on the eve of the 1914–18 war, it held one seventh of world reserves.[13]

Such a development was only possible because France enjoyed a surplus on its balance of payments: it could simultaneously export its

TABLE 1.2 *French Monetary Circulation at different times*

FFr millions

Date of monetary enquiry	*A stock of gold*	*B écus*	*C A + B*	*Stock of coin in circulation*	*Coin and banknotes in circulation*
14.08.1878	5000	3000	8000	6057	8380
15.07.1897	4200	1935	6135	3614	7231
15.10.1903	4800	1800	6600	4390	8721
16.10.1909	6000	1500	7500	5155	10 323

SOURCE Rist (1914)

capital and build up its gold reserves. Not only was the franc a reserve currency, but the foundation of this situation was also particularly solid: whilst the United Kingdom and Germany had more liquid external liabilities than gold reserves, the liquidity position of France was much stronger. The official reserves of gold and foreign currency of the Banque de France amounted to nearly three times the known liquid assets of other countries in francs.[14]

At the beginning of the period, in 1897, the 'monetary base' in circulation is known, thanks to the enquiry of 15 September of that year; silver money then represented a little less than half of the stock of coin in circulation. A little more than half of the total of gold and silver was in circulation with the public. Added to this was a more or less equivalent share of Banque de France banknotes.

The enquiries of 1903 and 1909 brought to notice (Table 1.2):

- in the stock of coin, the continual increase in the share of gold and the corresponding fall in that of silver ecus;
- in the part of the monetary base in circulation, the maintenance of the dichotomy between coin and banknotes.

As for the deposits in the banking system, they still amounted to only a little more than FFr1 billion in 1903 and FFr3 billion in 1909.

In comparison with other countries, France thus had an outmoded monetary structure: deposits in English banks were five times, and those in German banks twice, as large as those in French banks; but the total amount of banknotes in circulation in France was equal to eight times that of the English fiduciary circulation and twice that of the German.

This great contrast, in particular with the English financial system, was a paradoxical consequence of the rules governing the note issue in the two central banks. With the Banque de France the 'banking principle' authorised a large issue of banknotes against gold reserves, rediscounts of commercial claims, and advances against securities; with the Bank of England the 'currency principle', inspired by the memory of the inflationary crises and the exchange rate fluctuations experienced in the nineteenth century after the war with France, limited issues of notes to those against reserves of precious metals and a fixed amount of Treasury bills.

The French banks accordingly experienced a less vigorous development than their English or German counterparts. Their policy of granting credits was strictly inspired by the principles of the Banque de France. The essential part of the assets of the banks thus consisted of discounted short-term commercial claims, the development of the outstanding total of which closely followed the movements of business: there was thus no 'transformation' and there were no long-term credits in the banks' portfolios. This explains the volatility of the totals outstanding, which lacked the inertia that was to be provided much later, after the 1950s, by the rise in importance of long-term credits. We shall therefore see that, during the whole of the period up to the Second World War, the money stock experienced fluctuations which were often very sharp.

These extremely prudent orientations weakened any tendencies to 'overheating'. The Banque de France which, as we have seen, possessed a very considerable gold reserve was able to maintain its interest rates at very low levels and to control crises easily with rare and moderate variations in the discount rate: thus between 1898 and 1913 the discount rate was modified 14 times in France, within a range from 2 per cent to 4 per cent, while in Germany the rate was varied 62 times and in England 79 times, the fluctuations in the latter countries ranging between 3 per cent and 7 per cent and between 2.5 per cent and 7.5 per cent respectively.

The French banks were prudent and remarkably solid. It was already possible to distinguish banks which could be described as deposit banks, which constituted the major part of the balance sheet of the banking system and which modelled the principles of their lending operations on those of the Banque de France: the merchant banks; and several banking houses forming 'la haute banque', often family firms of Jewish or Protestant origin, which placed numerous foreign loans on the French market.

The banks were healthy, but at the same time dependent on the

Banque de France: they had a permanent shortage of cash, generated by the large size of the fiduciary circulation and aggravated by the competition with them of the Institut d'Emission, which managed sight deposits amounting to 7 per cent of total bank money (today 0.05 per cent).

THE GOLDEN AGE OF LONG-TERM SAVING

The *Belle Epoque* is considered as the golden age of the saver, particularly the French saver.[15] In fact only rarely have new issues of negotiable securities reached such a level in relation to national output or, therefore, to national savings – the current flow or the accumulated stock. France in those days placed hardly any of its negotiable savings in money, and only a little in savings bank deposits; she bought securities,[16] French and foreign.

Between 1900 and 1913 about FFr38 billion of securities were issued, that is, FFr20 billion by French issuers[17] and FFr18 billion by foreigners. The annual average thus corresponded to FFr2.7 billion (this was also the amount observed in 1913). In the same period savings bank deposits grew by only a few hundred millions and M2 by half a billion (FFr) each year.

Table 1.3, in which annual averages have been calculated for the period 1910–13, shows how far the financial structure of the French economy of the period was different from that which prevails even today.

THE MONETARY CONJUNCTURE

The monetary regime in force before 1914 thus permitted only limited excesses. Nevertheless, the rates of growth, real and nominal, registered during the *Belle Epoque* were not negligible.

Between 1897 and 1913 the index of industrial production calculated by Crouzet increased by 50 per cent. During the same period the index of wholesale prices in terms of gold grew by 45 per cent. As far as the money stock was concerned, it was FFr7.56 billion at the end of 1897; in June 1914, after seasonal adjustment, it amounted to FFr15.86 billion, that is, it had doubled. This corresponds to an average annual growth rate of some 4.1 per cent.

Thus there was a moderately increasing 'monetarisation' of the

TABLE 1.3 *Financing of the French Economy and Structure of Financial Investments 1910–13*
(average yearly flows in current FFr billion)

Sources of financing	
Budget balance	–0.2
Credits	
bank	1.84
other	0.4
Net issues of bonds by companies	4.6
Other uses of funds net	1.67
External	4.72
Financial investments	
Bonds	
French	5.35
foreign	5.58
Savings banks	0.15
M2	2.15

economy. The income velocity of money (the ratio of national income to M2 + gold and silver reserves) followed a gently declining trend until 1910, superimposed on which were fluctuations marking the phases of the economic conjuncture: a fall in velocity between 1900 and 1903 in a period of recession, a recovery from 1904–05 when production recovered strongly, and a renewed decline from 1906 which was appreciably accentuated in 1910. After this year the income velocity increased very sharply, at the same time as activity.

The phases of the conjuncture appeared relatively well-marked over the period. During three 'crises' (1900, 1907 and 1913), the money stock grew more slowly (1901) or flattened out (1908 and 1913); prices fell; and interest rates, particularly short-term rates, declined.

(a) In France the crisis of 1900 was moderate, and followed by a quasi-stagnation of activity up to 1905. According to the end-year statistics there was in fact only a slowing down of the growth of M2 (in 1901). Among the counterparts it was bank credits which virtually stopped increasing. From 1901 and up to 1904 this was also true of the credits granted by the Banque de France (which as we have noted

TABLE 1.4 *Summary of Monetary and Financial Data 1897–1913 (End-period totals, Annual Averages for Interest Rates)*

FFr billion

	1897	*1898*	*1899*	*1900*	*1901*	*1902*	*1903*	*1904*
M2	7.56	7.84	8.13	8.53	8.73	9.11	9.24	10.15
Specie in circulation	3.61	3.76[1]	3.92[1]	4.09[1]	4.32	4.35	4.39	4.44
Claims on the Treasury								
Banque de France reserves				3.2	3.5	3.7	3.6	3.7
Claims on the economy				5.0	4.9	5	5.4	6.4
Deposits in savings banks	4.27	4.28	4.19	4.36	4.43	4.39	4.31	4.44
(for reference, ceiling on deposits, in francs)	1500							
Discount rate	2	2.2	3.10	3.2	3	3	3	3
Yield on bonds (3% stock)	2.9	2.92	2.98	2.96	2.99	3.06	3.11	3.03
New issues of negotiable securities								
shares	0.47	0.73	0.86	0.83	0.49	0.51	0.35	0.36
bonds	0.51	0.94	1.47	0.94	1.25	1.30	0.84	1.39
National income[1]	27.1	26.20	28.90	30.60	31	31.10	32.10	34.6
Income velocity (national income/M2 + gold and silver reserves)		2.25	2.40	2.38	2.38	2.31	2.36	2.33

TABLE 1.4 *continued*

	1905	*1906*	*1907*	*1908*	*1909*	*1910*	*1911*	*1912*	*1913*
M2	11.03	11.41	11.27	11.71	12.75	13.94	14.36	15.39	15.88
Specie in circulation	4.49	4.66	4.88	5.05	5.16	5.36	5.52	5.74	5.93
Claims on the Treasury									
Banque de France reserves	4	4	3.7	4	4.5	4.12	3.97	3.87	4.16
Claims on the economy	6.6	7.4	7.8	8.1	9.2	10.45	11.66	12.52	12.29
Deposits in savings banks	4.66	4.77	4.97	5.12	5.47	5.64	5.61	5.70	5.82
(for reference, ceiling on deposits in francs)	1500	—	—	—	—	—	—	—	—
Discount rate	3	3	3.45	3	3	3	3.10	3.40	4
Yield on bonds (3% stock)	3.08	3.16	3.13	3.07	3.06	3.14	3.27	3.44	3.78
New issues of negotiable securities									
shares	0.78	0.98	0.45	0.93	1.28	1.19	1.76	1.41	1.41
bonds	1.78	2.04	1.40	2.03	2.07	3.12	2.55	2.37	2.71
National income[2]	34.80	35.4	36	36.1	37.5	37.5	45	49	49
Income velocity (national income/M2 + gold and silver reserves)	2.24	2.20	2.23	2.15	2.09	1.94	2.26	2.32	2.25

1. Linear interpolation
2. Figures from Sauvy, revalued at current (retail) prices.

was developing its commercial activities at this time). The gold reserves hardly increased during the four years from 1901 to 1904. As far as interest rates were concerned, the discount rate of the Banque de France, which had been lowered to 3 per cent in 1901, remained at this level until 1907. The rate for advances against securities went down.

(b) The recovery of 1905 was clear-cut (so much so that, as we have seen, some experts prefer to date the beginning of the long phase of expansion from this year). Credits to the cconomy and M2 recovered from 1904. At the beginning of 1906 order books were 'overloaded'.[18] Prices rose. Interest rates rose, until they went above what was later to be called the marginal efficiency of capital. The crisis broke in 1907. Bank credits and the money stock fell. Industrial production diminished.

(c) The outlines of the recovery were discernible in the monetary domain in 1910. However, activity regained its momentum only in 1911–12, a time when interest rates rose once more until they resulted, for both activity and the cost of credit, in a reversal – though a relatively slow one – in 1913. But the symptoms of a crisis were certainly there: a stagnation of credits to the economy and a marked deceleration in the growth of M2; a halt to the rise, or a fall, in production; and a slight easing of wholesale prices and interest rates.

NOTES TO CHAPTER 1

1. Rébérioux (1975).
2. In 18 years there were 15 presidents of the Council, some of them it is true for several terms, such as Briand (three terms).
3. The record for longevity must be that of G. Pallain as Governor of the Banque de France (1897–1920).
4. There are two opposed schools of thought on this point. For some (T. Markovitch, E. Malinvaud) the division is in 1896: thus Malinvaud 'contrasts a growth from 1870 to 1896 of 1.6% per annum with a growth after this date of 2.4%'. For others the division is in 1905. 'M. Levy-Leboyer finds a rate of 1.93% from 1885 to 1905 when building activity is included in his index, and 2.66% when it is excluded, whilst from 1905 to 1913 the rates are 4.19% and 4.42%'. Malinvaud 'admits that [his index] experiences an acceleration from 1905'. (Labrousse and Braudel, 1970–82, vol. 4/1, pp. 120ff.)
5. Crouzet (1970).
6. Without having worked out the theory the men of the time thus achieved the 'cyclically adjusted budget'!
7. Cf. White (1933).

8. Lescure (1932).
9. We quote from the 11th edition. Lysis was the pseudonym of two 'neo-Saint-Simonians', Vergeot and Letailleur (cf. Allinne, 1983 p. 8).
10. Marjolin (1941, p. 56).
11. Dauphin-Meunier (1936).
12. The proportion of silver in the reserves of the Banque de France fell progressively from 67 per cent in 1881 to less than 12 per cent in 1914 (Sédillot, 1971 p. 101).
13. Ramon (1929, p. 419).
14. Lindert (1969).
15. The opinion was often put forward at the time (and is sometimes found today in ill-informed works) that the French savings ratio at that time was exceptional, in comparison both with other countries and with the present time. In fact the French rate of that time, which oscillated from 1890 to 1914 between 8 per cent and 13 per cent of national income, was comparable with those of the other major industrial countries (cf. J. Bouvier in Labrousse and Braudel, 1970–82, vol. 4/1, p. 197); it was a little lower than that observed in the course of the last few years, which from a high of 18 per cent has just (1984) gone below 14 per cent.
16. 'During the three or four years before the war the French saver held nearly 40% of his wealth in negotiable securities' (Michalet, 1968, p. 102). This relates to the saver in average or easy circumstances, whose death gave rise to probate declaration.
17. The new issues break down as follows: FFr8.2 billion in shares and rather more than FFr11 billion in bonds, of which FFr5.6 billion was for local authorities and railways and FFr5.9 billion for industrial and commercial companies. 'Apart from the conversion effected by Rouvier in 1902 of the 3.5% stock to 3% perpetual, there was no financial operation on behalf of the State' (Crédit Lyonnais, 1963, p. 90). In fact we should note that in July 1914, that is to say on the eve of war, the State issued a 3.5 per cent redeemable loan of FFr805 million. The major credit institutions took up most of it initially, but it had not yet been registered as owned by the public when the conflict broke out (Théry, 1921, pp. 133–4).
18. Lescure (1932).

2 1914–18: The First World War

The Great War signified on more than one count the 'end of a world'[1]: 'the war shattered, at a single blow and definitively, the nineteenth century monetary system'.[2]

A NEW MONETARY STRUCTURE

J. Bouvier notes three great monetary consequences:

- the abandonment of the convertibility of banknotes into gold coin, which was never reestablished;
- the increase in the circulation of Banque de France banknotes, to the detriment of bank deposits – which involved, at any rate at the beginning of the period, a large increase in the share of the Banque de France in credits to the economy (20 per cent before the war, as much as one third in 1915);
- the preponderant share in the counterparts of the money stock taken by claims on the Treasury. In fact if one considers the sources of financing as a whole (see Table 2.3), the balance of the national budget forms the major part of it. In 1914 and 1915 bank credits *went down*.

We may add a fourth consequence, which was also to have a great future: the development of the role of the public sector. Thanks to the war, the Treasury became an 'immense deposit bank'. In the aftermath of the conflict this development was prolonged and consolidated by the establishment of postal cheques in 1918, and by the reorganisation in 1919 of the *banques populaires*[3] and of the Crédit National (the latter intended to finance reconstruction), and finally of the Banque Nationale du Commerce Extérieur (the modern BFCE).

(1) THE DECLARATION OF WAR AND THE DECISIONS WHICH FOLLOWED

The declaration of war had been preceded by a period of crisis of confidence, marked by withdrawals of deposits, during which the

TABLE 2.1 *Major Annual Statistics 1914–18*

	1914	*1915*	*1916*	*1917*	*1918*
Balance of payments (FFr million):					
Trade including colonies and precious metals			–39 527		
Income account			–24 252		
Capital account			28 773		
FFr/$	5.18	5.18	5.18	5.18	5.18
Prices (% change)					
Wholesale	2.0	37.5	34.3	39.1	29.6
Retail, Paris	2.6	15.1	21.8	29.6	28.5
M2 (% change)	11.7	16.4	14.9	31.6	35.6

SOURCES balance of payments – Meynial (1925); FFr/$ and wholesale prices – Statistique Générale de la France (1932); retail prices in Paris – Singer-Kerel (1961); M2 – authors' calculations.

Banque de France had been obliged to provide assistance to the banks. Also, with effect from 2 August a moratorium on current deposits and accounts[4] had been decided upon, and on 5 August Banque de France banknotes were made inconvertible[5] and the ceiling on the Banque's advances to the Treasury was raised – the latter increased from FFr4.1 billion at the end of 1914 to FFr17.3 billion at the end of 1918 (and FFr26 billion at the end of 1920). In December 1914 the stabilisation of the situation permitted the unblocking of bank accounts. But the war (and the postwar period) were unfavourable to the latter.[6] Several reasons can be found for this[7]:

- depositors had suffered the exceptional measures of 1914 which led them, initially at least, to show a certain mistrust of deposit banks; they preferred hoarding and above all the direct subscription of National Defence Bonds ('which brought them a remunerative rate of interest without immobilising their capital for too long');
- 'they addressed themselves . . . more than in the past to the Banque de France';
- for their part the large institutions 'desiring to be able to meet any new panic . . . resolved to ensure their liquidity themselves . . . not wishing to assume too great a responsibility towards their depositors they were rather timid and did nothing to attract deposits – particularly by not raising the return to the latter (the BNC was a rare exception)'.

The unpopularity of the commercial banks did not reach the same intensity during the Second World War, as we shall see later.

(2) THE FINANCIAL COST OF THE GREAT WAR

Rather than by a systematic recourse to the creation of money through advances from the Banque de France – 'a dangerous procedure which could bring in its train a monetary depreciation of which the collective memory of the French people retained a dreaded example, that of the "assignats" of the revolutionary period'[8] – the government (in this instance the minister of finance, Ribot – who was also president of the Council between March and November 1917) covered the budget deficit by borrowing. In the absence of the usual peacetime outlets for private savings (particularly foreign investment), the sums which the Treasury put into circulation against its expenditure returned to it in large measure in the form of subscriptions to its borrowings: the 'circuit' was thus partially closed.[9]

National Defence Bonds

When a bond issue failed,[10] Ribot and Pallain decided to address themselves to liquid savings, borrowing by very short-term Treasury bills, rebaptised, to ensure their success, as National Defence Bonds. These bonds, at 5 per cent interest, were renewable indefinitely every three months and were sold through public channels in denominations of FFr100, 500 and 1000. The National Defence Bonds and other liquid savings resources provided in total more than one third of the funds for the war. Between 1 August 1914 and the end of 1918, the floating debt was thus increased by FFr60 billion (it continued to increase subsequently, as we shall see). The external debt, which had been nil at the beginning of the period, exceeded FFr27 billion on 31 December 1918. The total increase of internal and external debt, FFr130 billion in round figures, was hardly less than the expenditure of the State during the 53 months of the war, at FFr160 billion (Table 2.2; see also the more detailed figures in Table 2.3).

The war had a double effect: it reduced supply – the North and East, particularly productive regions both agriculturally and industrially,[11] were occupied by the enemy – and it increased unproductive demand.

TABLE 2.2 *The First World War and its Financing (schematic table, in current FFr billion)*

Total expenditure from 1.8.14 to 31.12.18	*158.5*
Principal sources of financing	
Taxes	23.4
Consolidated debt	35.4
Domestic floating and term debt	60.6
External debt	27.3
Advances from the Banque de France	13.2

SOURCE Théry (1922).

Imbalances

In these conditions the acceleration in price rises is not surpising, nor is the decline in the external accounts:

- between July 1914 and November 1918 the general index of wholesale prices of 45 items went from 100 to 365 and that of retail prices in the large towns from 100 to 251;
- the decline in the external accounts was appreciable. The commercial deficit was only FFr1.5 billion in 1914. It reached FFr7 billion in 1915, FFr14 billion in 1916, and FFr21 billion in 1917.

Notwithstanding this, the franc remained stable in relation to other currencies throughout the whole of the war – at the beginning, thanks to the repatriation of assets from abroad and, as well as to the establishment of exchange controls in 1915, to sales of gold brought to the State by the French people; and, later, thanks to the Anglo-Saxon credits. In the middle of 1916 exchange agreements established 'complete solidarity between the British and French Treasuries'.[12] The denunciation of these agreements in 1919 was at the origin of the fall of the franc.

The monetary part of the internal financing of the war manifested itself as a multiplication of the money stock by three: M2 was a little over FFr15 billion on the eve of the war, and reached FFr46 billion on that of the armistice. Even this multiplication was insufficient, since a number of organisations (towns, savings banks, merchants' associations, and chambers of commerce) had to put into circulation payment vouchers or emergency notes.

The development of the counterparts highlights the 'explosion' of the money stock (Table 2.4):

TABLE 2.3 *The financing of the French economy, 1913–18 (FFr billion)*

	1913	*1914*	*1915*	*1916*	*1917*	*1918*	
Sources of financing							
Balance of State budget[1]	–0.02	5.52	16.80	22.86	28.36	34.28	
				107.84			
Credits				5.85			
Bank	–0.23	–0.92	–1.27	1.1	2.44	4.50	
Non-bank[2]	1.47		0.25	0.42	0.68		
				1.39			
External[3]	0.69			–35.01			
							Investments
	2.70		8.23	7.45	4.72	10.28	Bond subscriptions
				30.68			
		0.56	0.25	0.80	5.35	0.25	Net subscriptions of Treasury bills[4]
				7.23			
	0.07	–0.08	–0.38	–0.38	0.25	+0.50	Deposits in savings banks
				0.09			
	0.49	1.86	2.92	–4.55	9.52	10.79	ΔM2
				29.64			
	1.35			12.43			Residual

1. A surplus reduces the supply of financing (– sign); a deficit increases it (+ sign).
2. Including net issues of bonds by non-financial companies.
3. Balance of payments figures from Meynial (1925).
4. Estimates.

The aggregation of the data over several years is justified by the uncertainty attached to the annual figures, particularly with regard to the external item and the subscriptions of Treasury bills.

TABLE 2.4 *Counterparts of the money stock 1913–19*
(End-period, FFr billion)

	1913	*1914*	*1915*	*1916*	*1917*	*1918*	*1919*
Gold and foreign exchange	4.16*	4.51	6.42	6.09	6.37	8.12	7.14
Credits to the economy	12.29	11.37	10.10	11.34	13.31	16.47	21.45
(% share of Banque de France)	(18.4)	(39.5)	(33.5)	(28.6)	(24.0)	(19.9)	(14.2)
Claims on the Treasury	1.05	3.90	5.83	9.33	15.97	20.87	35.78
M2 (% change between the end of one year and that of the following)	3.2	11.7	16.5	22.0	37.7	30.2	46.7

* Not including specie in circulation.

SOURCE author's calculations.

• the maintenance of the external reserves, for the reasons noted above;
• the rise in importance of claims on the Treasury, which had been nil at the beginning of the period:
• the associated and relatively less rapid growth of claims on the economy. The lead given here by the Banque de France at the beginning of the war appears clearly, after which the situation returned to normal.

In spite of the sharp acceleration in the rise of prices, interest rates remained low. We have seen that the National Defence Bonds carried interest of 5 per cent. This was also the official discount rate of the Banque de France. The face-value interest rates for new bonds issued during the war hardly seemed high: 5 per cent in 1915 and 1916 and 4 per cent in 1917 and 1918. However, the issues were made below par and actuarial rates were a little, but not very much, more remunerative: 5.45 per cent (1914), 5.68 per cent (1915), 5.71 per cent (1916); the highest rate was reached during the 'terrible year' of 1917, at 5.83 per cent. On the other hand the yield on the Liberation loan of 1918 was only 5.65 per cent.

(3) THE ECONOMIC CONSEQUENCES OF THE WAR

The human consequences were the most terrible: by 11 November 1918 1 364 000 dead and 740 000 wounded had been recorded.

The non-human capital, particularly in the North and East, was devastated: 549 000 houses, 20 000 factories, 5000 kilometres of railways, 58 000 kilometres of roads, and 1 757 000 hectares of arable land were destroyed or required restoration.

The internal national debt went from FFr27.7 billion (only FFr1.6 billion of this representing floating or term debt) to FFr123.8 billion (FFr62.3 billion) at the end of 1918.

The external debt, nil on the eve of the war as we have said, reached FFr27.3 billion, half at term and half floating.

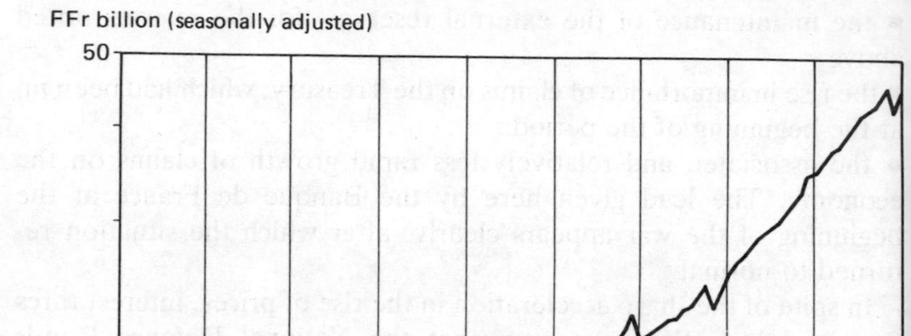

FIGURE 2.1 *Money stock 1910–18*

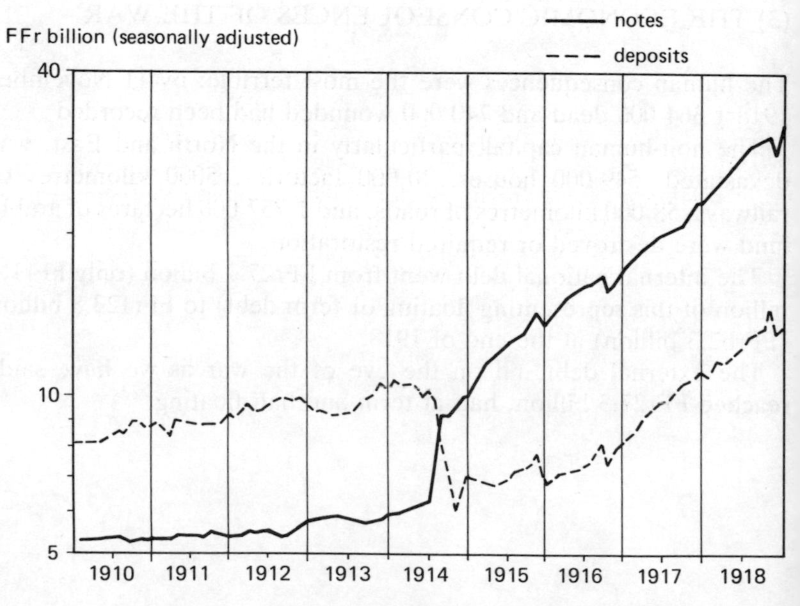

FIGURE 2.2 *Notes and bank deposits 1910–18*

NOTES TO CHAPTER 2

1. The title of the book by P. Bernard (1975)
2. J. Bouvier in Braudel and Labrousse (1970–82, vol. 4/1, p. 636).
3. The 'banques populaires' were organised in 1917 (the law of 13 March) to make it easier for small tradesmen and small businessmen to obtain discount credits. Mutual guarantee societies and banques populaires were envisaged at that time. The decrees for implementation were issued in 1918 (A. Théry, 1921, pp. 212–13).
4. The moratorium limited withdrawals to FFr250 plus 5 per cent of the remainder (E. Théry, 1922, p. 242). A. Théry (1921, pp. 139ff.) is a good guide for the period of financial and monetary 'crisis' at the beginning of the war.
5. The gold thus released was used in 1915 for the payment of indispensable imports supplied by the United States, until credits made it possible to avoid recourse to such shipments. The end of the credits, in 1919, led to new sales of gold.
6. In spite of inflation 'the deposits (at sight and at term) of the six principal banks, which stood at FFr5.9 billion at the end of 1913, regained this level only in the course of 1917. With FFr8.5 billion at the end of 1918, they represented in terms of purchasing power only half of their pre-war value' (Bouvier, ibid.). One sizeable exception was the development of the Banque Nationale de Crédit, which pulled itself up during the war into the fourth position among the very large banks.
7. We draw heavily on A. Théry (1921, pp. 200–01).
8. Bernard (1975, p. 38).
9. On the circuit, see Bloch-Lainé and de Vogüé (1960, pp. 271ff.): 'Reduced to its essence the art of public finance consists for the Treasury in trying to capture on the capital market the liquid assets put into circulation by the budget deficit, in order to ensure their return to its coffers. This policy evokes the idea of a closed circuit: if the Treasury succeeds in collecting via the "banking" sector of its operations sums equivalent to those which it expends via the "budgetary" sector, it succeeds in avoiding any recourse to the Institut d'Emission.'
10. Of a total of FFr800 millions offered to the public in July 1914, only FFr380 million had been placed by the beginning of September. However, during the conflict other long-term loans were placed, particularly in exchange for short-term bills which were thus consolidated. Overall in four years domestic 'long-term' debt had grown by FFr35 billion.
11. The French départements of Nord and Est produced before the war 90 per cent of linen thread and of iron ore, 80 per cent of steel, 70 per cent of sugar, 60 per cent of cotton fabric, 55 per cent of coal and 43 per cent of electric power, and paid 18.5 per cent of taxes (Gignoux, n.d., p. 16).
12. Gignoux (n.d., p. 21).

3 1919–26: The Failure of Monetary Deflation

As well as the two general elections, the results of which were the apparently indisputable victories of the Bloc National in 1919 (the 'bleu horizon' Chamber) and of the Cartel des Gauches in 1924, the whole period was dominated by political crises, national and international:

• the reparations crisis (together with the occupation of the Ruhr) and the related problem of the repayment of the French debts to the Allies, which led to differences with the latter and to wide fluctuations, in general downwards, in the franc relative to the dollar and to sterling;

• this same crisis made it clear that Germany would not pay: by this refusal it put completely in jeopardy the government's projections for the budget and for the repayment of its internal debt. The latter, as we saw in the previous chapter, was very largely short-term (National Defence Bonds). The stock of these developed in line with political events, and so weighed heavily on the domestic monetary situation;

• the 'strong men' (Clémenceau) had been discarded. Political instability returned, reaching a peak in 1925, hardly a year after the 'success' of the Cartel; thus France had seven different Ministers of Finance during these years. It is striking that the only periods when the franc was stable were those of the parliamentary recesses!

With the precious metals now definitely removed from circulation, the creation of money had two origins:

• the budget deficit: the financial circuit which had been brought into being during the First World War was no longer a closed one. The state experienced grave difficulty in placing its securities. It had to ask for advances from the Banque de France which it attempted to keep secret;

• the depreciation of the exchange rate: 1919–26 was the classic period of the 'hegemony of the exchanges' described by A. Aftalion. The fall in the franc stimulated the rise in prices and the money supply was adjusted to this.

The situation at the start of the period is entirely clear (at least with the benefit of hindsight). In January 1919 the money stock reached

TABLE 3.1 *Major annual statistics 1919–26*

	1919	*1920*	*1921*	*1922*	*1923*	*1924*	*1925*	*1926*
GDP (% change)	—	(65)*	−1.5	15.6	5.4	10.2	1.2	1.1
Industrial production (% change)	57(1913=100)	+8.8	−4.7	+41.8	+12.8	+23.9	−0.1	+16.7
Balance of payments (FFr million):								
Trade account	−16 740	−17 120	+1020	−1190	−1530	+1060	+1100	+1490
Income account	−9880	−13 440	+4850	+2880	+3050	+5520	+6810	+9400
Capital account	+10 020	+11 270	−5520	−3490	−3070	−8145	−9345	−13 135
FFr/$	5.18	5.18	13.49	12.33	16.58	19.32	21.23	31.44
Prices (% change)								
Wholesale	+5.6	+22.0	−32.1	−5.5	+28.8	+16.4	+12.8	+27.2
Retail, Paris	+22.6	+39.4	−13.2	−2.2	+8.9	+14.3	+7.1	+31.7
(Fontaine index)	(+35.4)	(+41.6)	(−18.0)	(+4.5)	(−5.3)	(+10.9)	(+4.0)	(+18.5)
Singer-Kerel	21.7	27.0	−15.6	−5.0	9.2	9.7	7.9	23.7
Balance of the State budget (FFr million)	−26 688	−17 139	−9275	−9761	−11 866	−7121	−1507	+1088
M2 (% change)	+12.4	+0.6	−0.7	+4.6	+8.7	+10.8	+25.4	+6.5

* (1929=100)

SOURCES GDP and industrial production – Carré, Dubois et Malinvaud (1972); exchange rates and prices – Statistique Générale de la France (1932); Fontaine (1966); Singer-Kerel (1961); balance of payments and budget – Sauvy (1984, vol. III); M2 – authors' calculations.

FFr49 billion, that is three times its level on the eve of war (FFr16 billion); the gold and silver reserves of the Banque de France represented FFr7.5 billion, against FFr4.5 billion in 1914; but before the war the public had held about FFr6 billion in coin whereas it possessed less than FFr2 billion at the time of the victory.

The gold backing of the note circulation plus bank deposits thus fell from more than 80 per cent in 1914 to 18 per cent in 1919. An easy but tempting comparison of these two backing ratios gives the ratio of 1 to 5, which is the ratio that eventually existed between the new gold value of the franc after the stabilisation of 1928 and that which had been assigned to it in 1914.

Two courses were open to the authorities: they could either ratify the situation and revise immediately the gold parity of the franc, an indispensable condition for the rapid reestablishment of its convertibility; or they could aim at a return to convertibility on the prewar bases.

The first solution was politically impossible for the time being: monetary stability has a mythical value in France, and, moreover, no 'expert' at that time dared to advocate such a policy, considered unworthy of a nation which had been until very recently 'everywhere in credit, nowhere in debt'.

The second solution accorded with national prestige. It was the course to which Britain was committed. It was not impossible, but a metaphor will allow its difficulty to be appreciated: it means getting nearer to the piano by moving the piano rather than the music-stool. Bringing the piano nearer consists in reducing the money in circulation in such a way that the ratio between this total and its gold and silver backing returns to a level which permits convertibility to be practised on the prewar bases.

Categorically renouncing the first way for the time being, the authorities committed themselves only partially to the second, and only after the money stock had increased by more than 35 per cent in 1919 and by 13 per cent during the first 11 months of 1920, this development being accompanied by a serious depreciation of the franc against the Anglo-Saxon currencies. A policy of deflation, aimed at reducing the money stock, was put into force from 1921 (see below), but (fortunately!) it did not have anything like the scope which revaluation to the prewar rate would have required; however, at least this deflation held back the depreciation of the franc on the exchange markets.

Deflation was interrupted from the second half of 1922, with a resumption of the granting of bank credits which resulted from, but also helped to sustain, a new crisis of confidence in the franc. In 1925 the money stock resumed a particularly rapid growth rate. With bond issues having become more and more difficult, notably during the 'black' years of 1924 to 1926, the needs of the Treasury and the needs of companies for funds combined to stimulate an accelerated creation of money (Table 3.2).

These two movements, monetary expansion and depreciation of the exchange rate, continued until July 1926; by that date the money stock had risen by 47 per cent in 20 months and the value of the dollar in francs had gone up by 150 per cent.

The creation of money benefited the banks only partially. During the war[1] the place of precious metals had been taken by Banque de France banknotes and not by bank deposits, the share of which in overall monetary assets had gone from more than 60 per cent in 1913 to 30 per cent in 1918. This percentage had risen only to 52 per cent in 1926.

The repeated phases of speculation led the credit institutions to emphasise treasury operations, international and domestic. The political instability and the fears of higher taxes, particularly the plans of the Cartel, could only encourage households and heads of companies to prefer banknotes.

This relatively unfavourable situation for the banks was exacerbated after 1929. During the 'crisis' the economy had less need of credit and non-financial agents, fearing the (real) difficulties facing the banks, continued to hold a large proportion of banknotes.

Returning to the period 1919–26, we can distinguish four phases:
(a) the immediately postwar speculative explosion, which terminated in a 'classic' reconversion crisis;
(b) this classic crisis was aggravated by the attempt at deflation in 1920–21; under the François-Marsal agreement the State committed itself to the progressive repayment of the Banque's advances, which was bound to entail a reduction in the money stock;
(c) however, from 1922 this deflation was put in question by the international crises;
(d) the situation became more acute with the Cartel des Gauches; it was then that 'the bubble burst'.

(1) THE EXPLOSION OF SPECULATION IMMEDIATELY AFTER THE WAR

The immediate postwar period can be defined as one in which people were 'carried away'[2] with inflationary euphoria: euphoria, because France was in the front rank of the victors – in 1919 France elected a 'bleu horizon' Chamber; and inflationary, because the reconstruction created intense needs which unbalanced the economy – demand exceeded supply, and whilst one part of the gap was filled by increased imports[3] which maintained that trade deficit, the rest brought about a marked acceleration in the rise of the prices of domestic and imported goods (both because the phenomenon was European and because the franc was depreciating heavily against the world currencies, the dollar and sterling). Domestic financing – issues of negotiable securities and the money stock – had to adapt to these developments.

1920 saw the peaks in the areas of production, the trade deficit, prices, negotiable security issues and the money stock:

- industrial production (not seasonally adjusted) rose by more than 10 per cent between the end of 1919 and the end of 1920;
- the trade deficit (n.s.a.) increased to FFr5.8 billion in the first quarter of 1919; a year later it reached FFr7.7 billion (+ 32 per cent), imports having nearly doubled;
- between November 1918 and April 1920 the general wholesale price index for 45 items went from 365 to 600 (+ 64 per cent); the retail price index for large towns reached its peak at 452 slightly later, in November (as against 261, it will be recalled, at the time of the Armistice, that is + 73 per cent)[4];
- new issues of French securities reached FFr43 billion in 1920, the average between 1919 and 1928 being FFr20 billion. Excluding the issues of the public authorities and those guaranteed by the State, the total was some FFr9 billion (against a prewar average of FFr5.4bn), FFr5.2 billion being for shares (against an average of FFr3.1bn). Companies broadened their capital bases and adapted their balance sheet structures to the new conditions[5];
- the money stock M2, which (s.a.) amounted to FFr46 billion at the time of the Armistice, reached a maximum of FFr78 billion in October 1920 (+ 69 per cent) at the point when the dollar reached the record rate of FFr17. Since the 'gold' counterpart was falling slightly (by around FFr1 billion between the first quarter of 1919 and the second quarter of 1920) and claims on the economy increased

only by some FFr7 billion, it was claims on the Treasury which explained the bulk of this growth (+ FFr26 billion between the end of 1918 and that of 1920, and +FFr18 billion between the first quarter of 1919 and the fourth quarter of 1920) for reasons which will become apparent.

'Germany will pay'

In 1919–20 the financing of the reconstruction did not seem to present any problem, for, it was thought, 'Germany will pay': the anticipated reparations made it unnecessary to go very far with the measures of domestic readjustment. At the very most there was a readiness to attack the epiphenomenon, the size of the circulation of Banque de France banknotes: by the François-Marsal agreement (29 December 1920), the State agreed to repay gradually to the Banque its wartime advances (by FFr2 billion a year from January 1921, up to 1935); there should follow a reduction in the money stock, which would restore the happy era of the Belle Epoque. For its part the United Kingdom attempted a similar exercise, with greater monetary success, since it re-established the prewar parity of sterling, but at what a cost in economic activity and employment!

As far as reparations were concerned, the precedent of 1871, when France paid without apparent problems the indemnity due to Germany, was so much in people's minds that very few in France had doubts about the ease with which the defeated country could discharge its obligations. The few who saw further into the future either did not dare to express themselves or were not listened to.

Once the principle of reconstruction was accepted, its budget was separated from the other expenditures of the State in a special account of 'recoverable' expenditure. The total was of course deeply in deficit, since the new expenditures were added to the insufficiency of supply, which was unfavourable to traditional fiscal receipts. In the expectation of payment of reparations, it was only natural that the deficit should be financed by borrowings at various terms. In the light of the commencement of the German payments in the near future, it seemed appropriate alongside the longer-term borrowings (those of 5 per cent in April 1920 and 6 per cent in November of the same year) to continue to have recourse to issues of Treasury bills, and particularly of National Defence Bonds. Consequently the floating debt increased continuously from the end of the war to the point where it created an 'overhang', the danger of which became apparent only with the return of instability. 'At the end of the war, 33 billions of bills were in circulation; three years later, in November 1921, they had become about 64 billion.'[6]

The instability was external. Just at the time when reconstruction called for increased imports, which generated a large payments deficit, the American and British allies 'pulled the rug away' by terminating the financial agreements which alone had allowed the franc to be maintained at its prewar parity in spite of much higher inflation. The franc was subjected to a strong depreciation. As Aftalion wrote, 'The dollar rate index (prewar base 100) which stayed at 105 during the latter months of 1918 and the early months of 1919 began to rise from March of that year',[7] that is, after the termination of the agreements. In April 1920 it reached a first maximum of 313. After some months of fluctuation, it reached a second maximum of 326 in December. The value of the dollar in francs thus went from 5.45 to 10.99 between March and December 1919.[8] At the same time there was a constant delay in the reparations, while the Allies were demanding payment of France's debts.

The instability was also internal. The 'Tiger' was 'thanked for his services' in January 1920. He was replaced by Millerand until September, and then, on Millerand's election as President of the Republic, by G. Leygues, who was in turn succeeded by Briand from January 1921.

(2) THE RECONVERSION CRISIS 1920–21

In the spring of 1920 the speculative euphoria gave place, in France as elsewhere, to a classic 'reconversion crisis',[9] and more restrictive policies added their effects to the inevitable correction of the earlier excesses.

Rigour restored

In France April 1920 marked the return of rigorous measures: fiscal rigour with the preparation of the François-Marsal agreement already mentioned, and monetary rigour with the Banque de France raising its discount rate to 6 per cent and maintaining it at this level until July 1921 when it was reduced to 5.5 per cent.

The crisis, which affected particularly the United Kingdom and even more harshly the United States,[10] had only a relatively limited effect on activity in France:

• the industrial production index, which was standing at 55 at the beginning of 1919, 60 at the end of that year and 82 at the end of 1920, went down to 70 in July-September 1921 (the lowest for the interwar period).

In France the structural effect of reconstruction partially offset the cyclical contraction. The other consequences of the crisis were:

• a reduction in prices: the wholesale price index of 45 items went down from 600, its level in April 1920, to a minimum of 313 at the beginning of 1922; the index of retail prices in large towns fell from 452 in November 1919 to 313 in August 1922;

• a return to equilibrium in the trade balance, that is, a surplus on the income account, but more than outweighed by the outflows of capital. Nevertheless, the dollar went down again in Paris, its index falling back from 326 in December 1920 to a minimum of 208 in April 1922;

• a slackening in the demand for credits to the economy; this demand rose to a maximum of FFr28 billion in the third quarter of 1920, and fell to a minimum of FFr22 billion five quarters later. Such a reduction facilitated the placing of Treasury securities: 'the crisis redirected liquid funds to Treasury securities',[11] which allowed the State to proceed with the first repayment of FFr2 billion provided for by the François-Marsal agreement; in fact the total of claims on the Treasury diminished by this amount between the fourth quarter of 1920 and the first of 1922. But the facility thus regained had the concomitant inconvenience that 'it created the dangerous illusion that this was an indefinite resource for the Treasury'.[12] In these conditions the State was able at the beginning of 1922 to reduce further (by half a point) the rate on National Defence Bonds, without harming their sales. In total M2 (s.a.) went down from FFr78 billion in October 1920 to a minimum of FFr70.3 billion in March 1922[13];

• finally, interest rates were lowered: the discount rate, reduced from 6 per cent to 5.5 per cent in July 1921, was again reduced, to 5 per cent, in March 1922; and the yield on 3 per cent government stock, which had also been disturbed by political developments, fell by a similar amount from a maximum of 5.54 per cent in October 1921 to a minimum of 4.98 per cent in August 1922.

(3) INTERNATIONAL CRISES AND THE HEGEMONY OF THE EXCHANGES 1922–24

In 1922 the 'crisis . . . tended to ease and a degree of stability started to reappear, after (. . .) the wild enthusiasms of the Armistice. It called on producers to equip themselves for the permanent markets which it was becoming possible for them to count on normally'.[14]

The 'hegemony of the exchanges'

Monetary developments were, however, less satisfactory. The period between the end of the first half of 1922 and the election which swept the Cartel des Gauches into power (11 July 1924) was in fact the first classic phase of what Aftalion described as the 'hegemony of the exchanges'.

The external crises – disagreements between the Allies over the attitude to adopt towards the evident 'ill-will' of Germany in the reparations problem, the occupation of the Ruhr at the beginning of 1923 – made it obvious that the forecasts of France's public finances had been excessively optimistic. The franc scarcely checked in its depreciation against the dollar, which stimulated domestic inflation.

The fall in the franc was, however, greater than the rise in prices (on average in 1923 the franc went down by a third, prices went up by a quarter), which was favourable to the external balance. But foreign exchange dealers were hardly aware of this point, which was in any case little known at the time; what they considered important was essentially inflation and the budget deficit. The unfavourable movement of both of these encouraged the fall in the franc. We shall recall here once more Aftalion's description of the phenomenon:

> At the beginning of 1922 the franc ceased its recovery and started a new depreciation which went further than at any previous period. The average monthly index of the dollar rate in Paris (base 100 in 1913), which had reached a minimum of 208 in April, then started to rise again. In December 1922 it reached 267; in December 1923, 373; in February 1924, 437. On 10 March 1924 the dollar rose to 28 francs or an index of 540, the maximum for the period.

Speculation against the franc did not arise from a loss of confidence by residents; essentially it was the action of people abroad who sold francs short; the very abundant supply of funds on the Paris money market allowed them to contract the loans eventually necessary to support their position. Consequently the Minister of Finance requested the French banks to limit their franc loans to non-residents[15]; in addition the Banque de France put up its discount rate to 5.5 per cent and then to 6 per cent in January 1924. When these measures had little effect, the authorities decided to fight speculation on its own ground, the foreign exchange market. In March 1924 the central bank carried out massive sales of foreign currency borrowed secretly from the Rothschild and Morgan banks.[16] These interventions were extremely effective, for between 10 March and 23 April the rate for the pound went down from 115.5 francs to 65.05 francs and the dollar from 28 to 18 francs.

The exchange crisis seemed to have been extinguished; indeed during the whole of the rest of 1924, the first months in office of the Cartel des Gauches (see below) were characterised by a situation of relative calm.

The internal consequences of these developments were as follows:

- a general rise in prices: the 45 item wholesale price index went from 313 in February 1922 to 555 in February 1924 (+77.1 per cent) and the large town retail price index from 313 in August 1922 to 401 in February 1924 (+28.1 per cent);
- an appreciable economic recovery: from 62 at the end of 1921 the general index of industrial production reached 113 in December 1924;
- a need by companies for credit: credits to the economy, which had stabilised at around FFr24 billion between 1920 and 1922, increased sharply; from FFr25 billion in the second quarter of 1922 they went to over FFr32 billion from spring 1924;
- renewed difficulties for the Treasury: the 'illusion' described in section (2) above evaporated. With the renewal of expansion and inflation, liquid savings turned away from Treasury bills and, more generally, from fixed interest securities. The circuit was no longer closed: the Treasury had once more to approach the Banque de France, and this at a time when by contractual agreement the ceiling on advances to the Treasury was being regularly lowered. From 1923 the Treasury had to modify its agreement with the Banque: its repayments were limited[17] and the Bank increased its purchases of bills; moreover, the Treasury had to resort to what in those days appeared to be secret advances: the second-rank banks bought bills, which they then rediscounted with the central bank.

Thus the requirements of the economy and the requirements of the Treasury combined to stimulate an increase in the money stock. The only factor weighing in the opposite direction was the outflows of foreign currency, which brought about an overall stability of the 'gold and foreign currency' counterpart. M2 (s.a.) rose from FFr70.3 billion in March 1922 to FFr75.6 billion in November 1923, then jumped to FFr81.7 billion in March 1924, that is a growth of nearly 30 per cent per year during the months of intense speculation against the franc, with the counterpart showing the greatest expansion being that of claims on the economy. During the same period savings bank deposits fell back slightly. The growth of the money stock slowed down strongly after the return to tranquillity on the foreign exchange market (April 1924).

The development of interest rates reflected only at a distance the serious tensions in the French economy. The discount rate of the Banque de France, which had stood at 5 per cent since March 1922, was still only 6 per cent two years later, but reached 7 per cent from the end of 1924 until July 1925. The yield on 3 per cent stock, which was 4.98 per cent in August 1922, reached 6 per cent in October 1924.

Contemporaries did not wait for Aftalion to note that this period of the 'hegemony of the exchanges' was damaging to the quantity theory. Thus the money market commentator in the recently introduced 'Annual Report' of the *Revue d'Economie Politique* wrote: 'In 1923, in contrast to what was seen in earlier times, an increase in the fiduciary circulation (. . .) did not precede but accompanied the rise in prices: far from being the cause of the latter, it was this time the result'.[18] As for the movements on the exchanges, another commentator considered that they were explained above all by what we nowadays call 'expectations'.[19]

(4) THE CARTEL DES GAUCHES

The political success of the Cartel des Gauches[20] was accompanied by a new period of serious instability. In France, between June 1924 and the call to Poincaré in July 1926, there were two Herriot cabinets, two Painlevé cabinets and a Briand cabinet. The financial situation was so difficult that there were no fewer than seven successive ministers of finance in 1925. In 1926 Caillaux, Minister of Finance in the new Briand cabinet, sacked Robineau and E. Moreau became Governor of the Banque de France.[21]

However, this period was rather favourable from the point of view of economic activity, apart from a certain loss of impetus in 1925, but this was international. Production resumed its growth from 1926.

Thus France experienced an economic recovery, but accompanied by inflation:

- the index of industrial production (n.s.a., 1923–25 = 100) rose from 86.6 at the end of 1923 to 107.2 at the end of 1924. It stagnated at 106.2 in 1925, but rose again to 124 in 1926;

- the budget deficit was reduced, and eliminated in 1925, thanks to supplementary fiscal charges introduced during the budget period;
- the income account was strongly in surplus, but the political situation led to outflows of capital which caused a deficit on the overall balance of payments. Savers were in fact disturbed by the tax plans of the Cartel, particularly by the plan for a tax on capital. The dollar resumed its appreciation against the franc. The index was 367 at the end of 1924, 358 in January 1925, and 790 in July 1926 (Aftalion).

As a result, whilst prices abroad went down again their rise in France accelerated:

- the 45 item wholesale price index, as we saw above, reached a first peak of 555 in February 1924. It went down only for two months, to 459 in April 1924, then rose again, at first slowly, to just over 520 at the beginning of 1925; after that its rise quickened to bring it to a new peak of 854 in July 1926;
- the large town retail price index was 401 in February 1924 and 395 in May, after which it rose continuously, the peak of 647 being reached in November 1926.

This conjuncture of severe pressures, real and/or nominal, in the economy maintained the difficulties of the Treasury, which was 'crowded out' of the market for liquid savings by the requirements of the company sector. The credits to the economy counterpart, which oscillated around FFr25 billion until mid-1923, reached FFr32 billion in 1924, exceeded FFr41 billion at the end of 1925 and reached a peak of FFr49 billion in the middle of 1926, that is, it doubled in three years!

The financial problems of the State were, however, at the heart of the problem and it is worth dwelling on these for a moment. The problems arose less from the size of the deficit, somewhat reduced in 1924 and 1925 when the economic recovery pushed up tax revenues, than from the crisis over the credit of the State.

This crisis was unfortunately inherent in the situation from the moment when the Left came to power with projects for fiscal reform (the capital tax) which terrified not only the business world but also the petite bourgeoisie; its concrete manifestation was a great reluctance to take up government securities of whatever term. Now from the beginning the government, warned by the Banque de France of the 'uncertain future' of the public finances, had to resort to the following procedure on a large scale: the Clémentel loan (Clémentel being the Minister of Finance in the new government) issued in November 1924 was provided with considerable fiscal advantages[22]; the result, in terms of the supply of fresh funds, was, however, disappointing. The danger was accentuated in 1925 by considerable surrenders of National Defence Bonds which significantly exceeded purchases.[23]

The government was thus quickly constrained to solicit advances from the Banque de France, but in order to get around the limit represented by the ceiling for the fiduciary issue it obliged those in charge of the Institut d'Emission at the time to manipulate the accounting position of the Banque.[24]

This artifice lasted until April 1925.[25] Its revelation could only reinforce the reluctance of savers to subscribe to Treasury bills (savings bank deposits also fell). Another unfavourable factor was the fear of a forced consolidation of Treasury bills: a parliamentary bill had actually been tabled with a view to enforcing a consolidation of those falling due on 8 December.

The situation of the public finances was further aggravated by the fact that a large amount of previously issued medium-term bills was due for redemption during the financial year 1925.[26]

The year 1925 and the first half of 1926 were thus particularly difficult: the total claims of the banking system on the Treasury, which had been stable at around FFr47 billion since 1920, went up to FFr61 billion at the end of 1925; claims on the economy, which contributed to the speculation against the franc (see below), grew by 26 per cent in 1925 and at a similar rate during the first half alone of 1926. The money stock, which had hardly varied between April and December 1924, increased by 47.5 per cent between the latter date and August 1926.

The depreciation in the exchange rate over the same period was considerable, but in contrast to what had been observed during the earlier crisis of November 1923-March 1924 the speculation was essentially by residents. The government implicitly recognised this since it offered savers a 4 per cent perpetual loan guaranteed against exchange rate fluctuations, but this too enjoyed hardly any success. The dollar rate went from 18 francs at the end of 1924 to more than 40 francs in August 1926.

The American banks refused to help, thereby showing that in their view the crisis was not a passing squall as in 1923–24 but a movement which owed its origin to 'crowd psychology' and could only be interrupted by the return of 'confidence'.

In spite of these developments interest rates did not 'explode'. The discount rate of the Banque de France, which had stood, it will be remembered, at 6 per cent since the beginning of 1924, reached a peak of 7 per cent at the end of that year, before returning to 6 per cent in July 1925. The yield on 3 per cent government stock went up to a peak of 7 per cent in June 1925 and was only at 6.35 per cent a year later. However, the net of tax yield on new bonds issued, which had oscillated around 6.5–7 per cent since 1921, rose to a peak of 9.45 per cent in February 1926. It was at 8.95 per cent in June.

BANK LIQUIDITY

During the war the factors governing bank liquidity had evolved profoundly. The fiduciary circulation had greatly increased, but the lending of the Banque de France to the Treasury, which had been nil in 1913, reached nearly FFr30 billion in 1919, in such a way that the net debt of the banks to the Institut d'Emission was only moderately increased: in relative terms this indebtedness was quite slight; the market was therefore practically 'outside the bank'.

This situation was little changed until 1924. From 1925 banking liquidity increased considerably and the money market 'went out of the bank', first in 1925, under the influence of a new injection of lending from the Banque to the Treasury, and then from 1926, because of the reversal of expectations about the franc and the resulting inflows of capital.

TABLE 3.2 *The financing of the French economy 1919–26 (FFr billion)*

	1919	*1920*	*1921*	*1922*	*1923*	*1924*	*1925*	*1926*
Sources of financing								
Balance of State budget[1]	26.63	17.14	0.28	9.76	11.87	7.12	1.51	−1.09
War damages	—	13.08	17.77	14.18	12.46	8.03	5.27	4.93
Credits								
Bank	8.68	−1.87	−0.39	1.2	4.46	1.99	8.87	−0.4
Non-bank[2]	3.7	5.20	6.50	2.50	4.80	3.20	2.08	3.22
External[3]	−4.21	−11.25	—	3.64	−0.44	5.04	—	14.32
Investments								
Bond subscriptions	9.67	33.86	18.81	22.91	21.20	9.72	2.24	7.12
Net subscriptions of Treasury bills by the public[4]		−13		14.99		10.40	−9.3	−1.55
Deposits in savings banks	1.71	0.95	1.51	1.14	0.70	0.44	1.79	1.87
ΔM2	21.28	4.5	1.15	0.19	4.68	3.68	22.21	13.59
* (of which banknotes)	(6.51)	(0.7)	(−1.09)	(−1.39)	(1.54)	(2.84)	(9.27)	(2.99)
Residual	5.13	−15.88	—	−2.18		1.14	0.79	0.04

1. A surplus reduces the supply of financing (– sign); a deficit increases it (+ sign).
2. Including net issues of bonds by non-financial companies.
3. Estimates according to Sauvy (1984).
4. Estimates.

TABLE 3.3 *Summary of monetary and financial data 1919–26 (end-period totals, averages for interest rates) (FFr billion)*

	1919	*1920*	*1921*	*1922*	*1923*	*1924*	*1925*	*1926*
M2	66.8	71.30	72.45	72.64	77.32	81.03	103.21	116.80
Net assets in gold and foreign exchange	7.2	6.44	6.42	6.40	6.42	6.43	6.43	10.05
Claims on the Treasury	36.85	46.74	46.11	46.13	47.12	47.47	60.90	61.63
	(+76.6%)	(+26.8%)	(−1.3%)	—	(+2.1%)	(+0.7%)	(+28.3%)	(+1.2%)
Claims on the economy	26.82	24.43	24.03	25.82	30.28	32.27	41	47.78
	(+73.4%)	(−8.9%)	(−1.6%)	—	(+17.3%)	(+6.6%)	(+27%)	(+16.5%)
Deposits in savings banks	7.23	8.18	9.69	10.85	11.56	12	13.79	15.66
(for reference, ceiling on deposits, in francs)	5000F (18 October)						7500 (25 April)	
Discount rate	5%	5.73%	5.79%	5.11%	5%	5.99%	6.33%	6.58%
Yield on bonds	5.18%	5.80%	6.10%	5.71%	5.99%	7.01%	9.11%	8.76%
New issues of negotiable securities:								
shares	3.61	10.05	4.81	3.01	4.39	7.84	5.60	5.56
bonds	9.64	33.86	18.81	22.91	21.20	9.72	2.24	7.12
(of which government bonds)	(6.16)	(27.76)	(8.73)	(16.04)	(15.30)	(6.47)	—	(3)
National income	—	143	115	137	162	213	230	315
Income velocity (national income/M2)	—	2	1.6	1.91	2.14	2.61	2.49	2.79

TABLE 3.4 *Factors affecting bank liquidity 1919–26 (FFr billion)*

	situation at end		*changes in*							*situation at end*
	1913	*1919*	*1920*	*1921*	*1922*	*1923*	*1924*	*1925*	*1926*	*1926*
A) Notes in circulation and accounts with the Banque de France[1]	−6.8	−41.1	−1.3	+2.2	+1.9	−1.6	−2.6	−10.6	−4.8	−58
B) Gold and foreign exchange	+4.2	+7.2	−0.8	—	—	—	—	—	+3.6	+10.2
C) Claims of the Banque de France on the Treasury	—	+28.8	+0.4	+0.9	−1.2	—	−1	+14.1	−0.9	+39.5
D) Miscellaneous[2]	+0.3	+1.3	−0.5	−0.6	−1.3	+0.5	+1.4	−1.8	+2.1	−1.1
E) Portfolio of the Banque de France[3]	+2.3	+3.8	+2.2	−0.8	+0.4	+1.1	+2.2	−1.7	—	+7.2
F) (for reference) Banks' reserves and deposits at the Banque de France	—	2.2	+1.2	−2.3	+2.3	+0.3	+0.4	+2.3	+0.8	7.4
F-E) Free liquidity of the banks (+) or net indebtedness to the Banque de France (–)	−2.3	−1.6	−0.9	−1.5	+1.9	−0.8	−1.8	+4	+0.8	+0.2

A + sign indicates a positive effect on banking liquidity, a – sign a negative effect.
1. Including the deposits of the banks.
2. Elements accounted for under the 'miscellaneous' heading of the Banque de France's accounts, and in particular foreign exchange operations.
3. Credits to banks, companies and private individuals.

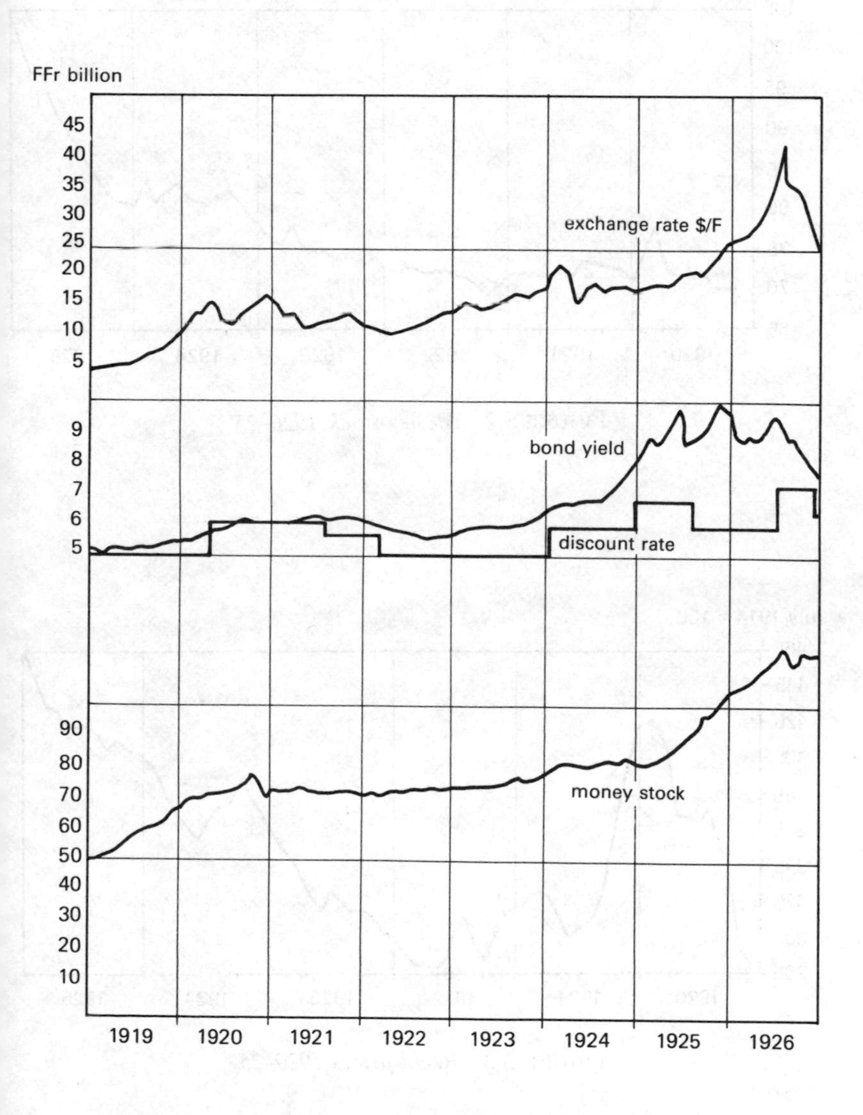

FIGURE 3.1 *Exchange rate, interest rates and money 1919–26*

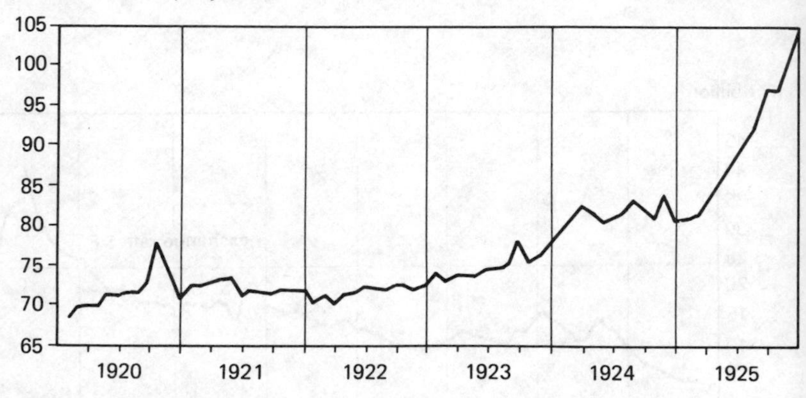

FIGURE 3.2 *Money stock 1920–25*

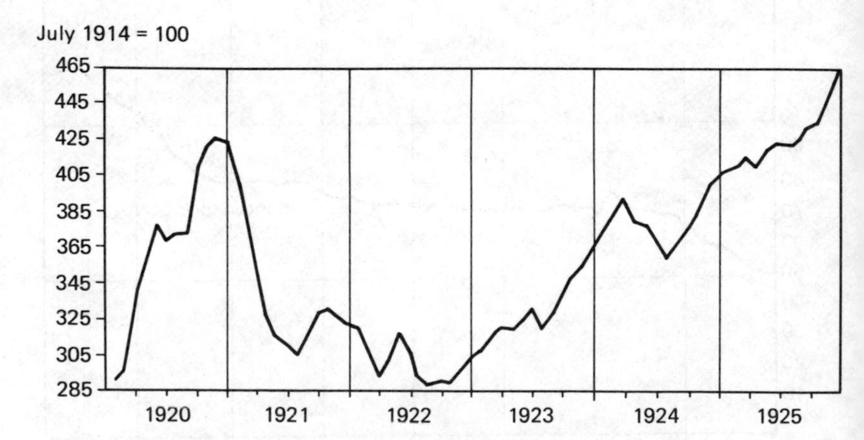

FIGURE 3.3 *Retail prices 1920–25*

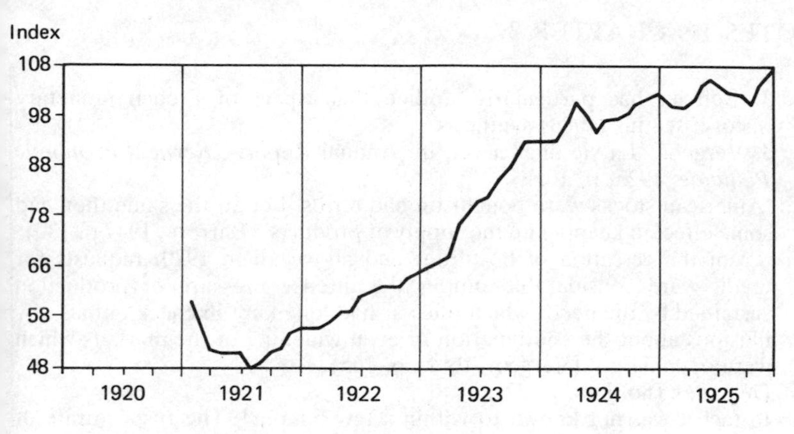

FIGURE 3.4 *Turnover tax 1920–25*

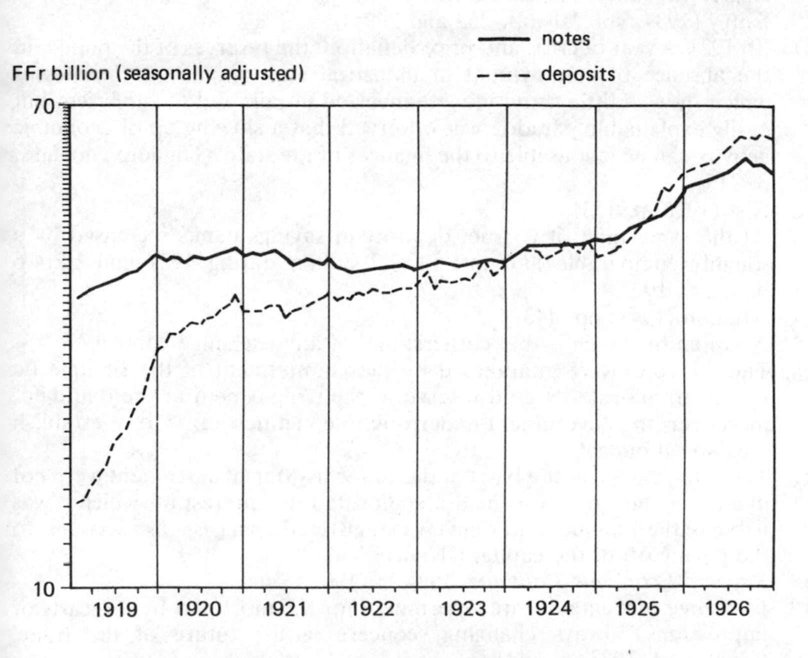

FIGURE 3.5 *Notes and bank deposits 1919–26*

NOTES TO CHAPTER 3

1. J. Bouvier has particularly studied this aspect of French monetary history; see his (1984) synthesis.
2. J. Vergeot, 'La vie financière', in 'Annual Report', *Revue d'Economie Politique*, 1923, p. 165.
3. 'American stocks were bought on bad terms, but all the same they had some effect in keeping up the supply of products' (Barrère, 1947 p. 130).
4. 'From the cessation of hostilities and above all in 1920, requests for credit were considerable, under the intense pressure of production sustained by the needs which the war had long kept in check but also by illusions about the continuation or even widening of the markets which were opening up' (Vergeot, ibid., p. 165).
5. Delanney (no date, p. 22).
6. In fact it was not known to within a few billions! 'The Inspectorate of Finances asserted that it was in error by 7 billions too much' (Gignoux, no date p. 215).
7. Aftalion (1948, p. 438).
8. The gold equivalent of the franc thus weakened, unofficially since convertibility was still suspended, from 276mg to 137mg.
9. According to the definition (itself classic) of Barrère (1947 p. 15), a reconversion crisis is 'a crisis which arises when the war economy is transformed into a peace economy'.
10. Sauvy (1984, vol. III, pp. 253 and 269).
11. 'In 1921, a year of crisis and price deflation, the reserves of the public, in the absence of employment in industrial and commercial businesses which showed little activity, were invested in bills and the apparent but easily explainable paradox was observed that a slowing up of economic activity can be favourable to the finances of the state' (Gignoux, no date, p. 215).
12. Rist (1926, p. 153).
13. At the same time, it is true, deposits in savings banks increased by a roughly comparable amount: FFr2.7 billion during 1921 and FFr4.6 billion in 1922.
14. Aftalion (1948, pp. 443–4).
15. A limitation which is the 'cornerstone' of any exchange control.
16. These credits were guaranteed by the commitment of the Banque de France to allocate its gold reserve to their repayment at the due date; moreover, the government undertook to enact new taxes to re-establish a balanced budget.
17. The repayments on the basis of the François-Marsal agreement were not in any way effective, for the State allocated the interest for which it was liable to the Banque, and which was registered on a suspense account, to the paying off of the capital advances.
18. *Revue d'Economie Politique*, 1924, p. 190.
19. Exchange movements 'are determined for the most part by forecasts or impressions, always changing, concerning the future of the franc' (Guébhard, 1923, p. 143).

20. Success but not victory. The Cartel proper held only 287 seats, whilst a majority in the Chamber was 291. It had to look for additional support from the centre (Jeanneney, 1982, p. 14).
21. Moreau (1954). See also Bredin (1980).
22. Its effective yield was 8.6 per cent.
23. Were some of these surrenders 'organised'? In October 1924 the Prefect of Savoie reported a proposal by the Bishop of Maurienne on the organisation by the Catholics, on a concerted date, of a collective surrender of National Defence Bonds (Jeanneney, 1982).
24. It was essentially a question of manipulating the accounting lags between the branch accounts and the head office account so as to reduce the peaks in the circulation at the ends of the months, a procedure to which earlier governments had had recourse, but not continuously and in order to avoid speculation against the franc. Another expedient which did not impair the accounting regularity of the balance sheet consisted of raking in the maximum number of banknotes in the banks and public offices and returning them to the central bank.
25. The secret was too heavy to bear for Robineau, who disclosed it to the Council of Regents of the Banque in December 1924. The latter remonstrated sharply with the government, which in order to try to regain the confidence of savers took it into its head to suppress the 'coupon slip' instituted by the previous Bloc National government to counter fraudulent declarations of interest on negotiable securities. To justify this suppression, which was surprising on the part of a left-wing government, the public authorities invoked 'Mélanie the cook, who put her savings into securities and has the right not to know how to read!' (Sauvy).
26. The left accused the governments in power before them of having planted these time bombs in a Machiavellian way in anticipation of its electoral success.

4 1926–31: The Strong Franc

THE 'POINCARÉ STABILISATION'

Over and above the essential element of the return of confidence[1] – which was marked by an upward correction of the franc-dollar rate from an annual average of FFr31 to the rate of FFr25 that was then maintained through the whole period – the 'Poincaré stabilisation' was, on the technical plane, above all the result of the intensification of the already restrictive stance of fiscal policy and of a consolidation of the floating debt.

The budgetary surpluses recorded in 1926 and the following year were equally the consequence of the highly inflationary conjuncture of 1925. In addition there were new taxes, mainly indirect, to reassure investors.[2]

The government of 'national union'[3] applied the recommendations of the Committee of Experts[4] which had proved a stumbling-block to its two precursors (the cabinets of Briand and Herriot). First Moreau and then Poincaré were not straightaway convinced of the harmfulness of a policy of deflation of the kind pursued in Britain. Quesnay, director of studies at the Banque de France, and C. Rist had to wage a long siege. Let us recall the main outlines of the policy which was adopted:

(a) the stabilisation of the currency was the condition *sine qua non* for the consolidation of the floating debt.[5] This stabilisation involved the following points:

- the balancing of the budget, in fact the move into surplus, which allowed a reduction in the advances of the Banque de France, thus exerting a contractionary influence on the money stock;
- the balancing of the external position, attained by internal effort and the return of previously exported capital, attracted in particular by high interest rates: the Banque's discount rate was thus raised to the unprecedented level of 7.5 per cent;
- the consolidation of the floating debt, rendered more solemn by the passing on 7 August 1926 at Versailles by the two chambers in

TABLE 4.1 *Major annual statistics 1927–31*

	1927	*1928*	*1929*	*1930*	*1931*
GDP (% change)	−1.2	5.7	8.7	−3.0	−4.1
Industrial production (% change)	−12.7	15.4	9.5	0.4	−11.4
	—	—	(10.8)	(0.0)	(−14.1)
Balance of payments (FFr million):					
Trade account	−304	−4480	−10 011	−12 973	−13 262
Income account	7746	5720	4489	308	−3012
Capital account	−7746	−5720	−4489	−308	+3012
(of which reparations)	(4200)	(5180)	(6700)	(7084)	(2600)
FFr/$	25.48	25.50	25.53	25.48	25.51
Prices (% change)					
Wholesale (45 articles)	−12.3	0.6	−1.7	−12.8	−15.0
Retail, Paris (13 articles)	0.4	−1.3	11.3	0.5	−0.4
Singer-Kerel	9.7	−2.0	6.0	2.5	−0.9
Balance of the State budget (FFr million)	217	3929	4934 (15 months)	−4918	
M2 (% change)	6.4	24.8	5.7	5.6	−0.7

SOURCES GDP – Carré, Dubois et Malinvaud (1972); industrial production – Statistique Générale de la France (1932), between brackets construction-inclusive index, with 1938 weights – INSEE (1966); balance of payments – Meynial (1925), annual reports of the *Revue d'Economie Politique*, reproduced in Sauvy (1984, vol. III); exchange rates and prices, Statistique Générale de la France (1932), Singer-Kerel (1961); budget – Sauvy (1984, vol. III; including the 'extraordinary' or 'special' elements); M2 – authors' calculations.

Congress together of a constitutional law setting up a 'Caisse (autonome) de gestion des Bons de la Défense Nationale et d'amortissement de la dette publique'. This agency benefited from the allocation of certain fiscal receipts (essentially those of the tobacco monopoly as well as the *eventual* budgetary surpluses).[6]

(b) The *de facto* stabilisation of the exchange rate, achieved from December onwards, was a necessary prelude to the return to gold convertibility. As the inflows of floating capital persisted and were in danger of bringing about an overvaluation of the franc, stabilisation of the parity by law was decided upon in August 1928. 'Putting the old bimetallism out of its misery, the provisions (of the law) were that the franc should henceforth weigh 65.5 mg of gold of millesimal fineness 900. This parity was established by the introduction of convertibility for ingots of gold (and not coin).'[7] The gold reserve had to be equal to at least 35 per cent of the monetary base. In addition the Banque de France reserved the right to buy precious metals and foreign currency in the market, even if this led to the issue of banknotes above the legal ceiling. This is what happened particularly in 1928, causing a rapid growth of money under this heading.

However, this year appears to be an exception for this period. Overall, the return to stable prices and the 'crisis', which lowered tax receipts, led to a renewal of bond issues and a quasi-stagnation of the money stock.

In parallel with this, and throughout the period, savings bank deposits increased considerably – at an average of 25 per cent a year between 1926 and 1930 as against 8.5 per cent during the three previous years.

BEFORE THE CRISIS

As far as economic activity, prices and money were concerned, three subperiods can be distinguished between July 1926 and 1931:

- a first subperiod of a twelvemonth, between the arrival of Poincaré in office and the middle of 1927, during which budgetary restrictions led to diminished activity (the unadjusted monthly index went from 128 in December 1926 to 115 a year later); to price reductions (the 45 item wholesale price index fell from 854 in July 1926 to 600 in October 1927 and the large town retail price index from 647 in November 1926 to 522 in February 1928); and to a decrease in credits to the economy and, to a more limited extent, in the money stock:

M2 (s.a.) was reduced from FFr119.6 billion in August 1926 to FFr114.4 billion in May 1927. Within the counterparts an inflow of external capital was offset to the extent of some FFr15 billion by a fall in claims on the economy, due to the halt to speculation on the franc and the inflow of liquid funds from abroad;

- a second subperiod, of recovery, covered 1928 and 1929: the index of industrial production (n.s.a.) was 144 at the end of 1929 as against 115, as we have seen, two years earlier; wholesale prices were at 653 in March 1929, and retail prices at 593 in November of that year; finally M2 (s.a.) increased, although less and less rapidly, until the summer of 1930, reaching FFr173.3 billion in August of that year (that is a rise of about 50 per cent since mid-1927). In face of the sterling crisis and the stock exchange collapse in New York, capital continued to flow into Paris. The gold counterpart increased continuously, but until the end of 1929 credits to the economy grew at a similar rate;
- during the third subperiod, from 1930, France was struck by the 'crisis'[8]: the index of industrial production went from 144 in December 1929 to 134 12 months later and to an average of 96 for 1932; wholesale prices were at 498 in December 1930, and retail at 569 in February 1931; they then rose under the impact of the protectionist measures introduced to support agricultural prices; the demand for credits by companies diminished and M2 (s.a.) went down, from FFr173 billion in August 1930 to FFr163.8 billion in December 1931. In particular the banking system, which was affected by a series of bankruptcies,[9] contracted – an unfavourable situation for bank deposits – whilst there was an increased hoarding of Banque de France banknotes (their share in M2 went in a single year, 1931, from 44 per cent to 51 per cent) and of deposits in savings banks. At the end of 1928, in a period of confidence, the total of savings bank deposits (both ordinary and postal savings banks) stood at FFr27 billion. It was FFr31 billion a year later, FFr40 billion in 1930 and more than FFr50 billion in 1932, and, partly reflecting a considerable raising of the deposit ceiling, peaked at around FFr60 billion in 1933. The demands of the State, hitherto small, increased once more. Claims on the Treasury went from FFr12 billion, their level in 1928–30, to FFr18.9 billion in 1931 and FFr26–29 billion from 1932 to 1935. New issues of government bonds, according to the statistics of the Crédit Lyonnais, reached their lowest level in 1930–31 (FFr0.5 billion per annum); they went up to FFr5 billion in 1932, FFr12.4 billion in 1933, FFr10.8 billion in 1934 and FFr7.3 billion in 1935.

TABLE 4.2 *The financing of the French economy 1927–31 (FFr billion)*

	1927	*1928*	*1929*	*1930*	*1931*	
Sources of financing						
Balance of national budget[1]	−0.22	−3.93	−4.93	−0.01	−4.92[2]	
War damages	4.78	3.12	3.3		2.08[2]	
Credits				5.38		
Bank	−1.37	+37.54	12.23	−5.59	−16.57	
Non-bank[3]	5.60	6.27	9.8	15.65	12.6	
External[4]	16.40	8.28	4.65	11.85	10.50	
						Investments
	9.98	17.72	4.99	15.77	13.35	Bond subscriptions
	−6.44	−1.78	11.28	7.10	−14.80	Net subscriptions of Treasury bills
	5.62	5.77	4.92	6.63	12.27	Deposits in savings banks
	14.65	29.73	0.45	8.78	−5.51	ΔM2
	(3.11)	(6.30)	(5.11)	(8.38)	(9.16)	* (of which banknotes)
	1.38	−0.16		−4.74		Residual

1. A surplus reduces the supply of financing (– sign); a deficit increases it (+ sign).
2. Displaced financial years, from March to March, until 1933.
3. Including net issues of bonds by non-financial companies.
4. Assets in gold and foreign exchange of the Banque de France, excluding the effect of the devaluation of 1928.

TABLE 4.3 *Summary of monetary and financial data 1927–31 (end-period totals, averages for interest rates) (FFr billion)*

	1927	*1928*	*1929*	*1930*	*1931*
M2	131.55	161.17	161.53	170.21	164.70
Net assets in gold and foreign exchange[1]	32.67	63.65	68.45	80.30	90.80
Claims on the Treasury[1]	47.14	14.24	12.50	12.47	18.92
	(−23.5%)	(−69.8%)	(−12.2%)	—	(+51.7%)
Claims on the economy	46.79	86.12	99.60	92.94	75.17
	(—)	(+84.1%)	(+15.7%)	(−6.7%)	(−19.2%)
Deposits in savings banks	21.28	27.05	31.97	38.60	50.87
(for reference, ceiling on deposits, in francs)	7500 F (25.4.25)				20 000 F (31.3.31)
Discount rate	5.22	3.53	3.50	2.72	2.11
Yield on bonds	6.58	5.33	4.80	3.82	3.70
New issues of negotiable securities					
shares	7.86	14.06	18.26	10.85	5.39
bonds	9.28	17.72	4.99	15.77	13.35
(of which government bonds)	(3.25)	(10.76)	—	(0.43)	(0.68)
National income	318	337	393	395	361
Income velocity (national income/M2)	2.62	2.21	2.48	2.35	2.17

1. Taking account of the devaluation of the franc on 25 June 1928, which produced a capital gain on the gold reserve of FFr 16.6 billion, allocated to the repayment of the advances made to the State by the Banque de France.

As far as interest rates were concerned, their movements were less erratic. The inflow of capital and then the lower level of activity favoured a relatively constant rate of decline: the Banque de France's discount rate, which had returned to 6.5 per cent in December 1926, went by stages to 3.5 per cent in June 1928, 3 per cent a year later, and finally to 2.5 per cent, its trough, in 1931. The yield in Paris for fixed-income securities had approached 10 per cent in November 1925 (9.97 per cent); it ended 1926 at 7.70 per cent, 1927 at 6.07 per cent, 1928 at 5.13 per cent, 1929 at 4.25 per cent and 1930 at 3.95 per cent. It reached its trough of 3.48 per cent in August 1931.

THE NEW PRESENTATION OF THE ACCOUNTS OF THE BANQUE DE FRANCE

The monetary law of 25 June 1928 was the occasion of a clarification of the method by which the accounts of the Banque de France were presented. Over the years this presentation had become burdened with various headings, which were often far from explicit, and which moreover represented operations of doubtful liquidity.

An initial reorganisation dealt with the headings representing operations in gold and with abroad. The item 'Gold Reserve' [Encaisse-or], which was substituted for the item 'Banque's reserves' [Encaisse de la Banque], comprised the entire stock of gold in the possession of the Banque, including therefore that purchased to stabilise the franc in 1927 and 1928 which had hitherto been accounted for under a 'miscellaneous' item on the assets side.

The stock of silver no longer appeared in the reserve; it was handed over (under the assets item 'Demonetised silver coin for remelting' [Pièces d'argent démonétisées à refondre]) to the State which was the issuer of metal coin; the Banque put these coins into circulation; its claim on the State in this connection was recorded under the item 'silver and other coin' [Monnaies d'argent et de billon].

An item 'liquid assets abroad' [Disponibilités à vue à l'étranger] was created; it collected together the foreign currency assets acquired by the Banque, most of which had previously been accounted for within the 'miscellaneous' item on the assets side.

One heading disappeared, the 'Treasury bills discounted as State advances to foreign governments' [Bons du Trésor escomptés pour avances de l'Etat à des gouvernements étrangers], a completely irrecoverable claim, which was taken over by the newly created Caisse Autonome d'Amortissement; the latter issued, on this occasion, three month cash vouchers negotiable at the Banque.

A clarification of the relations between the Banque and the State was then brought into operation. The 'Advances to the State' [Avances à l'Etat] were amortised thanks to the accounting appreciation produced by the revaluation of the gold reserve, but an interest-free loan to the State of FFr3.2 billion was agreed, which was to be repaid on the expiry of the Banque's privileged position as bank of issue. The other relationships with the State were simply and clearly redefined, on the assets side by the minimal but permanent advance which was represented by the Banque's assets in postal chequing accounts, on the liabilities side by the current account of the Treasury. Still on the liabilities side, the current account of the Caisse Autonome d'Amortissement brought together the various accounts for the amortisation of advances to the State.

BANK LIQUIDITY

The situation sketched out in 1926 was confirmed and amplified. Until 1928 massive inflows of capital were recorded, which largely compensated for the State's repayment of its indebtedness to the Banque de France; the movements of the fiduciary circulation had overall a moderately restrictive effect. In 1928 the net indebtedness of the banks to the Institut d'Emission was practically nil.

From 1929, the restrictive effect of the fiduciary circulation (and secondarily that of the deposits of companies and individuals with the Banque de France) was considerably strengthened: the economic crisis accentuated the preference of economic agents for material (or 'official' – meaning accounts with the Banque de France) forms of money. However, the inflows of capital persisted throughout the period, the franc being considered as a currency of refuge. Moreover, in 1931 the assistance given by the Banque de France to the Treasury increased once more, and finally from this year business stagnation led to a contraction in bank credits, the banks thus accumulating amongst their assets large quantities of unused liquid funds. In addition in 1931 the banks were overall net creditors of the Banque de France.

TABLE 4.4 *The old presentation of the accounts of the Banque de France*

BANQUE DE FRANCE & SUCCURSALES

SITUATION HEBDOMADAIRE

ACTIF		*AU 5 AVRIL 1928 MATIN*	*AU 29 MARS 1928 MATIN*
Encaisse de la Banque		5.886.779.283 42	5.886.782.745 42
Disponibilités et Avoir à l'étranger: Créance sur la Banque de l'État Russe (Convention du 26 Octobre 1917, art. 3.)		mémoire	mémoire
Disponibilités et Avoir à l'étranger: Disponibilités à l'étranger		59.940.364 61	56.592.232 41
Achats d'or, d'argent & de devises (Loi du 7 Août 1926)		2.432.147.700 50	2.430.143.244 99
Effets échus hier à recevoir ce jour		2.938.809 75	2.885.060 71
Comptes courants postaux		358.824.007 93	433.950.254 98
Portefeuille de Paris: Effets sur Paris	598.273.251 61	611.905.523 59	681.949.305 91
Portefeuille de Paris: Effets sur l'Étranger	12.733.564 66		
Portefeuille de Paris: Effets du Trésor remis à l'encaissement	898.707 32		
Portefeuille des Succursales: Effets sur place	1.970.591.564 86	1.997.967.899 »	1.663.084.394 »
Portefeuille des Succursales: Effetsdu Trésor remis à l'encaissement	27.376.334 14		
Avances sur lingots & monnaies à Paris		»	»
Avances sur lingots & monnaies dans les Succursales		»	»
Avances sur titres à Paris		205.380.710 99	201.594.179 49
Avances sur titres dans les Succursales		1.520.724.451 »	1.509.214.181 »
Avances à l'État (Loi du 9 Juin 1857, Convention du 29 Mars 1878, Loi du 15 Juin 1878) prorogée, lois des 17 Nóvembre 1897, 29 Décembre 1911 et 20 Décembre 1918).		200.000.000 »	200.000.000 »
Avances à l'État (Lois des 5 Août et 26 Décembre 1914, 10 Juillet 1915, 16 Février et 4 Octobre 1917, 5 Avril et 7 Juin 1918, 5 Mars et 17 Juillet 1919, 22 Avril et 31 Décembre 1920, 31 Déc. 1922, 27 Déc. 1923, 31 Déc. 1924, 15 Avril, 27 Juin, 23 Novembre & 4 Décembre 1925, 7 Août 1926, Décret du 13 Juin 1927 et Convention du 28 Décembre 1927).		24.200.000.000 »	23.150.000.000 »
Bons du Trésor français escomptés pour avances de l'État à des Gouvernements étrangers (Lois des 1 or Avril et 29 Décembre 1915, 15 Février et 4 Août 1917, 22 Mars et 20 Décembre 1918 et 15 Mars 1928).		5.930.000.000 »	5.930.000.000 »
Rentes de la réserve: Loi du 17 Mai 1834		(*a*) 10.000.000 »	(*a*) 10.000.000 »
Rentes de la réserve: Ex-Banques départementales		(*b*) 2.980.750 14	(*b*) 2.980.750 14
Rentes disponibles		212.436.430 90	212.436.430 90
Rentes immobilisées (Loi du 9 Juin 1857) (y compris les 9.125.000 de la réserve)		(*c*) 100.000.000 »	(*c*) 100.000.000 »
Hôtel et mobilier de la Banque		(*d*) 4.000.000 »	(*d*) 4.000.000 »

Immeubles des Succursales	214 491.821 03	214.350.612 88
Dépenses d'administration de la Banque et des Succursales	46.645.971 27	42.746.877 93
Emploi de la réserve spéciale	(*e*) 8.156.464 98	(*e*) 8.156.464 98
Divers	26.755.736.365 17	26.001.287.502 11
	70.761.056.554 28	68.742.154.237 85
PASSIF		
Capital de la Banque	182.500.000 »	182.500.000 »
Bénéfices en addition au capital (Lois des 9 Juin 1857 et 17 Novembre 1897)	272.696.110 93	272.696.110 93
Réserves mobilières — Loi du 17 Mai 1834	(*a*) 10.000.000 »	(*a*) 10.000.000 »
Réserves mobilières — Ex-banques départementales	(*b*) 2.980.750 14	(*b*) 2.980.750 14
Réserves mobilières — Loi du 9 Juin 1857	(*c*) 9.125.000 »	(*c*) 9.125.000 »
Réserve immobilière de la Banque	(*d*) 4.000.000 »	(*d*) 4.000.000 »
Réserve spéciale	(*e*) 8.407.444 16	(*e*) 8.407.444 16
Compte d'amortissement (Lois des 26 Décembre 1914 & 20 Décembre 1918)		
Garantie d'amortissement (Convention du 26 Octobre 1917, article 3)	mémoire	mémoire
Excédent affecté à l'amortissement des avances à l'État	383.923.701 72	372.562.705 01
Cte annexe d'intérêts du c[te] d'amortissement (Loi du 20 Décembre 1918)	19.412.089 01	19.412.089 01
Billets au porteur en circulation	60.293.025.525 »	58.580.245.890 »
Arrérages de valeurs transférées ou déposées	75.250.612 12	61.660.094 03
Billets à ordre récépissés payables à Paris et dans les Succursales	349.297 15	371.228 70
Compte courant du Trésor	21.615.275 52	4.726.900 61
Comptes courants et Comptes de Dépôts de fonds à Paris	6.317.029.997 86	6.713.727.302 58
Comptes courants et Comptes de Dépôts de fonds dans les Succursales	1.635.046 600 »	1.672.969.429 »
Dividendes à payer	3.995.558 »	4.236.028 »
Escomptes et intérêts divers à Paris et dans les Succursales	53.315.233 84	49.145.251 62
Réescompte du dernier semestre à Paris et dans les Succursales	9.159.213 »	9.159.213 »
Divers	1.459.224.145 83	764.228.801 06
	70.761.056.554 28	68.742.154.237 85

Certifié conforme aux écritures:

Le Gouverneur de la Banque de France,

E. MOREAU.

TABLE 4.5 *The new presentation of the accounts of the Banque de France*

BANQUE DE FRANCE
SIÈGE CENTRAL & SUCCURSALES

SITUATION HEBDOMADAIRE

ACTIF		AU 6 JUILLET 1928	AU 29 JUIN 1928
Encaisse-or (monnaies et lingots)		29 175 976 951.82	28 990 033 416.24
Monnaies d'argent et de billion		200 342.19	202 686.92
Comptes courants postaux		476 682 422.88	325 690 193.77
Disponibilités à vue à l'étranger		15 920 276 401.20	15 559 114 146.25
Devises en report		7 819 849 288	8 935 623 918
Avances sur lingots et monnaies d'or		71 802 058.85	53 069 413.08
PORTEFEUILLE COMMERCIAL ET D'EFFETS PUBLICS:			
Effets de commerce escomptés sur la France.	2 188 379 693.30	2 206 391 461.29	3 582 658 512.38
Effets de commerce escomptés sur l'Étranger.	18 011 767.99		
Effets négociables achetés en France	»	12 684 965 222.87	11 686 441 030.75
Effets négociables achetés à l'Étranger	12 684 965 222.87		
Avances sur titres		1 961 855 174.95	1 837 039 991.62
Bons négociables de la Caisse autonome d'amortissement *(Convention du 23 Juin 1928).*		5 930 000 000	5 930 000 000
Prêts sans intérêts à l'État *(Loi du 9 Juin 1857; convention du 29 Mars 1878; loi du 13 Juin 1878 prorogée, lois des 17 Novembre 1897, 29 Décembre 1911, 20 Décembre 1918 et 25 Juin 1928).*		3 200 000 000	3 200 000 000
Rentes pourvues d'affectations spéciales *(Loi du 17 Mai 1834; décrets des 27 Avril et 2 Mai 1848; loi du 9 Juin 1857).*		112 980 750.14	112 980 750.14
Hôtel et mobilier de la Banque et immeubles des succursales		219 399 246.02	219 353 460.32
Piéces d'argent démonétisées à refondre		732 115 960.42	732 115 930.42
Divers		1 329 676 752.55	1 308 662 573.47
Total		81 842 172 033.18	82 472 986 023.36

PASSIF

Capital de la Banque		182 500 000	182 500 000
Bénéfices en addition au capital		272 696 110.93	272 696 110 93
(Lois des 9 Juin 1857 et 17 Novembre 1897).			
Réserves mobilières légales		22 105 750.14	22 105 750.14
(Loi du 17 Mai 1834; décrets des 27 Avril et 2 Mai 1848; loi du 9 Juin 1857).			
Réserve immobilière		4 000 000	4 000 000
ENGAGEMENTS A VUE:			
Billets au porteur en circulation		60 295 093 855	60 628 093 645
Comptes courants créditeurs:			
Compte courant du Trésor public	5 989 389 694.42		
Compte courant de la Caisse autonome d'amortissement	620 317 175.34	12 400 979 215.03	11 781 992 390.02
Comptes courants et comptes de dépôts de fonds	5 487 773 510.46		
Dispositions et autres engagements à vue	303 498 834.81		
Engagements provenant de reports sur devises		7 819 849 288	8 935 623 918
Divers		844 947 814.08	645 974 209.27
Total		81 842 172 033.18	82 472 986 023.36

Certifié conforme aux écritures:
LE GOUVERNEUR DE LA BANQUE DE FRANCE,
E. MOREAU.

TABLE 4.6 *Factors affecting bank liquidity 1927–31 (FFr billion)*

	situation at end 1926	*changes in*					*situation at end 1931***
		1927	*1928*	*1929*	*1930*	*1931*	
A) Notes in circulation and accounts with the Banque de France[1]	−58	−8.5	−2.1	−5.4	−11.5	−20.8	−106.3
B) Gold and foreign exchange	+10.2	+22.6	+15.4*	+3.8	+11.9	+10.5	+90.2
C) Claims of the Banque de France on the Treasury	+39.5	−15.3	−11*	+0.6	−1	+8.8	+5.8
D) Miscellaneous[2]	+1.1	+4.4	−5.2	−2.7	−0.3	+4.2	+1.5
E) Portfolio of the Banque de France[3]	+7.2	−3.2	+2.9	+3.7	+0.9	−2.7	+8.8
F) (for reference) Banks' reserves and deposits at the Banque de France	7.4	+3.2	−4.3	+0.2	+2	+12.8	21.4
F-E) Free liquidity of the banks (+) or net indebtedness to the Banque de France (−)	+0.2	+6.4	−7.2	−3.5	+1.1	+15.5	+12.6

A + sign indicate a positive effect on banking liquidity, a − sign a negative effect.

1. Including the deposits of the banks.
2. Elements accounted for under the 'miscellaneous' heading of the Banque de France's accounts, and in particular foreign exchange operations.
3. Credits to banks, companies and private individuals.

* Not taking account of the revaluation of the gold reserve and of its allocation of the amortisation of the Banque de France's advances to the State.

** Accounting figures, after revaluation of the gold reserve.

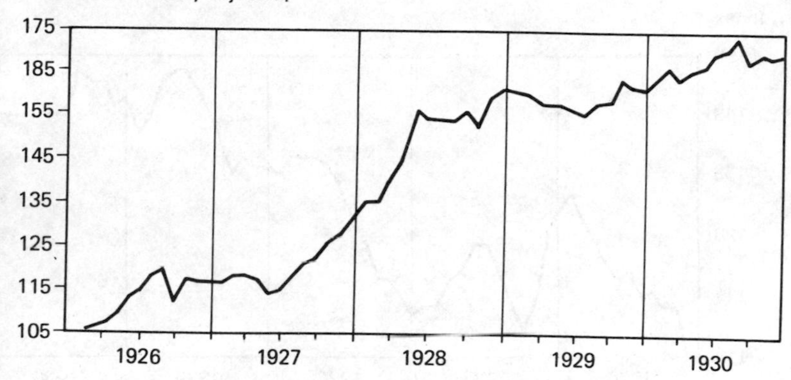

FIGURE 4.1 *Money stock 1926–30*

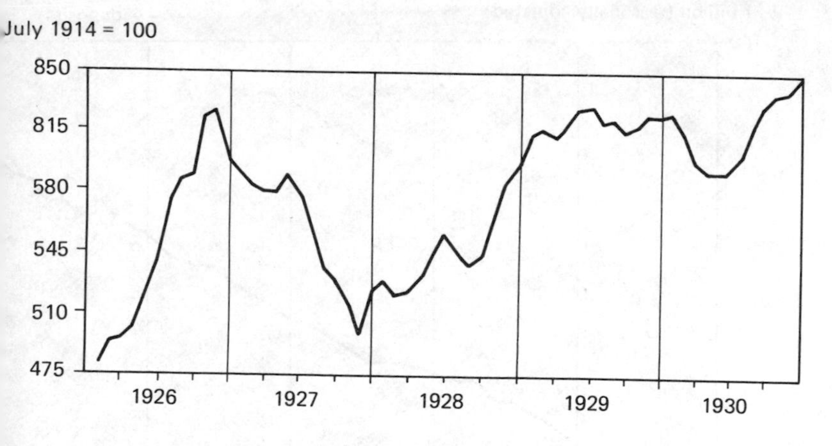

FIGURE 4.2 *Retail prices 1926–30*

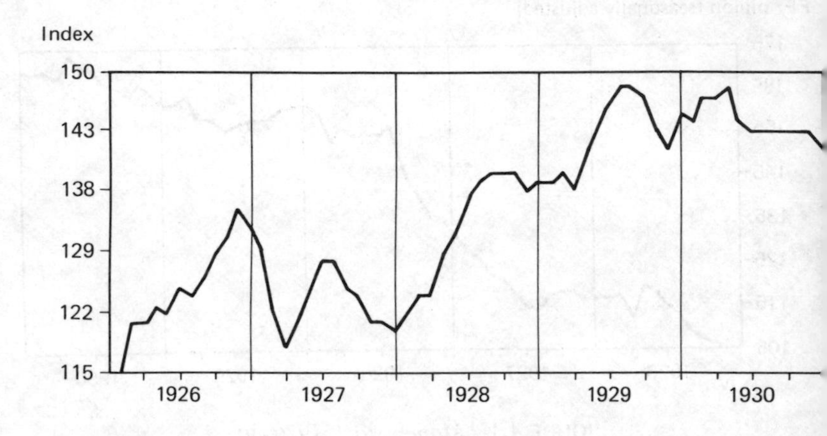

FIGURE 4.3 *Turnover tax 1926–30*

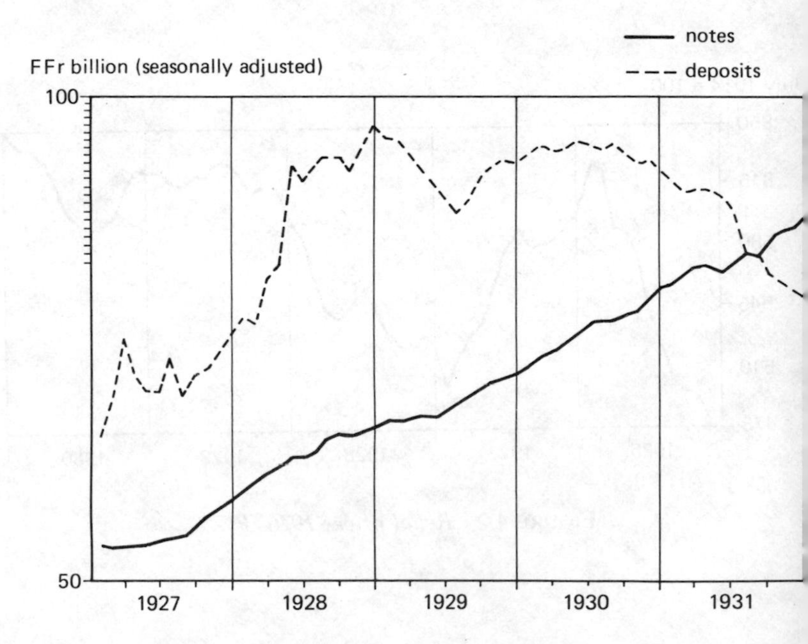

FIGURE 4.4 *Notes and bank deposits 1927–31*

NOTES TO CHAPTER 4

1. For this episode as a whole see Miquel (1984) and Moreau (1954).
2. At the same time death duties were reduced, as were income tax rates.
3. Neither the socialists nor the communists took part.
4. A Committee of Experts was set up by Briand at the beginning of June 1926. It was chaired by Sergent, the President of the BUP, and G. Jèze and C. Rist were prominent members. Its report was ready on 3 July.
5. Jèze (1934).
6. These surpluses, accumulated from 1927 mainly by Poincaré, formed what was called at the time 'Father Gaspard's treasure'. Chéron, his successor in the Ministry of Finance under several ministers, and then Germain-Martin resisted appeals in vain. In particular pensions for war veterans were created in 1930 (Germain-Martin, 1936, p. 40).
7. Sauvy (1984, Vol. I, p. 69).
8. Until 1930 contemporaries do not seem to have been specially anxious. Thus W. Oualid considered that it was a question of a 'passing crisis' or of the 'sign of an economic stabilisation following on the monetary and financial stabilisation' (Foreword to the 'Annual Report' of the *Revue d'Economie Politique*, 1930, pp. 433 ff.). France's demographic situation rendered it 'sheltered from unemployment'. Nevertheless, from 1931 a different note was sounded. Rist, who was responsible for the 1931 'Annual Report', wrote, 'We are concerned with a financial and credit crisis of a violent and widespread nature such as history has never known' (*Revue d'Economie Politique*, 1931, p. 465).
9. The bankruptcies affected essentially the smaller establishments (such as the Banque Adam). Large banks (for example, the CIC) profited by it to increase their deposits and to expand their branch networks.

5 1931–36: To Deflate or Devalue

MONETARY DISORDER AND POLITICAL DISORDER

The stability of the previous period was followed by a new period of monetary disorder, this time of an international kind. As for the French franc, it was maintained at its Poincaré parity with gold, and appreciated continuously under the effect of the depreciation of the currencies of France's principal partners.

The period began on 21 September 1931 with the devaluation of sterling, which was itself followed by that of a number of 'satellite' currencies. This devaluation 'brought everything into question again',[1] interrupting in particular the recovery under way in other countries. In April 1933 the abandonment of the gold standard by the United States and the subsequent depreciation of the dollar completed the disorganisation of the international monetary system and made the currencies of the gold-bloc countries, among them the French franc, appear overvalued, thus aggravating the economic recession in the countries belonging to the bloc.

The dilemma was therefore to deflate or to devalue. Certainly prices went down in France, with all the negative economic consequences which this implied, but they did so to an insufficient extent.

The political disorder did not make the economic choices any easier. The period was marked by growing international tensions: the advent of Nazism, the remilitarisation of the left bank of the Rhine by Germany, and the sanctions crisis following the Italian aggression against Ethiopia.

In France, the Union des Gauches, the reincarnation of the Cartel, won the elections of 1932. But Herriot, scarred by his collision in 1924 with 'the wall of money', showed considerable prudence. The rioting of 6 February 1934, provoked by the Stavisky affair,[2] brought back a brief national unity under the leadership of Doumergue.

Finally, just as the Chamber of the Cartel had ended by enthroning Poincaré, that of the 'Bloc' in 1935 called upon Laval, to whom it gave exceptional powers, which the new President of the Council

TABLE 5.1 *Major annual statistics 1932–36*

	1932	*1933*	*1934*	*1935*	*1936*
GDP (% change)	−4.3	4.5	0	3.2	1.1
Industrial production (% change)	−14.0	8.8	−6.8	−4.4	7.6
Balance of payments (FFr million):					
Trade account	−10 015	−9000	−6850	−6000	− 9175
Income account	−4815	−2950	−1250	−700	− 3050
Capital account	4815	2950	1250	700	3050
FFr/$	25.46	20.57	15.22	15.15	16.71
Prices (% change)					
Wholesale (45 articles)	12.0	−4.7	−5.7	−8.1	16.7
Consumption (1930=100)					
Retail, Paris	7.5	−5.3	−3.7	−7.4	−5.0
Singer-Kerel	−5.1	−6.7	−5.1	−4.7	3.5
Balance of the State budget (FFr million)	−4628 (9 months)	−11 509	−8813	−10 383	−16 896
M2 (% change)	−3.2	−1.2	4.9	−1.3	−0.5

SOURCES GDP – Carré, Dubois et Malinvaud (1972); industrial production – INSEE (1966); balance of payments – annual reports, *Revue d'Economie Politique*; exchange rates, prices and budget – Sauvy (1984, vol.III); M2 – authors' calculations.

used to organise deflation by decree.[3] This was a failure. It happened too late, both politically – it was less than a year away from the legislative elections which were to bring the Popular Front to power – and economically – the deflation was implemented just as prices started to recover in France under the influence of some resumption of activity.

Moreover, Belgium had dislocated the gold bloc by devaluing the belga (its franc at that time) in March 1935.

As we saw in the last chapter, France was affected by the Crisis in 1930. The vague stirrings of international recovery having been shattered by the devaluation of the British pound and its satellites, in 1931 all the indices now pointed to the Crisis.[4]

Nevertheless, a check to the difficulties, as much in other countries as in France itself, is discernible in 1932. It was not perceived at the time, the less so because a year later a relapse took place, concomitant with the devaluation of the dollar and particularly serious in the countries of the gold bloc.

Internally the public finances, which had been so good up to 1930, fell victim to the depression. The latter naturally weighed heavily on tax revenues, whereas the previous period had brought great parliamentary generosity in the way of expenditure, particularly in transfer payments (such as the institution of war veterans' pensions in 1930) which were later to become a heavy burden. 'Father Gaspard's treasure', which Tardieu in his celebrated plan for national retooling proposed to spend productively, was largely squandered. When the 'plan' was taken up again, to help in the struggle against the Crisis, it was no longer on the scale required. Overall the budget deficit continued to increase. As the depression brought a falling-off in the demand for credits, the temptation to have recourse to liquid savings to finance the deficit got the upper hand. The short-term debt, which should gradually have been consolidated, resumed its 'progress' (but largely financed by the banks).

THE EFFECT OF THE PUBLIC FINANCES ON THE ECONOMY

The political disorder made this debt again unstable. Together with the outflows of capital, which resumed in 1935 with the break-up of the gold bloc, there followed rises in interest rates, which could only further crowd out the private economy. Before Keynes and in the

Swedish tradition, Charles Rist described clearly the consequences of this crowding out: 'the most severe brake on French economic recovery for several years has been the constant rise in the interest rate due to the continual calls that the State has been obliged to make on the capital market in increasingly unfavourable conditions. Far from following the fall in the other elements of the economy, the interest rate has not ceased to rise'.[5]

Let us consider the matter. The discount rate of the Banque de France underwent wide variations. It touched its minimum, 2.2 per cent, in January 1935, rose to 6 per cent in May-June before falling again and then, a year later, regained the 6 per cent level. The return on bonds (measured by the capitalisation rate for fixed income securities) went from 3.48 per cent in August 1931[6] to 6.37 per cent the day after 6 February 1934; went down again to 4.61 per cent in February 1935; and was at 5.89 per cent in April 1936. However, as we shall see, prices fell almost continuously during the period, in any case up to the second half of 1935.

Faced with the reluctance of savers to subscribe to State securities, the government arranged in February 1935 that the Banque de France should buy in (subject to a repurchase option) Treasury bills. According to Sauvy this was followed by a renewed creation of money, which until then was falling strongly.[7] This renewal, the author considers, could only further undermine the experience of deflation. The statistics which we have established do not allow us to be so definite, at least as far as 1935 is concerned, a period during which the Treasury bill portfolio of the Banque de France remained limited since it increased by only FFr3.9 billion, going from FFr40 million in March to FFr3.94 billion in December. It was only in 1936 that the portfolio was considerably inflated, reaching just over FFr15 billion in June.

In fact the overall increase of claims on the Treasury was hardly more rapid during 1935 than in 1934. These claims did not really increase until after the establishment of the Popular Front government.

The table showing the financing of the economy (Table 5.3), although relying heavily on estimates, gives us a striking picture of the deflation which characterised the year 1935: for the first time, and the last during the period being considered, the demand for funds was negative in spite of the budget deficit, capital outflows adding their restrictive effect to that of the diminution of banking credits. The money stock fell strongly and even savings bank deposits experienced a reduction in the first half-year. In the reports of their operations the banks were reduced to congratulating themselves on the excellent liquidity of French banks: this however, was sharply reduced during the year 1935, under the effect of massive outflows of capital, and at the end of the year the assets in reserve and in accounts with the Banque de France represented no more than about 14 per cent of the deposits, against almost 20 per cent 12 months earlier. The money market went back 'into the bank' for some time, an entirely exceptional situation for this period.

Another subject of bitterness among the banks was the small amount of capital obtained on the capital market by the private sector. Like Rist, they saw it as a direct responsibility of the State, which was exerting a crowding out effect by the excessive volume of its security issues. In fact it was share issues which plummeted (being less than 1 per cent of the national income on average for the period, against 3 per cent between 1926 and 1931).

AN ALMOST UNINTERRUPTED FALL IN THE MONEY STOCK

M2 hardly ceased to fall during the period from the middle of 1931 to the beginning of 1936 (Table 5.2). The brief revival of activity in 1932 was marked only by a check in its decrease. This resumed in 1933 and was particularly strong between the middle of this year and that of 1934. A slight recovery was then noted, which was followed from the beginning of the second quarter of 1935, by a new very steep fall.

- The gold and foreign currency counterpart reached its peak in 1932, went down sharply in 1933, then recovered, but the cracking-up of the gold bloc and the French domestic situation led once more to outflows of capital; the French franc ceased to be a refuge currency. In spite of these unfavourable developments, the movements of gold and foreign currency were the only relatively expansionary element of the money stock. It was their strengthening in 1934 which led to the temporary improvement in liquidity: among the counterparts the item 'gold and foreign exchange' constituted 51 per cent of the total at the end of 1934, against 38 per cent four years earlier.
- On the other hand the recession weighed heavily upon credits to the economy, which represented no more than 32 per cent of the counterparts in 1934, against 55 per cent in 1930. Among the total of these credits, the share financed by the Banque de France, which had

TABLE 5.2 *Sources of the change in the money stock M2 1931–36 (FFr billion)*

	1931	*1932*	*1933*	*1934*	*1935*	*1936*
						•
Gold and foreign exchange	+2.54	−2.09	−9.06	+4.74	−15.60	−5.47
Domestic credit*	−8.11	+1.14	−1.37	−3.79	8.64	+24.30
(of which claims on the Treasury)	+6.45	+9.35	−1.02	+0.46	+2.83	+17.06
(bank credits)	−17.77	−9.93	−7.94	−3.99	−8.45	+12.94
ΔM2	−5.57	−0.95	−10.43	+0.95	−6.96	+18.83
(% change)	−7.9	−0.6	−6.4	+0.7	−5.5	+12.9

* approximate.
• accounting figures.

been stable since the beginning of the crisis at about 10 per cent, increased considerably to reach nearly a quarter in 1935. The crisis was also a crisis for the commercial banks,[8] marked by the withdrawal of deposits, in favour of the Banque de France and the savings banks. This situation aggravated the decline in banking which started in 1914.[9]

• From 1931 claims on the Treasury expanded, strongly until 1933, less strongly from 1933 to 1934 (notably under the influence of the efforts made towards budgetary economies, which allowed the deficits to be stabilised). As noted above, they did not resume significant growth until 1936.

At the beginning of 1936 M2 ceased to decline; the renewed growth of credits to the economy and above all that of claims on the Treasury, exceeded the outflows of foreign currency, and the counterpart structure was reversed.

A recovery in production and prices was noted, in fact, from the second half of 1935: as with earlier recoveries, it was international. In France,

• the index of industrial production (1923–35 = 100) stood at 91.5 at the end of 1934; it rose to 94.4 a year later (and to 98.3 in December 1936);

• the 45-item wholesale price index stood at 498 in December 1930; it reached a minimum of 334 in July 1935 and stood at 372 in June 1936. For retail prices, measured by the price of 34 items in Paris (1914 = 100), the index was at 594 in April 1930; its minimum was 420 in August 1935; and it rose to 461 in June 1936;

TABLE 5.3 *The financing of the French economy 1931–36 (FFr billion)*

	1931	*1932*	*1933*	*1934*	*1935*	*1936*	
Sources of financing							
Balance of State budget[1]	10.10		11.51[2]	8.81	10.38	16.90	
		21.61					
Credits							
* Bank	−17.71	−9.93	−7.94	−3.99	−5.71	10.20	
* Non-bank[3]	15.50	16.83	12.10	10.02	8.29	5.70	
External	10.50	−1.09	−8.06	+4.74	−15.60	−17.58[4]	
							Investments
	17.10	23.14	24.81	23.22	14.49	5.1	Bond subscriptions
		−19		−0.4		−3.2	Net subscriptions of Treasury bills
	12.27	6.41	1.58	1.18	2	−1.14	Deposits in savings banks
	−5.51	−0.91	−10.44	0.95	−8.56	18.83	ΔM2
	(−4.63)	(−0.49)	(−2.11)	(+1.30)	(−1.36)	(+6.17)	* (of which banknotes)
		−17.64		−5.37	−10.57	−4.37	Residual

1. A surplus reduces the supply of financing (− sign); a deficit increases it (+ sign).
2. Displaced financial years, from March to March, until 1933.
3. Including net issues of bonds by non-financial companies.
4. Diminution of the gold and foreign exchange reserve, disregarding the devaluation of 1 October 1936, which changed the definition of the franc in terms of gold from 65.5mg (at 900 mils. fineness) to 43–49mg. (at 900 mils. fineness). The capital gain thus produced was allocated, to a limit of FFr10 billion, to the Fonds de Stabilisation des Changes created by the same law of 1 October 1936, and for about FFr2 billion to the amortisation of the advances made by the Banque de France to the State.

TABLE 5.4 *Summary of monetary and financial data 1932–36 (end-period totals, averages for interest rates) (FFr billion)*

	1932	*1933*	*1934*	*1935*	*1936*
M2	163.76	153.32	154.27	145.71	164.54
Net assets in gold and foreign exchange[1]	88.71	71.65	84.39	68.79	63.32
Claims on the Treasury	28.27 (+49.4%)	27.25 (−3.6%)	27.71 (1.7%)	27.80 (0.3%)	47.60 (71.2%)
Claims on the economy	65.24 (−13.2%)	57.30 (−12.2%)	53.31 (7%)	47.60 (−10.8%)	57.80 (+21.4%)
Deposits in savings banks	57.28	58.86	60.04	62.04	58.90
(for reference, ceiling on deposits, in francs)	20 000	20 000	20 000	20 000	20 000
Discount rate	2.50	2.50	2.70	3.40	3.67
Yield on bonds	4.73	5.74	5.61	5.31	5.86
New issues of negotiable securities:					
shares	3.07	2.52	2.02	2.05	1.41
bonds	23.14	24.81	23.22	14.49	5.10
(of which government bonds)	(5.18)	(12.45)	(13.79)	(7.35)	(0.73)
National income	307	295	247	245	261
Income velocity (national income/M2)	1.89	1.85	1.62	1.63	1.72

1. Taking account of the devaluation of 1 October 1936. The new definition of the franc in terms of gold was not fixed but floating (43–49 mg. of gold, against 65.5 mg.: the capital gain can be estimated at FFr12 billion, but only about FFr2 billion were allocated to the repayment of the Banque's advances to the Treasury.

- finally the money stock M2 (s.a.) which continued to decrease until January 1936 (its minimum), going from FFr163.8 to FFr142.4 billion, recovered to FFr151.7 billion in June 1936.

BANK LIQUIDITY

Bank liquidity remained easy, although the factors which affected it varied appreciably. The fiduciary circulation was less restrictive. The outstanding total of notes in circulation even went down on several occasions in 1932, 1933 and 1935, as did also the total money stock.

On the other hand from 1932 the movements of capital were

TABLE 5.5 *Factors affecting bank liquidity 1932–36 (FFr billion)*

	situation at end 1931	*changes in* 1932	1933	1934	1935	1936	*situation at end 1936***
A) Notes in circulation and accounts with the Banque de France[1]	−106.3	+2.6	+8.4	−2.3	+7.6	−12.6	−102.6
B) Gold and foreign exchange	+90.8	−2.1	−9.1	+4.7	−15.6	−12.4*	+63.3
C) Claims of the Banque de France on the Treasury	+5.8	+2.5	−1.5	−0.6	+3.5	+24.5*	+28
D) Miscellaneous[2]	+0.9	+0.4	+0.3	−1.2	+1	−2.5	−1.9
E) Portfolio of the Banque de France[3]	+8.8	−3.4	+1.9	−0.6	+3.5	+3	+13.2
F) (for reference) Banks' reserves and deposits at the Banque de France	21.4	−0.6	−7.5	−0.6	−5	+0.5	8.2
F-E) Free liquidity of the banks (+) or net indebtedness to the Banque de France (−)	12.6	+2.8	−9.4		−8.5	−2.5	−5

A + sign indicates a positive effect on banking liquidity, a − sign a negative effect.

1. Including the deposits of the banks.
2. Elements accounted for under the 'miscellaneous' heading of the Banque de France's accounts, and in particular foreign exchange operations.
3. Credits to banks, companies and private individuals.

* Not taking account of the FFr7 billion revaluation of the reserve allocated to the repayment of advances to the State.

** Accounting figures, after revaluation of the gold reserve.

reversed and became more and more unfavourable, the net flows being of great volume in 1935 and 1936; but their negative effect on bank liquidity was counterbalanced in 1935 and 1936 by the growth of the lending provided by the Banque de France to the Treasury. Finally the liquid reserves of the banks remained at a high level.

Overall, in 1936 the liquidity of the banks had only slightly deteriorated and the net indebtedness of the banks to the Institut d'Emission was only slight.

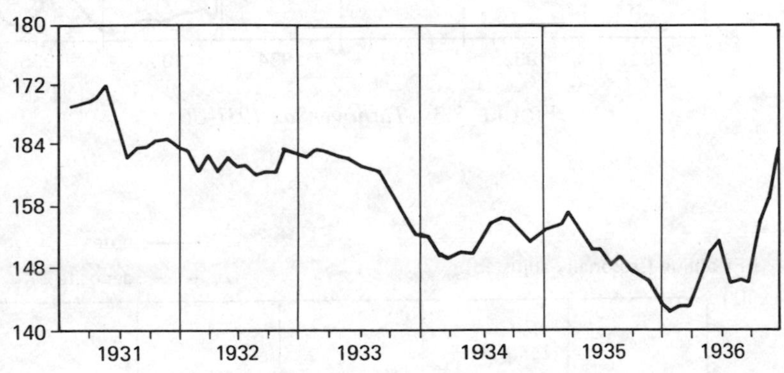

FIGURE 5.1 *Money stock 1931–36*

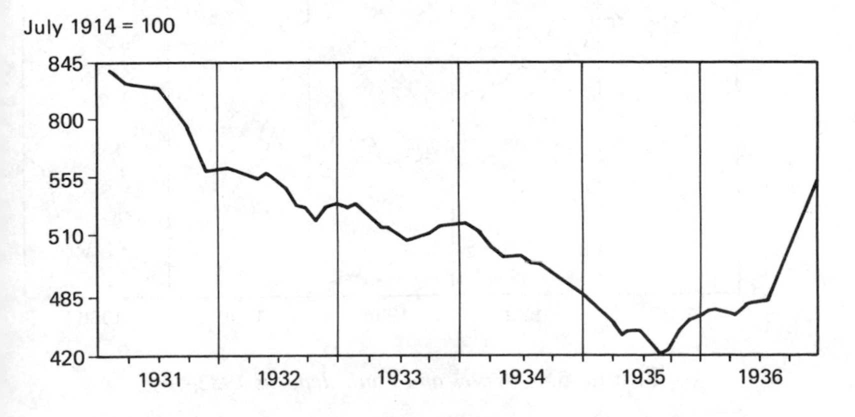

FIGURE 5.2 *Retail prices 1931–36*

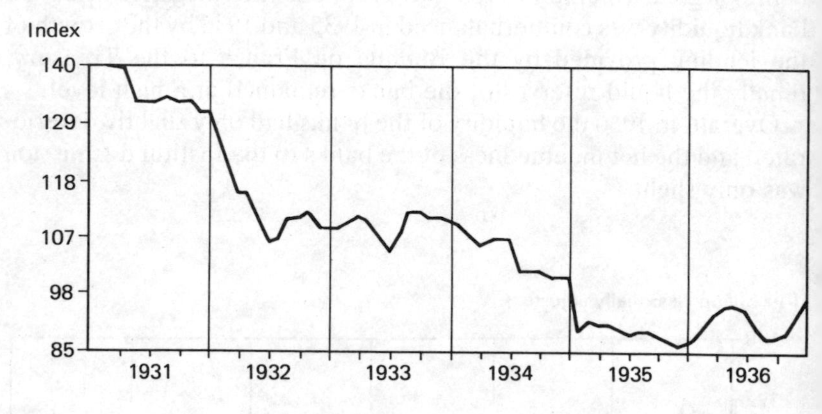

FIGURE 5.3 *Turnover tax 1931–36*

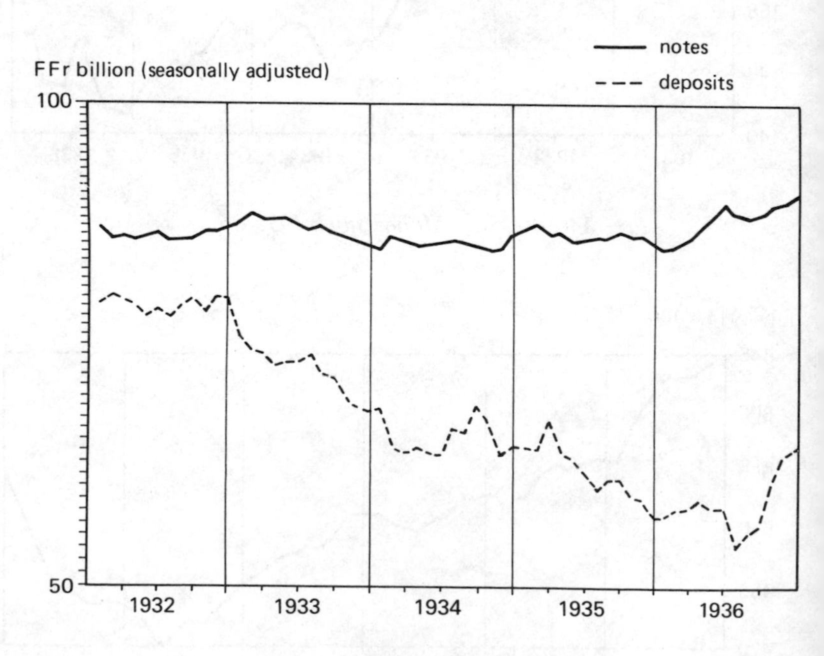

FIGURE 5.4 *Notes and bank deposits 1932–36*

NOTES TO CHAPTER 5

1. Sauvy (1984, vol. I, p. 97).
2. It will be recalled that the Crédit Municipal de Bayonne, founded by this adventurer, had issued more than FFr200 million's worth of bogus cash vouchers, and that Stavisky had appropriated the funds. Some members of the government of the time (headed by Chautemps) had supported Stavisky. (Dubief, 1976, pp. 74–5).
3. The decrees involved essentially a general cut of 10 per cent on virtually the whole range of public expenditure, including pensions and the floating debt; new taxes on high incomes and on defence contractors. 'It was expected that a FFr11 billion improvement in the budget would result from this enormous effort; after which it was hoped that, with government stock regaining parity despite the cut in the coupon, a new conversion would succeed: finally with the situation rendered more healthy, it would then, but only then, be possible to carry out a moderate devaluation of the currency.' (Gignoux, n.d. pp. 222 ff.)
4. Sauvy (1984, vol. I, p. 100).
5. C. Rist, foreword to the 1936–37 'Annual Report' of the *Revue d'Economie Politique*, p. 491. He had already written two years earlier, 'A debt which represents a charge of 45% of the budget, which itself represents 30% of a (national) income . . . is beyond the powers of the Nation . . . The nominal return of the industrial, commercial and agricultural undertakings, on the net product of which this charge must be raised, is today no longer sufficient to meet this' (foreword to the 'Annual Report' in the *Revue d'Economie Politique*, 1937, p. 547).
6. The particularly low level of interest rates recorded in 1931 led the authorities to prepare a conversion. It was deferred to September 1932 by political events both international (the Lausanne conference on reparations) and domestic. Seven per cent Treasury bills, and 5 per cent and 6 per cent stock of 1915, 1916 and 1928, were converted at par to 4.5 per cent. FFr80 billion out of a possible total of FFr85.5 billion were converted (Germain-Martin, 1936 pp. 167 ff.).
7. Sauvy (1984, vol. I, p. 223).
8. After the Banque Adam (which passed into the control of Oustric), the fraudulent bankruptcy of which compromised Tardieu, the Custodian of the Government Seals, and other personalities of the first order (Dubief, 1976, p. 16), a series of other institutions got into difficulty: those of the Vincent group (Banque Nationale de Crédit and Comptoir Lyon-Allemand), and the Banque d'Alsace et de Lorraine (cf. Germain-Martin 1936, pp. 79–88). 'The BNC was liquidated by amicable agreement at the beginning of 1932 and transformed into the BNCI with the help of the major banks.' As for the Banque d'Alsace-Lorraine, it was taken over by the Alsatian branch of the CIC. Lastly, the 'BUP came within a hairsbreadth of catastrophe' (J. Bouvier in Braudel and Labrousse, 1970–82, vol. 4, p. 713).
9. Cf. Bouvier (1984).

6 1936–39: The Relapse

THE ECONOMIC POLICY OF THE POPULAR FRONT

The government of the Left under Léon Blum came into office at the beginning of June 1936 with a diagnosis and a cure clearly stated and understood at the time. It decided to 'abandon the policy of deflation pursued, almost without interruption, since the beginning of the crisis. The balancing of the budget is no longer considered to be the paramount element in straightening out the public finances. It should result from the economic recovery which, stimulated and encouraged by a policy of increasing the purchasing power of the masses, should ultimately lead to an increase of budgetary resources and in particular of tax revenues'.[1]

Several authors have explained the reasons why the cure thus put into operation did not come up to the standard of the 'Keynesian' quality of the diagnosis:

- A. Sauvy laid stress on the error of applying rigidly the 40-hour principle, which significantly restrained the recovery of supply and, in conjunction with the boosting of demand, precipitated an exceptional degree of inflation and a deterioration of the external balance. Far from improving, the budgetary situation worsened, and brought back the expedients of the 1920s: borrowing guaranteed against exchange rate fluctuations and the creation of money;
- more generally, the phenomena of confidence operated against the Blum government. The franc was once more the chief victim. Progressively, like the earlier Chambers of the 'left', the Assembly resulting from the 1936 elections slipped to the 'right', from Blum to Chautemps, from Chautemps to Daladier. The latter welcomed Paul Reynaud as Finance Minister. Reynaud repudiated what a contemporary called 'the fantasies of romanticised economics'. But his task of management was interrupted by the international crises, which stimulated rearmament.

TABLE 6.1 *Major annual statistics 1937–39*

	1937	*1938*	*1939*
GDP (% change)	5.4	0	4.2
Industrial production (% change)	5.6	8.0	13 (7 months 38/ 7 months 39)
Balance of payments (FFr million):			
Trade account	−16 340	−13 772	—
Income account	−6 200	338	—
Capital account	6 200	−338	
FFr/$	25.14	34.95	37.85
Prices (% change)			
Wholesale (45 articles)	39.0	13.7	7.6
Consumption: Retail, Paris	24.9	13.7	(8 months 38/ 8 months 39) 13.1
Singer-Kerel	24.2	17.6	(8 months 38/ 8 months 39) 4.5
Balance of the State budget (FFr million)	−23 713	−27 692	—
M2 (% change)	11.3	10.0	—

SOURCES GDP – Carré, Dubois et Malinvaud (1972); industrial production 1937 and 1938 – INSEE (1966); exchange rates, budget and balance of payments – Sauvy (1984, vol.III); prices – Statistique Générale de la France; M2 – authors' calculations.

RESUMPTION OF MONETARY EXPANSION

The money stock grew almost continuously from the end of the summer of 1936 up to the declaration of war, increasing by 35 per cent between the low point of September 1936 and the end of 1938. With the 'gold and foreign exchange' counterpart on the whole declining until the arrival of Paul Reynaud, it was essentially the requirements of the Treasury which explained the rapid growth of the money stock:

- credits to the economy increased only to a limited extent, by FFr8 billion or 13 per cent, and this in two years, from the end of 1936 to that of 1938;
- on the other hand claims on the Treasury grew by nearly FFr30 billion or 44 per cent, between December 1936 and September 1938. The Reynaud devaluation then permitted a purely accounting reduction in claims on the Treasury, whilst the 'gold and foreign exchange' counterpart expanded.

As for the fundamental causes of the movements thus noted, they appeared to be of three kinds:

(1) The rise of costs and prices in France: the only policy of the Popular Front – the raising of wages by 7 to 15 per cent, the introduction of paid holidays, and then the progressive introduction of the 40-hour week – must have increased the costs of French companies by 40 to 50 per cent.[2] The average annual rate of rise in retail prices went up from 5 per cent in 1936 to 25 per cent in 1937 and 13.6 per cent in 1938.

(2) The second factor is the additional rise in costs and prices due to the decline in the franc, which led France to 'import inflation'.

It is useful to pause for a moment on this dramatic fall of the franc which amounted, between September 1936 and November 1938, to a devaluation of nearly 60 per cent in its gold value.

After the devaluation of 1 October 1936, the franc could move between 43 and 49 mg. in gold value, that is, a bracket of devaluation from 25 per cent to 34 per cent. A Fonds de Stabilisation des Changes was created which received as its first endowment FFr10 billion of the capital gain in accounting terms which resulted from the devaluation.

To support the franc the Fonds sold gold, or foreign currency, which it bought from the Banque de France, thanks to its initial endowment, or which it procured from foreign central banks in exchange for gold. It transferred to the Banque de France the gold and foreign currency which exceeded its current requirements. The operations of the Fonds were thus not in fact secret; but their repercussions in the balance sheet of the Banque de France were delayed.

After several weeks of improvement, the capital outflows recommenced; they were interrupted by the pause announced by Léon Blum,[3] but this respite was once more short-lived: the Banque's gold reserve fell to FFr49 billion in the second half of the year, that is, a decrease of FFr14 billion since December 1936.

A new parity adjustment was therefore made in June 1937, but in the form of the abolition of the limits between which the Fonds de Stabilisation des Changes had to maintain the parity of the franc: the franc was therefore 'floating'; however, on 21 July the gold reserve was revalued on the basis of 43 mg. of gold of millesimal fineness 900 to the franc.[4]

The year which followed was characterised by a continuous depreciation in the franc's exchange rate against foreign currencies: thus the rate for the pound sterling went from FFr129 in June 1937 to FFr179 in April 1938, and that of the dollar from FFr26 to FFr38.

On 4 May the government declared that the rate for the pound would not go beyond FFr179. This *de facto* stabilisation thus ratified a very substantial devaluation. The following months marked a return of confidence in the franc and in November the Reynaud government revalued the gold reserve on the basis of 27.5 mg.[5]

It is evident from these developments that the 'fundamental factors' played very little part, either in the depreciation of the franc or in its stabilisation from spring 1938. In fact, the devaluation of October 1936 had eliminated the price 'differential' between France and its major foreign partners; at no time in the future did this differential reappear.[6] It was thus a crisis of confidence from which the franc suffered for nearly a year and a half; the turnround observed during the second half of the year being similarly much more psychological in origin. The depreciation of the franc was thus not the logical consequence of economic imbalances but a perverse phenomenon, causing inflation.

(3) Finally, the third factor in the increase of the money stock was the worsening of the budgetary deficit which led to an appeal to the Banque de France. The ceilings were raised. The advances of the Banque de France to the Treasury had been stabilised at FFr3.2 billion in 1928. They increased by FFr19 billion in the second half of 1936, by another FFr12 billion in 1937, and in September 1938 they reached a total of more than FFr53 billion. In 1938 Daladier resumed the issue of (short-term) National Defence Bonds.

EXPANSION AND INFLATION

In spite of its relatively rapid growth, the money stock increased by less than did transactions. Its 35 per cent rise in three years compares with:

- an increase of 20 per cent in industrial production (98 in July 1939 against 82 three years earlier);
- a virtual doubling of wholesale prices: the 45-item index was at 372 in June 1936 and reached its peak of 693 in May 1939;
- a rise of the order of one quarter in retail consumption prices.

The undeniable acceleration in the velocity of money reflected the economic recovery.

During the period two short phases were recorded in which the money stock did not increase rapidly. They corresponded to periods of slackened growth of activity: the first was the spring of 1937, when

TABLE 6.2 *The financing of the French economy 1936–39 (FFr billion)*

	1936	*1937*	*1938*	*1939*	
Sources of financing:					
Balance of State budget[1]	16.90	28.3	27.7	86.8	
Credits:					
* Bank	10.20	2.55	5.13	2.60	
* Non-bank[2]	5.70	4.53	2.94	3.26	
External	–17.58	–2.74	–1	+10.12	
					Investments
	5.1	19.29	10.46	8.26	Bond subscriptions
	–3.2	3.07	5.58	12	Net subscriptions of Treasury bills
	–1.14	2.46	2.22	3.16	Deposits in savings banks
	19.44	11.20	27.09	52.61	ΔM2
	(6.17)	(5.01)	(18.07)	(39.80)	* (of which banknotes)
	–4.37	–3.38			Residual

1. A surplus reduces the supply of financing (– sign); a deficit increases it (+ sign).
2. Including net issues of bonds by non-financial companies.

the Blum government issued a major loan with an exchange rate guarantee (issued at 98 with a coupon rate of 4.5 per cent, that is, a yield of 4.6 per cent; it brought in FFr8 billion). It was also at this moment that the beginning of the revival stimulated by the boosting of purchasing power ran out of steam (for Sauvy, this was because it came up against the ceiling of the 40-hour week, which had now become general).

The second phase was at the beginning of 1938, with the departure of the Socialists from the government and the slackening of industrial production: credits to the economy fell back slightly.

Blum's return in March brought a resumption of advances from the Banque de France. The arrival of Daladier a month later was marked by new measures in favour of the economy – notably the interest rate subsidies for housing and supplementary credit facilities for industry and commerce. Expenditure on armaments increased. Some relaxations were introduced to the 40-hour week. Industrial activity in fact improved considerably.

It should be noted that substantial variations occurred in the structure of the money stock, the phases of crisis, domestic or

TABLE 6.3 *Summary of monetary and financial data 1937–39 (end-period totals, averages for interest rates) (FFr billion)*

	1937	*1938*	*1939*
M2	175.74 (−6.8%)	202.83 (+15.4%)	255.40 (+25.9%)
Net assets in gold and foreign exchange	60.58[1]	87.26[1]	97.38
Claims on the Treasury	56.72 (+19.2%)	53.02[2] (−6.5%)	93.68 (+76.6%)
Claims on the economy	60.35 (+4.4%)	65.48 (+8.5%)	67.08 (+2.4%)
Deposits in savings banks	61.37	63.62	66.75
(for reference, ceiling on deposits, in francs)	20 000	20 000	20 000
Discount rate	3.81	2.76	2
Yield on bonds	6.12	6.10	4.97
New issues of negotiable securities:			
shares	2	1.68	1.73
bonds	19.29	10.46	8.26
(of which government bonds)	(14.73)	(7.52)	(5)
National income	338	380	433
Income velocity (national income/M2)	2	2.22	1.90

1. Taking account of the devaluations of 21 July 1937 and 12 November 1938, which produced capital gains to the reserves of about FFr7 billion and FFr31.5 billion respectively.

2. After the repayment of FFr31.5 billion of advances from the Banque de France to the State, as the result of the capital gain produced by the devaluation of November 1938.

external (particularly Munich), leading to a preference for banknotes at the expense of bank deposits. The development of savings bank deposits was much more regular.

LOW RATES OF INTEREST

In the spirit of the time and in spite of the marked rise in prices, rates of interest remained relatively low during the whole of the period.

After the tension due to the victory of the Popular Front and the expectation of devaluation, the Banque de France, which had put its discount rate up to 6 per cent, brought it back to 2 per cent on 15 October 1936. The continued outflows of gold compelled a return to 4 per cent at the beginning of 1937. The second foreign exchange crisis in June 1937 took it up to 6 per cent. It went to 3 per cent at the end of 1937, to 2.5 per cent in March 1938 and 3 per cent at the time

TABLE 6.4 *Factors affecting bank liquidity 1937–39 (FFr billion)*

	situation at end 1936	*changes in*			*situation at end 1939***
		1937	*1938*	*1939*	
A) Notes in circulation and accounts with the Banque de France[1]	−102.6	−8.9	−23.5	−30.5	−165.5
B) Gold and foreign exchange	+63.3	−2.8	−4*	+9.3	+98.3
C) Claims of the Banque de France on the Treasury	+28	+10.9	+24.7*	+24	+58.2
D) Miscellaneous[2]	−1.9	+0.8	+2.5	−0.2	+1.3
E) Portfolio of the Banque de France[3]	+13.2	—	+0.3	−3.2	+10.3
F) (for reference) Bank's reserves and deposits at the Banque de France	8.2	+1.6	−0.3	+2.7	12.2
F-E) Free liquidity of the banks (+) or net indebtedness to the Banque de France (–)	−5	+1.6	−0.6	+5.9	+1.9

A + sign indicates a positive effect on banking liquidity, a – sign a negative effect.

1. Including the deposits of the banks.

2. Elements accounted for under the 'miscellaneous' heading of the Banque de France's accounts, and in particular foreign exchange operations.

3. Credits to banks, companies and private individuals.

* Not taking into account the FFr20.5 billion from the revaluation of the gold reserve allocated to the repayment of advances to the State.

** Accounting figures after the revaluation for the gold reserve.

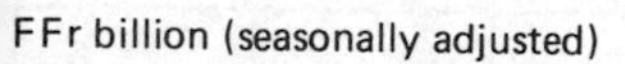

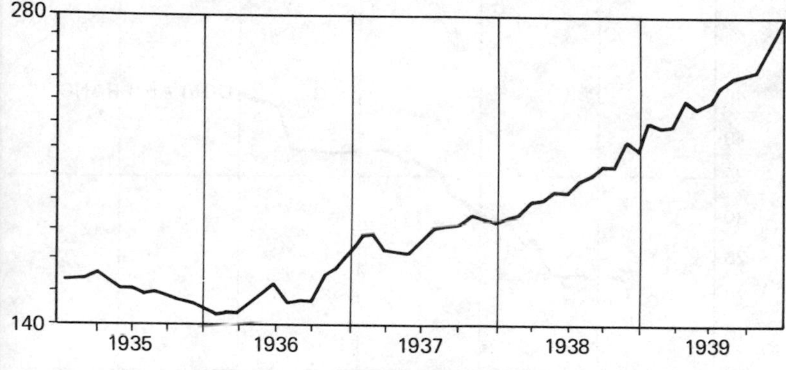

FIGURE 6.1 *Money Stock 1935–39*

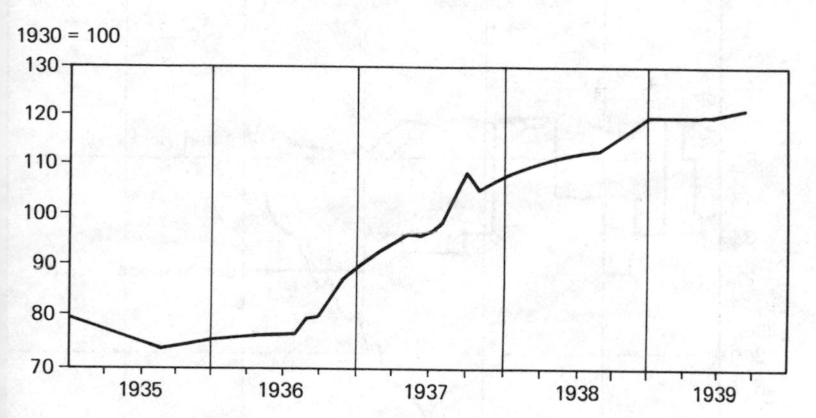

FIGURE 6.2 *Consumption prices 1935–39*

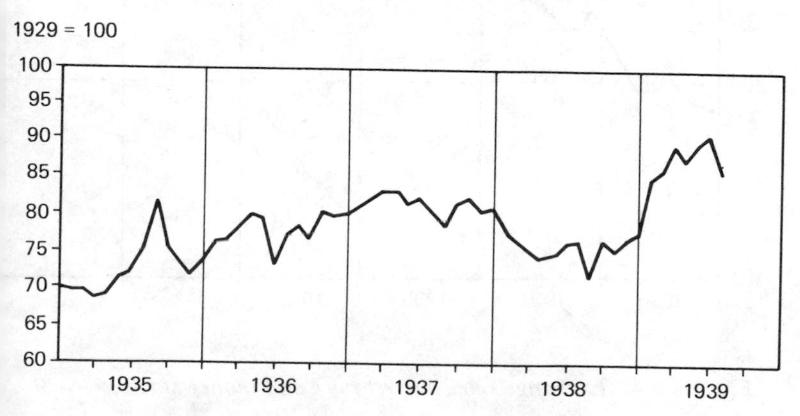

FIGURE 6.3 *Industrial production 1935–39*

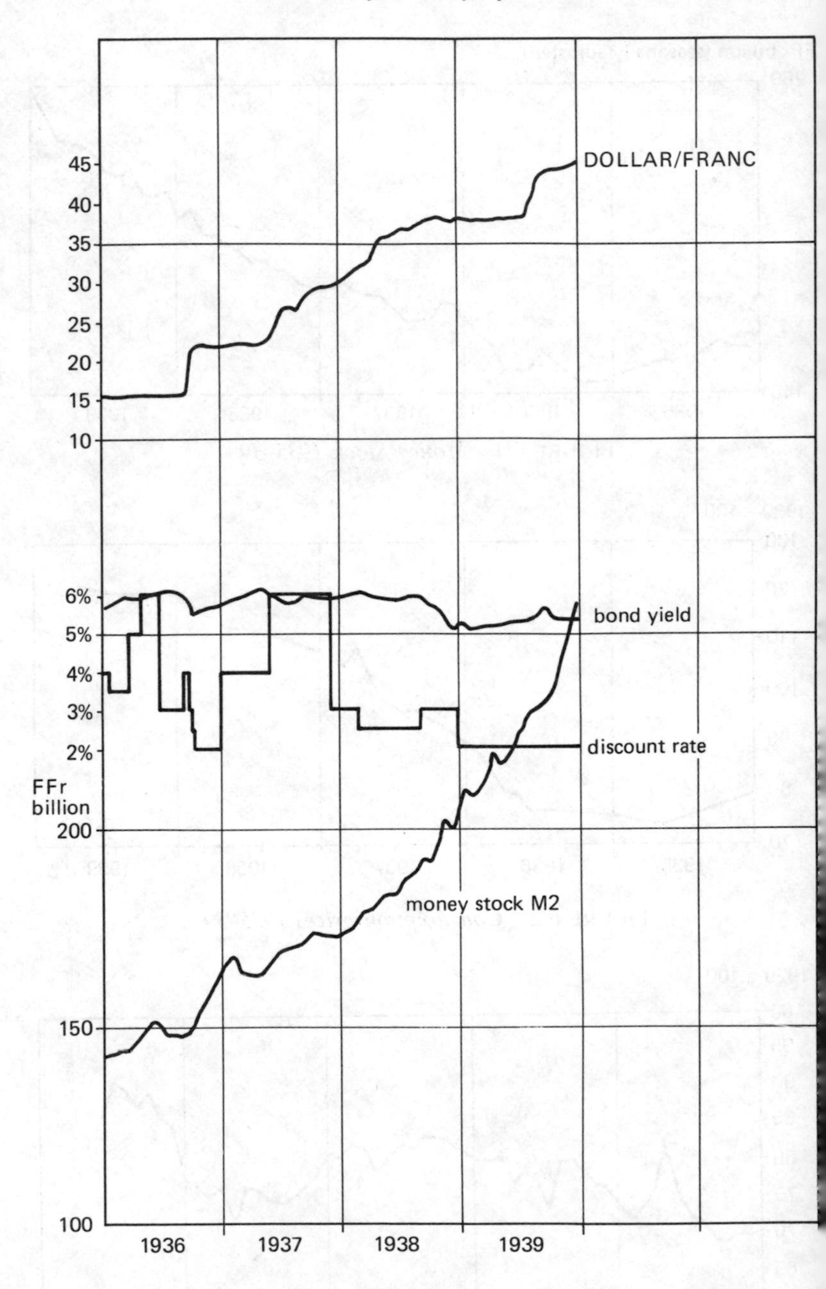

FIGURE 6.4 *Exchange rate, interest rates and money stock 1936–39*

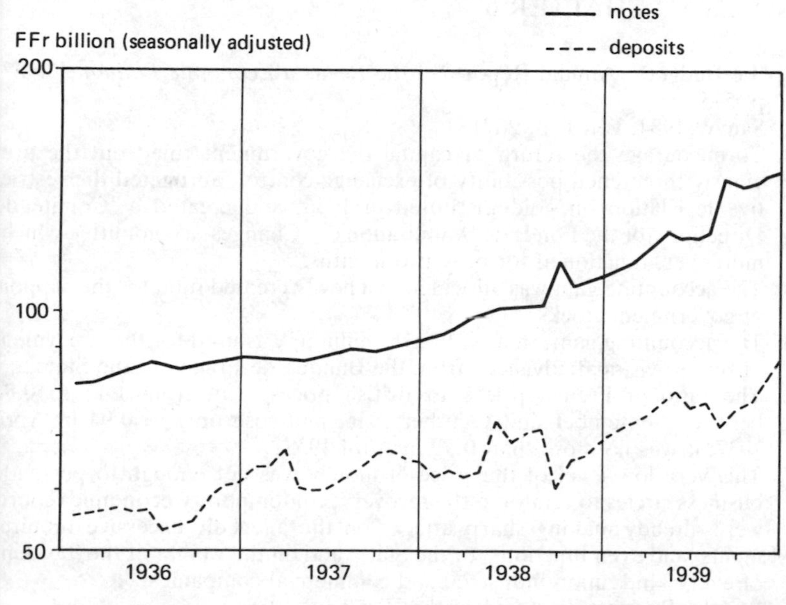

FIGURE 6.5 *Notes and bank deposits 1936–39*

of Munich. On 3 January 1939, the discount rate was brought down to the 'exceptionally low figure of 2%'.[7]

Bond yields (the net capitalisation rate for fixed income securities), which went up to 6.28 per cent in August 1936, against 3.48 per cent (see above) in August 1931, oscillated between 5.3 per cent and 6.6 per cent until November 1938[8]; and went below 5 per cent at the beginning of 1939.

BANK LIQUIDITY

The period was characterised by a considerable increase in the fiduciary circulation, connected with the political uncertainties. The movements of gold and foreign exchange were more or less neutral over the three years, weak outflows in 1937 and 1938 being offset by an inflow in 1939. But there was an important growth in the Banque de France's lending to the Treasury, particularly in 1938 and 1939.

The net effect of these movements was a slight reduction in the Banque de France's portfolio of private credits. The liquidity position of the banks therefore remained very comfortable; at the end of 1939 they were again net creditors.

NOTES TO CHAPTER 6

1. 'Le Budget', 'Annual Report' of the *Revue d'Economie Politique*, 1937, p. 575.
2. Sauvy (1984, vol. I, p. 267).
3. To encourage the return of capital the government ruled out the previously threatened possibility of exchange control, abrogated the restrictive legislation on gold instituted in 1936, and created a 'Comité de Direction' for the Fonds de Stabilisation des Changes, a committee which, moreover, functioned for only two months.
4. The accounting gain was allocated to a newly created fund for the support of government stocks.
5. The accounting gain, that is, FFr31.5 billion, was used for the repayment of the provisional advances from the Banque de France to the State.
6. The ratio of French prices to British prices went from 1.15 to 0.86 between September and October 1936, and rose only to 0.94 in April 1937; it was no more than 0.72 in April 1938.
7. This very low level of the price of money was not enough to persuade business circles to reinforce the recovery; contemporary economic reports were already making sharp attacks on the allegedly excessive requirements 'and even functions' of the State, and on the weight of the 'burdens of every kind' upon industrial and commercial companies.
8. See the Rapport d'activité of the BNCI for 1938.

7 1939–44: The Second World War

In some respects the monetary conjuncture in France during the Second World War was surprisingly similar to that observed during the 1914–18 war: the money stock was inflated to the same degree, being multiplied by 2.9 from the end of 1914 to the end of 1918 and by 3.3 between the end of 1939 and the end of 1944; and there was the same tendency to hold material forms of money, to the detriment of bank deposits, the share of notes in circulation in M2 rising from 57 per cent in 1939 to 66 per cent in 1944, whilst between 1914 and 1918 it had risen from 41 per cent to 69 per cent.

Finally, among the sources of the money supply, claims on the Treasury took a predominant place during both these periods. Elsewhere, however, appreciable differences appear, which reflect the significant deterioration of the French economy between 1939 and 1944.

The first difference relates to the ratio between the growth in the quantity of money and the development of production. Whereas during the 1914–18 period production was multiplied by 2.1 and the money stock by 2.9, the corresponding increases between the end of 1939 and the end of 1944 were respectively 1.3 and 3.3. The estimated rates of growth of production during the second war obviously underrated the reality since prices were maintained at an artificially low level, inflation being measured less by indices than by the lengths of the queues outside the shops and the prices on the black market. Nonetheless, a significant hiatus existed between the rate of growth of liquid assets and that of the value of transactions. A considerable reserve of inflation was built up in this way, the effects of which were to be felt after the Liberation, illustrating a simple but almost mathematical quantity theory relationship.

A second difference from the conjuncture of the First World War, one of degree rather than of kind, lies in the disproportion between the sources of the money supply. In 1918 claims on the Treasury represented 44.5 per cent of the counterparts of M2, certainly a very large proportion, especially when they stood at zero in 1914, but claims on the economy continued to play an important role, at 38.3 per cent. In June 1944 the monetary indebtedness of the Treasury

TABLE 7.1 *Major annual statistics 1940–44*

	1940	*1941*	*1942*	*1943*	*1944*
National income (% change)	–17.8	–20.5	–10	–6.4	–15.3
Industrial production (% change)	–39 against 1938			–11.5	–29.7
Balance of payments (FFr billion):					
Trade account	–28.26	–9.16	+4.11	+21.45	+15.79
Prices (% change)					
Wholesale	+31.4	+22.5	+17.2	+16.1	+12.6
Retail, Paris	+17.8	+17.5	+20.3	+24.2	+76.9
Balance of the State budget (FFr billion)	–212	–183	–193	–296	–283
M2 (% change)	+45.1	+20.8	+31.8	+25.7	+14.3

contributed more than 82 per cent of the creation of money and claims on the economy less than 8 per cent. Moreover, these figures give only a partial picture of the fall in productive activity, since the claims on the Treasury were financing, not as in the 1914–18 war expenditure which encouraged economic activity, but to a very large extent the levies of the army of occupation on national production.

After briefly describing the situation on the eve of war, we shall distinguish two subperiods: from September 1939 to May 1940, the first wrong turnings; and from June 1940 to August 1944, the Occupation.

THE ECONOMIC AND MONETARY SITUATION OF FRANCE ON ENTERING THE WAR

In economic terms France, after an almost continuous decline which began in 1931, had seemed for some months to be on the way to a definite recovery.

Between September 1938 and July 1939 industrial production had increased at an annual rate of 26 per cent, unemployment had regularly fallen, and retail prices after a spurt in December 1938 had subsequently remained remarkably moderate. Certainly external trade remained heavily in deficit, but war preparations were responsible for this; on the other hand capital movements were in a favourable direction and between the end of 1938 and September 1939 the Banque de France had increased its gold reserves by an amount equivalent to FFr10 billion.

It is difficult to detect what, in this recovery, was due on the one hand to the measures taken by the Reynaud government, in particular the lifting of the freeze on working hours and the devaluation of the franc on 12 November 1938; and on the other hand to the rearmament which had taken on a new momentum after the Munich crisis; elements of the answer can doubtless be found in the different aspects of monetary development.

As we have seen, the French economy was emerging from a long period of monetary deflation: from 1929 to 1936 the money stock, apart from minor fluctuations, had slightly diminished; a renewed growth at the end of 1936 was interrupted in 1937; however, from the middle of 1938 monetary expansion was lively and practically uninterrupted, this resumption coinciding with a halt in the decline of production followed by a swift rise.

The resumption is equally marked for savings bank deposits, which in June 1938 stood at FFr63.2 billion, that is hardly 3 per cent more than in June 1935, and which at the end of 1939[1] reached FFr66.9 billion in spite of two periods of exceptional withdrawals occasioned by the Munich crisis and the declaration of war.

By far the most important source of monetary expansion was the growth of the monetary financing of the Treasury, which without doubt shows the relatively small size of the spontaneous recovery and the importance of the expenditure on armaments. In a general way, the development of the public finances was the determining factor for the period in which we are interested.

SEPTEMBER 1939 TO MAY 1940: THE FIRST WRONG TURNINGS

At the beginning of the war, the government had to take a certain number of safety measures, but it certainly did not go far enough in taking the steps required by the situation.

Comprehensive exchange controls were established,[2] with the creation of an exchange office, at first administered by the Banque de France, responsible for centralising all foreign currency earned and issuing the foreign currency necessary for authorised imports. The export of foreign capital was prohibited, and operations in gold were made subject to authorisation by the central bank. However, even though a decree made it incumbent on all French people resident abroad to declare the major part of their assets to the exchange office, no requisitioning was decided upon. Foreign currency assets therefore remained limited to the reserves of the Banque de France and the Fonds de Stabilisation des Changes on the eve of the war, that is, 2833 tonnes of fine gold, representing at the rate of that time (27.5 mg. of millesimal fineness 900) about FFr115 billion. These reserves might have appeared comfortable since they represented in weight of gold more than twice what the Banque possessed in its assets in April 1914 (1200 tonnes); in reality they were smaller than those effectively available at the beginning of the First World War, a time when, with gold circulating freely, a vast reserve existed outside the vaults of the Institut d'Emission, which was not the case in 1939. At the beginning of the Second World War private holdings of the yellow metal reflected secret hoarding, and there was for that reason little chance of its being placed at the disposal of the government.

Furthermore, France in 1914 possessed an extensive portfolio of external claims, a large part of which was used for international settlements; this portfolio was very small in 1939.

The government augmented the nominal value of its reserve by proceeding in February 1940 to a new devaluation, made necessary by economic developments, which brought the exchange value of the reserves up to FFr135 billion (see below).

The foreign exchange resources of the United Kingdom being also very limited, an agreement was signed between the two countries (4 December 1939) providing in particular for a fixed parity between the two currencies for specified renewable periods, a co-operation between the two exchange stabilisation funds, unlimited reciprocal credits without guarantee, the facility for each of the two countries to invest its reserves in securities issued by the other government (Treasury bills), the joint issue of loans on foreign capital markets, and finally a common policy for the purchase of war *matériel*.

If as a result the government's foreign exchange policy was coherent, domestic arrangements were more lax: although legally frozen in September, prices still recorded a rise of about 20 per cent between this date and June 1940.

The causes of this drift obviously lay in the imbalance between the supply of and demand for goods and services; no measures of rationing having been taken during the 'phony war', private sector demand had to be added to the greatly inflated demand of the State. From 1939 the public finances were in fact to play a determining role in the economy.

Intended to be more or less in balance, the 1939 budget turned out to be in deficit by FFr87 billion (21 per cent of the national income), the financing of half of which was effected by monetary means: essentially the lending of the Banque de France which made available to the government provisional advances renewable every three months at a rate of 1 per cent; and the purchase of Treasury bills by the banks.

Since the financial sphere was functioning as a 'closed vessel', the offset to the measured supply of money from external leakages was only slight, and the growth of the money stock accelerated from the autumn of 1939, reaching 38 per cent at an annual rate between the end of September 1939 and the end of May 1940.

Obviously production did not follow a comparable pattern of growth; the circuit was far from being closed, as is shown by the summary calculation of Table 7.2, which compares for the year 1939 an estimate of the demand for funds and the distribution of invest-

TABLE 7.2 *Financial flows 1939 (FFr billion)*

Sources of financing		*Investments*	
Budget deficit	87	Bonds	8.3
Bank credits to the economy	1.6	Savings banks	3.2
Other credits (including issues of bonds by companies)	4.5	Treasury bills	37.5
		Notes	39.5
	93.1	Bank money	13.3
net external flows	+9.5	Residual	0.8
	102.6		102.6

ments between economic agents. The holding of banknotes amounted to more than the subscriptions to Treasury bills; this break in the circuit could only widen.

The acceleration in the rise of prices still further reduced the potential development of French exports; given the enormous requirements for military *matériel*[3] a fresh devaluation was decided upon in February 1940, reserves in gold and foreign currency being calculated on the basis of 23.34 mg. of gold of millesimal fineness 900, instead of 27.5 mg. (the parity of 12 November 1938). The capital gain from this revaluation was allocated to the repayment of FFr15 billion of advances from the Banque de France to the State. Linked with this operation, an agreement stipulated that the Banque de France would cede to the Fonds de Stabilisation des Changes a stock of gold representing FFr30 billion and would receive as counterpart FFr30 billion in renewable three-month Treasury bills.

THE OCCUPATION – JULY 1940 TO AUGUST 1944

This period was characterised by a striking fall in production, brisk inflation and a surplus on the balance of trade artificially created by the pillage organised by the occupying power.

The overall index of industrial production recorded a fall of 55 per cent between June 1940 and May 1944: over the same period the rise in retail prices was assessed by the INSEE index as 155 per cent: imports fell by 90 per cent but exports by only 50 per cent, so that at the beginning of 1944 France's exports amounted to 280 per cent of her imports. This situation reflected the constraints operating on the

French economy directly, from the restrictions against imports and the levies made by France's principal 'partner' at that time, Germany; and indirectly, from the German government's fixing of a rate of exchange of 20 francs to the Reichsmark (RM), which significantly undervalued the franc and rendered French products extremely attractive to the army of occupation. For example, at the declaration of war the rate of exchange was FFr16 = RM1 and during the war the rate on the Zurich foreign exchange market, which though narrow was free, did not move far from FFr17 = RM1.[4]

These conjunctural developments must be set in a context of particularly brisk monetary expansion, at the origin of which was the situation of the public finances.

The development of the public finances

The budget deficit increased from 21 per cent of the national income in 1939 to 57 per cent in 1943 (Table 7.3). The cause of this sharp rise was a growth of expenditure almost entirely attributable to the charges imposed by Germany. In fact, in spite of a striking increase in subsidies intended to restrain the rise in prices (representing 1 per cent of the national income in 1940, 5 per cent in 1943 and 11 per cent in 1944), the Vichy government made an effort to limit the growth of conventional budgetary expenditure, an effort which was, of course, facilitated by the almost total absence of public capital expenditure during this period.

On the other hand the German authorities imposed charges of three kinds which ultimately fell on the budget:

- occupation charges for the German army, initially at a rate of FFr400 million a day, reduced to FFr320 million in 1941, then raised to FFr500 million in 1942 when the 'free' zone was invaded; to this tribute was added, also from 1942, occupation costs for the Italian army amounting to FFr1 billion a month;
- the financing of the bilateral 'clearings': a clearing office was made responsible for receiving the equivalent value in francs of the Reichsmarks necessary for French imports and paying to French exporters the franc equivalent of their sales in Germany. Obviously this office never received a single Reichsmark in payment for imports of French goods by the Germans and the French government had to advance the sums necessary to pay for the exports. Thus the French balance of trade 'surplus' observed at this time had particularly perverse effects,

TABLE 7.3 *Development of the budget deficit and the methods of financing it 1939–44 (FFr billion)*

	1939	*1940*	*1941*	*1942*	*1943*	*1944*
'Conventional' expenditure	150.1	204	121	133	135	213
Occupation indemnities (Germany and Italy)		80	130	124	220	142
Clearing and miscellaneous			12	33	63	52
Total expenditure	150.1	284	263	290	418	407
Receipts	63	72	80	97	122	124
Deficit	87	212	183	193	296	283
Deficit as % of national income	21.1%	47.5%	44.2%	43.6%	56.7%	52.5%
Financing of the deficit						
Long term borrowings	5		10	14	49	137
Monetary resources[1]	44.3	124.3	91.3	117.2	153.9	62.6
Other means of finance	37.7	77.7	81.7	61.8	93	83.4
(of which Treasury bills issued to the public and subscribed by the CDC)		(63)	(69.4)	(48)	(82)	(69)

NOTE 1. Advances from the Banque de France, Treasury bills subscribed by the banks, postal chequing accounts, coin.

since it reduced the supply of available goods and, in spite of the exchange controls, was expressed in an immediate contribution to monetary growth;

- other miscellaneous charges, in particular the indemnities paid to the owners of premises occupied by the German army and the compensation for requisitions.

Thanks to an astonishing increase in fiscal pressure, during this period taxes covered an almost constant proportion (about 30 per cent) of expenditure.

The financing of the deficit was achieved in what can be considered an honourable proportion by savings resources, some rather exceptional – deposits by industrialists in blocked accounts at the Treasury of their rights to tax deductions,[5] payment of certain public expenditures by drafts accepted by the Crédit National; and others more orthodox – long-term borrowings which in 1943, a particularly black year, yielded nearly FFr50 billion, Treasury bills which the public and the Caisse des Dépôts et Consignations subscribed to at an average of FFr70 billion a year.

In spite of these efforts, the break in the circuit remained wide open and the public authorities had to finance their deficit by monetary resources in a proportion which was never less than 50 per cent, except in 1944, with the great success of the Liberation bond issue (see below).

Interest rates, it is true, were not particularly attractive: for bonds they fell from 5.71 per cent in 1939 (annual average) to 3.78 per cent in 1944 (that is, a real pre-tax rate of – 18.5 per cent!); for Treasury bills the decline was not so steep, but the levels were derisory: 2.75 per cent in 1939, 2.21 per cent in 1944.

Would the government have had more success in tapping the liquid funds put into circulation if it had agreed to more attractive remunerations for savings?

This seems doubtful: in a country which remained very rural and where a 'wait and see' attitude to the course of the war was predominant, the 'roving flood'[6] was, in the absence of sufficient employment on consumer goods, bound to be invested in almost constant proportions in public securities and monetary assets.

The monetary situation and credit policy

The long-term tendency towards expansion of M2 was brought about by the financing of a monetary nature which the Treasury derived mainly from its borrowings from the Banque de France, but also from the subscriptions of bills by the banks and finally, but marginally, from the growth of the assets of individuals and companies in postal chequing accounts.

The conjunctural fluctuations of the money stock should not be linked to economic variables, or indeed to an autonomous behaviour of economic agents. They depended more on the rate at which the authorities and the armies of occupation made use of the tribute paid to them.

As in all the occupied countries, the Germans installed in France branches of the Reichsbank, the Reichskreditkassen (RKK), banks which issued money destined for the German army and administration.

But whilst in some countries the RKK effected a genuine independent creation of Reichsmarks, these operations were limited at that time in France. After July 1940 the Banque de France resumed its normal functions and progressively substituted its own banknotes for those, denominated in Reichsmarks, which had been issued by the RKK for France. The RKK then received, by credit to its account in the books of the Banque de France, the occupation indemnities denominated in francs which it redistributed to those whom it administered.

However, the RKK did not succeed in the early years in utilising the whole of the enormous tribute which was paid to it and considerable sums accumulated on its account with the Banque de France: a part of the monetary creation due to the advances of the Banque de France to the State, in order to permit it to pay the indemnities, thus found itself sterilised in the liabilities of the Banque. At the end of 1941 the sums not used reached FFr61 billion, or nearly 30 per cent of the occupation costs paid by France since July 1940.

Thus the increase in M2 which had reached 44 per cent in 1940 went down again to 22 per cent in 1941. From the end of that year, however, it accelerated, the RKK having ceased to accumulate reserves. The administration had more or less to empty its account in the course of 1942, and the increase in M2 rose again to 33 per cent in that year. It then slowed a little (25 per cent at an annual rate during the first half of 1943); but after this, essentially because of the growing weight of payments imposed by the occupying power, it returned to an annual rate of 30 per cent which was maintained practically until August 1944 in spite of a relatively important issue by the State on the bond market.

In all, between the end of 1939 and August 1944, the money stock increased by 250 per cent. Savings bank deposits increased somewhat less rapidly, at 167 per cent overall, but with a spectacular acceleration: a growth of 1.3 per cent in 1940 as a result of the disorganisation of the country, 13 per cent in 1941, 21 per cent in 1942, 32 per cent in 1943 and 46 per cent in 1944. The ceiling on deposits, which had remained at FFr20 000 (200 1959 francs) since 1931, had been raised to FFr25 000 in October 1941, FFr40 000 in October 1942 and FFr60 000 in August 1944. These successive rises were not irrelevant to the growth of deposits, but the very considerable increases in 1943 and 1944 also reflected the more and more complete disorganisation of the economic circuits of production and distribution, and the more and more pronounced wait-and-see attitude of the population.

In total, the aggregate which approximates to M3 (without Treasury bills, the outstanding amount of which is unfortunately very difficult to determine) increased by 233 per cent between the end of September 1939 and August 1944.

The reconciliation of this monetary expansion with the development of the principal economic indicators is illuminating in some respects, misleading in others.

The velocity of circulation of money (income velocity: national income/M2) diminished considerably, going from 2.1 in 1939 to 0.9 in 1944, a movement which revealed the creation of a disturbing reserve of inflation.

Figure 7.1 shows the divergence which was developing between the rate of growth of money and that of the retail price index, whilst production fell continuously.

Until 1942 the time path of injections of money accompanied fairly closely the fluctuations in the price index, but from 1943 the rise of the index became very erratic and its representative accuracy is more and more open to question.

Among the counterparts of the money stock the contraction of the share of claims on the economy reflected that of economic activity: 27 per cent at the end of 1939, 20.6 per cent at the end of 1940, 18 per cent at the end of 1941, the decline then becoming much sharper, to 9 per cent at the end of 1943 and 7.7 per cent at the time of the Liberation, almost a third of these claims being furthermore in the portfolio of the Banque de France in this period, against 10–15 per cent on average on the eve of war.

Regarding the behaviour of the public in the choice of monetary assets held, it was banknotes that were most obviously preferred.

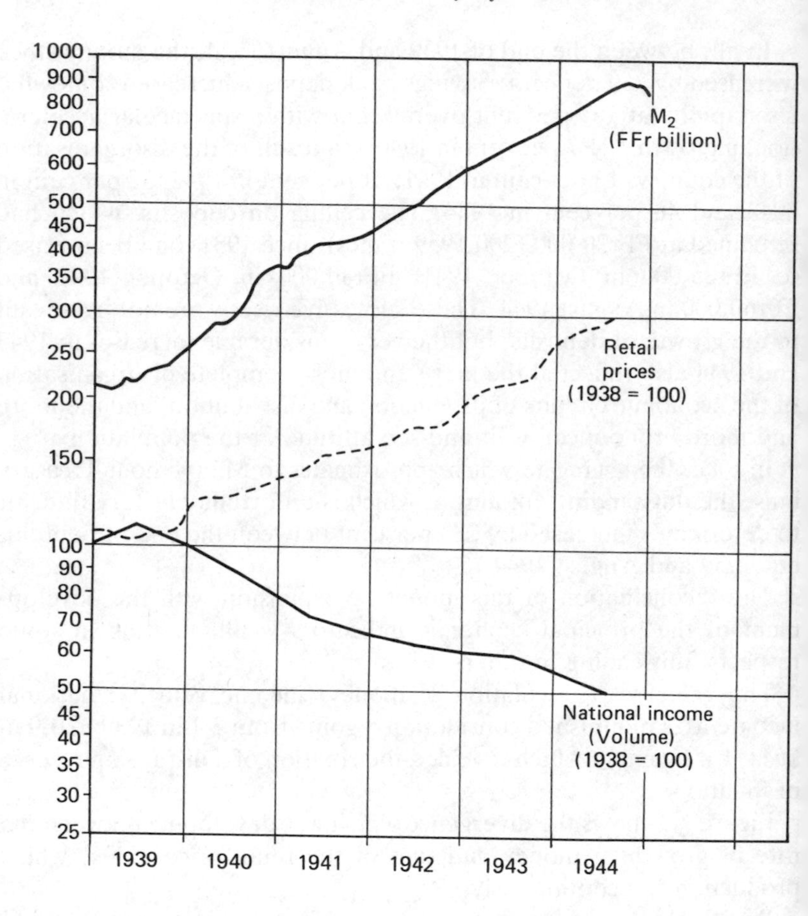

FIGURE 7.1 *Money, prices and national income 1939–44*

There was an increase of more than 300 per cent between the end of 1939 and August 1944. At the Liberation every French citizen held on average FFr15 500 in notes, against FFr3800 on the eve of war. The relative unpopularity of deposit money especially affected the banks, whose deposits increased by 'only' 147 per cent during this period; on the other hand postal chequing accounts enjoyed a considerable growth of 237 per cent, though one must recognise in this the effects of the State's taking over an increasingly large share in the allocation of resources and of goods and services through the organisations for the direction of production and for rationing set up at the beginning of the war.

On the monetary level it is obviously a matter of indifference whether liquid assets take the form of notes or deposits; but the government was preoccupied with this marked preference for forms of money which were material – and anonymous. This preoccupation was part of the inspiration for the laws of 13 and 14 June 1941 which laid the foundations of a corporate regulation of the banking system, intended to limit competition but at the same time to give security to depositors: the classification of banks, the creation of the category of 'financial establishments' which could not receive deposits from the public, and the setting up of the Commission de Contrôle des Banques. In spite of the modifications made in 1945 and 1967 this legal framework was to last for more than 40 years.

To conclude on this period, it is striking that the rise in prices was not more rapid since, particularly from 1942–43, all the conditions were present together for a galloping inflation of the type which Germany experienced in 1923: a considerable flood of monetary creation, an increasingly obvious disorganisation of production, and sharp practice and breaking of the rules being considered as a patriotic duty.[7]

Three essential reasons seem to have prevented such an inflation: the still largely rural structure of the population, and the feeling that 'a sou is a sou' – indeed this enormous mass of banknotes was very little used; the freezing of wages, which rose by only 63 per cent between 1939 and August 1944, relative to prices which rose by 180 per cent; and finally the totalitarian regime which put a brake on the natural mechanisms of the acceleration of inflation.

BRIEF MONETARY HISTORY OF FREE FRANCE

On 28 June 1940 General de Gaulle was recognised by the British government as the head of the Free French. The Free French movement had very soon to face up to financial and monetary problems: the maintenance of the troops who were continuing to fight, and also the organisation of monetary arrangements in the numerous and large colonial territories which joined the movement from the summer of 1940.

It was appropriate to set up an issue of money to replace that which had hitherto been current in the territories and which was under the strict control of metropolitan France; in fact the authorities in Paris could easily have disorganised the economic life of these colonies, for example, by massive injections of currency.

Moreover, it was necessary to finance the public expenditure of Free France and finally to ensure the settlement of its financial transactions with its allies.

Several agreements were signed with the British government (7 August 1940, March 1941): the British agreed to a permanent advance to Free France, thus ensuring a counterpart to its expenditure; moreover, the exchange agreements signed in 1939 were confirmed: the maintenance of the franc/pound exchange rate at FFr176.63 and the holding of foreign exchange reserves in common.[8]

The Caisse Centrale de la France Libre (CCFL) was created in December 1940 (becoming in 1943 the Caisse Centrale de la France d'outre-mer, and in 1945 the Caisse Centrale de Coopération Economique), which was to play the role of a genuine central bank[9] for the territories under the control of Free France.

In fact the CCFL was in the first place a bank of issue, issuing its own banknotes or having them issued for its account by the existing colonial banks. The counterpart of this issue consisted of gold and foreign currencies, bought from the local treasuries of the colonial territories, and of the notes of the colonial banks withdrawn from circulation.

The CCFL was also a banker for the Free French State. In this area, however, it could be said that it played at the same time the role of a central bank, granting advances to the Free French government, and the role of a treasury, since it proceeded to make regular issues of Treasury bills in the name of Free France, a situation obviously entirely out of the ordinary and which would be 'sacrilege' in normal circumstances.

Finally the CCFL was also an exchange office, centralising the assets in gold and foreign exchange and playing the role of a clearing house for the various territories of Free France. It was at this time that a system of correspondents' accounts was set up which is the ancestor of the operational account which today regulates the relations between the countries of the franc zone.

But the most important monetary problems which confronted Free France arose as the various stages of the Liberation were achieved.

(1) The monetary problems associated with the Allied landing in North Africa

When the Allies landed in North Africa in December 1942 the CCFL had just extended its authority to the territories of French West Africa.

The Allies provided their troops with special military banknotes to which they accorded a very favourable rate of exchange, 75 francs to the dollar (instead of the official rate of FFr43.80) and 300 francs to the pound sterling, which was thus in violation of the Franco-British exchange agreements. These parities had to be rapidly revised, but this was the occasion of a renegotiation of the Franco-British exchange agreements; as a result of these agreements in February 1944 the exchange rates of 200 francs to the pound and 50 francs to the dollar were in force throughout the territories answerable to the French Committee of National Liberation.[10]

(2) Monetary reform in Corsica

After the liberation of Corsica the provisional government put into effect there an original monetary policy which included:

- the withdrawal from circulation of banknotes issued by the Banque de France and their exchange for new notes, but within the limit of FFr5000 per person presenting them (plus FFr3000 per employee for the heads of companies). This deflation thus sterilised for the time being about one third of the fiduciary circulation. When the question of a monetary reform was also raised after the Liberation of metropolitan France, some people invoked the Corsican experience, but the government did not embark on this course (see below);
- a temporary blocking of assets in banks and savings banks;
- finally the opening of an account, in the books of the branch of the Banque de France in Ajaccio, in the name of the central treasury in Algiers, which foreshadowed the approaching return to the Banque of the character of a central bank.

In addition and to complete these particularly effective stabilisation arrangements, the issue of bearer securities was forbidden, and a tax was instituted on increases in wealth recorded since 1939.

(3) The liberation of the metropolis

The essential problem arose from the introduction by the Allies of a currency which was said to be French (there was thus a difference from the introduction of military banknotes in North Africa in 1943) but was different from that which was legally current in the country, and allocated to the expenditure of the campaigning armies. This measure was very badly received by General de Gaulle, who saw in it the sign of the assimilation of France, in the minds of the Allies, to

TABLE 7.4 *Summary of monetary and financial data 1939–44 (end-period totals, averages for interest rates) (FFr billion)*

	1939	*1940*	*1941*	*1942*	*1943*	*1944*
M2	255.4	370.6	447.4	589.3	741.6	847
Net assets in gold and foreign exchange	97.38	114.66		114.64	114.64	105.19
Claims on the Treasury	93.68	175.14	248.38	412.66	578.37	644.6
	(+76.6%)	(+87%)	(+41.8%)	(+66.1%)	(+40.2%)	(+11.5%)
Claims on the economy	67.08	75.03	81.18	63.46	69.13	95.48
	(+2.4%)	(+11.9%)	(+8.2%)	(–21.8%)	(+8.9%)	(+38.1%)
Deposits in savings banks	66.75	67.69	76.59	92.50	122.32	178.26
(for reference, ceiling on deposits, in francs)	20 000		25 000 (31/10)	40 000 (27/10)		60 000 (9.8.44)
Discount rate	2	2	1.80	1.75	1.75	1.75
Yield on bonds	4.97	4.80	3.60	3.45	3.59	3.39
New issues of negotiable securities:						
shares	1.73	0.70	5.69	7.40	6.51	5.56
bonds	8.26	1.29	16.68	21.86	52.63	144.06
(of which government bonds)	(5)	–	(9.83)	(14.11)	(49.12)	(137.05)
National income	433	419.3	391.7	424.1	493	738.5
Income velocity (national income/M2)	1.90	1.31	0.93	0.80	0.73	0.87

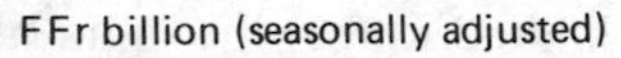

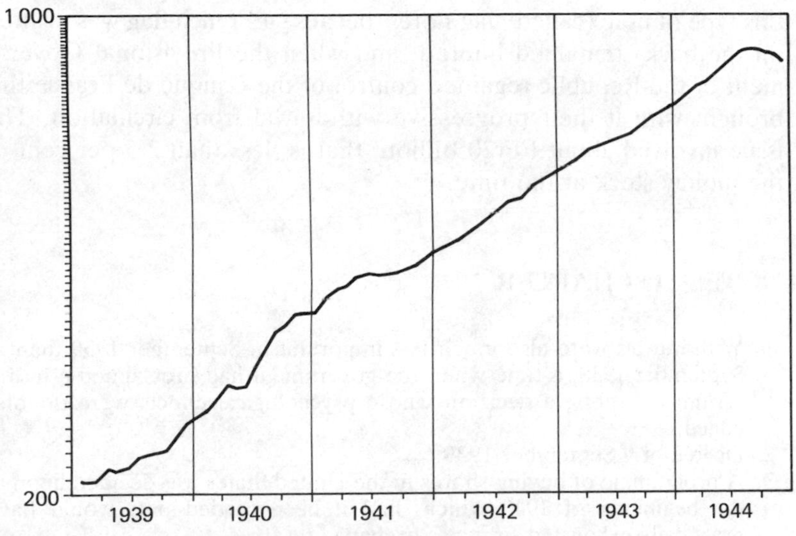

FIGURE 7.2 *Money stock 1939–44*

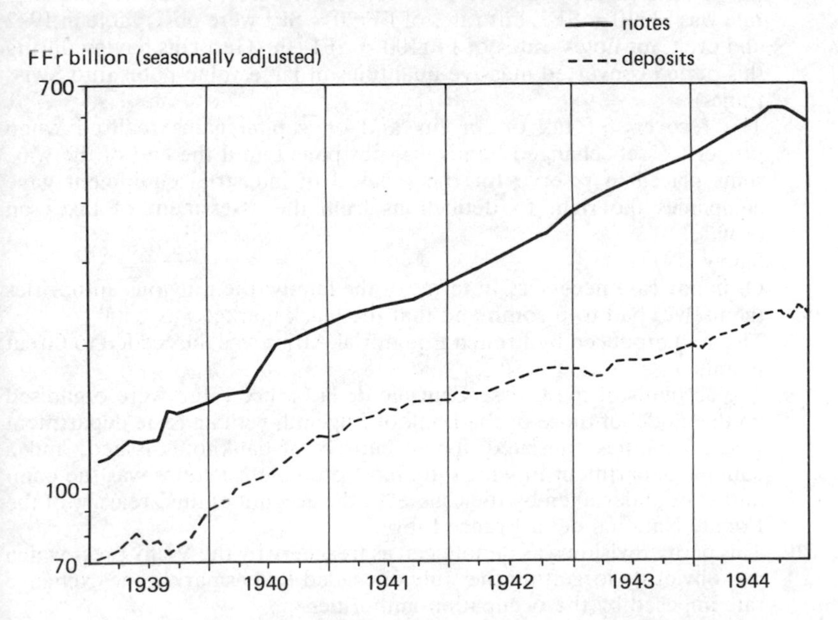

FIGURE 7.3 *Notes and bank deposits 1939–44*

some occupied territory, and only had a limited range; the issue of this type of note (called 'flag notes' because a French flag was printed on the back) remained limited, and when the Provisional Government of the Republic regained control of the Banque de France this brought with it their progressive withdrawal from circulation. The issue involved about FFr20 billion, that is, less than 2.5 per cent of the money stock at the time.

NOTES TO CHAPTER 7

1. Withdrawals were also much less important in September 1939 than in September 1938, a time when the government had proclaimed a moratorium on debts, a decision whose psychological effects were double-edged.
2. Decree of 9 September 1939.
3. A programme of buying shares in the United States was decided upon at the beginning of 1940 which, had it been carried out, would have practically exhausted France's exchange reserves.
4. On the same market the rate for the French franc against the Swiss franc (SF) on the other hand underwent very considerable variations; the base rate was FFr10 = SF1, but rates of FFr20 = SF1 were observable in 1942 and even, for notes, rates of FFr100 = SF1 (the Germans having during this period converted massive quantities of large value notes into Swiss francs).
5. The recovery of tax on profits and on capital gains realised when property assets changed hands was postponed until the end of the war; sums placed in reserve for the renewal of industrial equipment gave companies the right to deductions from the assessment of taxes on profits.
6. Sauvy (1978).
7. Or in any case necessary in terms of the family: the religious authorities themselves had to recommend that the black market was 'vital'.
8. The gold produced by French Equatorial Africa was thus ceded to Great Britain.
9. The accounts of the Caisse Centrale de la France Libre were organised on the model of those of the Bank of England, with an issue department whose liabilities consisted almost entirely of banknotes issued, and a banking department in which the most prominent feature was the commitments undertaken by the Caisse for the account of the Treasury of the Comité National de la France Libre.
10. This parity revision was denounced as treachery by the Vichy press which was obviously forgetting the truly one-sided Reichsmark/franc exchange rate imposed by the occupation authorities.

Part II
1944–73

8 1944–45: The Liberation

This short period is important: the choices made then in financial and monetary matters were to have their consequences in the years to follow.

At the end of the month of August 1944 the country was in large part liberated and found itself in a situation apparently much more serious than after the First World War. In demographic terms the losses were certainly less than half those due to the earlier conflict[1]; but in economic terms the ruins of the war, the levies and the destruction due to the occupying power (evaluated in 1946 at FFr5000 billion, or several years of the national income at that time) had weakened an apparatus of production and distribution the situation of which was already hardly brilliant in 1939.

However, there were some favourable factors: a clear increase in the birthrate had been in operation since 1941 and the future appeared promising; the very scale of the destruction called for complete renewal; and the mentality of those who now had political responsibility, haunted by the Malthusianism which had plunged the French economy before the war into lethargy, was imbued with dynamism and the spirit of enterprise. In fact these men laid the foundations of a remarkable economic recovery, in the nationalisation of the major tools of production and the introduction of economic planning. In the financial sphere ideas were more hesitant or at any rate more discordant. Certainly it could be said that the government of the time did not have the courage to take certain unpopular measures which we shall examine in the following paragraphs, but it is clear that the ardent desire to see the economy free itself from stagnation and archaism could only encourage the concealment, tacit or explicit, of financial constraints.

MONETARY DEVELOPMENT AND THE CHOICE OF FINANCIAL POLICY

As we saw in the preceding chapter, the French economy was excessively liquid in the middle of 1944, the years of occupation having been characterised by a large growth of the money stock, the essential counterpart of which was the financing of the budget deficit, while production declined. The liquidity ratio (M2/national income) which had been 0.55 in 1939 was 1.46 in 1944.

First orientations: August 1944 to December 1945

The first deliberations of the government on the liberated territory were faced with the question of how to reabsorb this vast reserve of liquidity. However, those who supported the exchange of banknotes in circulation for new notes of smaller value (called exchange with a freeze), which had already been tried in Corsica, had to recognise a substantial obstacle to their plan. There were no reserves of new banknotes to enable this operation to be carried out successfully.[2] It was thus necessary to issue a loan, which was extremely successful, bringing in FFr164 billion at the time. The Treasury could thus repay the provisional advances that the Banque had agreed to extend to it between September 1938 and March 1940, which stood in September 1944 at FFr71 billion. However, the underlying rate of growth of money was such that the decrease in the money stock was only FFr35 billion, or 4 per cent.[3] It was clear that the problem of excess liquidity was not solved. At this time, however, by raising wages and family benefits by 50 per cent the government made a rigorous solution particularly difficult. To try to avoid setting off the spiral, the authorities decreed a price freeze on 17 November, which obviously called for compensation at the level of the producers: the subsidies were to represent 20 per cent of budgetary expenditure in 1945.

The debate on the freeze

In January 1945, taking advantage of the low interest rates, the government embarked on a vast operation of consolidation of its debt; covering FFr100 billion, this conversion consisted of the replacement of the 4 per cent 1918 stock and the 4.5 per cent 1942 stock by a 3 per cent loan repayable in 60 years.

At the same time the Banque de France had new banknotes at its disposal; so started the debate, which still continues today: is money the cause or the consequence of inflation?

Those who favoured a severe reduction of the money stock in circulation by the exchange of banknotes for a lower value were obviously considered as naive quantity theorists who took no account of the velocity of money and accorded to the creation of means of payment a very debatable causative role.[4]

General de Gaulle appeared himself to be favourable to exchange with a freeze, some of his words and writing showing a real understanding of the problem.[5] However, he pronounced in favour of exchange pure and simple, without confiscation, wishing not to 'upset the substance and the activity . . . of a sick and wounded country'. The circumstances were certainly hardly propitious to such a course; the two successful experiences of such a policy on a national scale at the time were that of Belgium, a country whose overall economic policy was very orthodox and which had the advantage of vast reserves of foreign exchange gained during the war by their exploitation of the Congo, and several years later the German monetary reform imposed by the Allies.

A decision to impose a freeze could not in any case be taken in isolation; it was not in fact coherent with the other 'wing' of the government's economic policy, its policy on wages. Following a series of meetings between the government, trade unions and employers' organisations, wage rises came one after the other between 17 April 1945 and the end of the year. Taking account of the readjustments already decided upon in the autumn of 1944, wages were thus raised between spring 1944 and October 1945 by 135 per cent for professional workers and 127 per cent for manual workers; large-scale rises in controlled prices were also decided upon.

The exchange of banknotes for new notes took place from the month of June 1945.[6] The operation was interesting in itself because it allowed an idea to be obtained of the amount of 'ill-gotten' banknotes which the holders no doubt would not dare present for exchange; in fact some FFr30 billion were not presented, to the benefit of the Treasury.[7]

On the other hand the exchanges provided an opportunity for presenters to be encouraged to subscribe to Treasury bills or to deposit their money in bank accounts. These two aims were achieved; subscriptions of Treasury bills reached nearly FFr100 billion and the share in the money stock of deposits in banks and postal current accounts rose from 33 per cent in April to 47 per cent in July.[8]

This operation made only a small dent in the mass of liquidity in circulation. The latter continued to grow rapidly and for 1945 as a whole it expanded by 21 per cent.

This rate of increase was little different from those of the years of occupation. But in contrast with the earlier situation it accompanied a marked recovery of production, in volume and in prices. The supply of financing was the result not only of the budget deficit, which

TABLE 8.1 *The financing of the economy, 1945 (FFr billion)*

Sources of financing		*Investments of non-financial agents*	
Budget deficit	311	Bonds	49
Bank credits	74	Savings banks	91
Non-bank credits[1]	35	Treasury bills and other short term investments	74
External	–31	Deposits[2]	176
		Notes and coin	2
		Residual	–3
	389		389

1. Including net issues of bonds by the private sector.
2. Banks, postal chequing accounts, and special funds accounts at the Treasury (Fonds Particuliers).

SOURCES Banque de France studies; reconstituted monetary statistics; Mouvement économique France (INSEE).

had been relieved of the occupation charges but inflated by subsidies, but also of credits, essentially from the banks, to the private sector (Table 8.1).

The velocity of circulation of money, which in 1944 had fallen to 0.7, rose to 1.1 and the liquidity ratio of the economy (M2/national income) went from 1.46 in 1944 to 0.9. Should this be considered satisfactory? Was it not rather the trigger for runaway inflation? The future was to confirm this pessimistic prognosis and, according to a classic sequence, during the following years monetary creation, although abundant, was in retreat compared to the growth in transactions, which was strongly inflated by the rise in prices.

ECONOMIC DEVELOPMENT AND THE READJUSTMENT OF THE PARITY OF THE FRANC

The index of industrial production (base 100 in 1938) had fallen to 19 in August 1944; in spite of the handicaps represented by the paralysis of many centres of production and the deprivation of a million and a half workers who were still prisoners in Germany, and in part thanks to a significant recovery in the production of armaments of all types, the index rose fairly rapidly to reach 67 in January 1946.

This output was still quite insufficient to satisfy a demand stimulated by the dishoarding of cash accumulated during the war and by the large wage increases decided upon in the autumn of 1944 and the spring of 1945: in spite of the introduction of price control the rise in the cost of living reached 48.4 per cent in 1945 (against 22.2 per cent in 1944).

Such a development could only be unfavourable to the country's meagre export capacity; this caused little trouble during the earlier months, in view of the size of domestic demand and the almost total stoppage of imports between August 1944 and the spring of 1945, a number of large ports having been destroyed or being still occupied by the Germans. From the ending of hostilities, however, purchases from abroad grew rapidly, and in December they exceeded in volume the 1938 level, although they had represented no more than 10 per cent of it in May.

On the other hand exports remained at a very low level and for 1945 as a whole the ratio of exports to imports was only 19.9 per cent, the deficit reaching FFr45.6 billion.

The reserves of gold and foreign exchange, which had varied little during the occupation, since they amounted to FFr75.2 billion in December 1944[9] against FFr84.7 billion in May 1940, were in danger of being rapidly exhausted.

The government attended to the most urgent matters first, signing a series of agreements, particularly with Switzerland and Britain, which granted France credits. In addition it negotiated with the Export-Import Bank a credit of $550 million.[10] These various borrowings did not prevent very substantial inroads being made into the gold reserve, and a readjustment of the value of the franc became imperative. Exchange rates had changed very little during the war: they were FFr43.80 = $1 and FFr176.62 = £1 in 1940, and FFr49.63 and FFr200 respectively in 1945, when the rates were fixed by an inter-Allied agreement. These new parities substantially overvalued the franc since, during these five years, prices had multiplied by four in France whereas they had increased by only 70 per cent and 40 per cent in Britain and the United States respectively.

As long as the Allied troops were stationed in France, the authorities considered it preferable to let this situation continue: an overvalued currency dissuaded them from making too massive purchases.

However, the parity amendment had to come before 1 January 1946 in conformity with the agreements France had signed at Bretton Woods in joining the International Monetary Fund, which stipulated that the member countries of this organisation must before that date declare the parity of their currency, either in terms of gold or in terms of a currency convertible into gold.

On 26 December the government fixed at FFr480 the rate for the pound sterling and at FFr111.107 the rate for the dollar, a franc being made equivalent to 17.773 mg. of fine gold. The gold reserve was consequently revalued and on 26 December amounted to the equivalent of FFr183.4 billion (for 958 tonnes, against FFr92 billion and 2407 tonnes in September 1939) instead of FFr65.15 billion a week earlier; the capital gain thus produced was used to the extent of nearly FFr54 billion as an advance to the Fonds de Stabilisation des Changes to allow it to pay 400 tonnes of gold in settlement of France's imports, which brought back down to FFr127 billion the value of the reserve recorded in the Banque's assets; and the remainder of the capital gain was used to benefit the Treasury, the indebtedness of which to the Institut d'Emission went between one week and the next from FFr563 billion to FFr505 billion.

These parities might appear realistic in view of the differences in the rates of inflation observed during the war; but the underlying rate of growth of prices was then some 5 per cent per month, which meant that in a few weeks the French franc would again be overvalued.

Economics textbooks teach that an overvalued currency helps to moderate inflation, while an undervalued currency sustains it. If one looks at the experiences of France and Germany, countries which started their postwar economic process, the first with an overvalued currency and the second some years later with a manifestly undervalued currency, one must admit that these factors are secondary in comparison with other parameters such as incomes policy, the psychology of economic agents, distribution channels, and the stock of liquidities in circulation, which the Allies reduced in the proportion of 10:1 at the time of the monetary reform in Germany, thus making that country an extremely handsome present.

The devaluation of the franc in December 1945 necessarily marked the breakup of the monetary unity of the French Empire. Whilst up to this date the currencies of the various parts of overseas France had always undergone depreciations identical with those of the franc, it was no longer the same from this date onwards. Parity was maintained with the francs in circulation in North Africa and the Antilles, but the franc in circulation in French black Africa, in Madagascar, in Reunion and in the French Somali Coast (or the CFA franc – Colonies françaises d'Afrique), countries where the rise in prices had been much weaker than in France, was worth, no longer one metropolitan franc, but FFr1.70 after the devaluation, while the franc in circulation in New Caledonia, Polynesia and the New Hebrides was worth FFr2.40.[11]

THE REFORM OF THE FINANCIAL STRUCTURES

At the same time France implemented a profound transformation of its financial machinery.

The general inspiration was in fact the idea that the distribution of credit was too important for economic activity for it to be allowed to develop spontaneously: it was a lever which could be controlled only by public authority.

In consequence, by the law of 2 December:

- the Banque de France, already reformed in 1936, was completely nationalised (2 December 1945)[12];
- the ownership of the four largest deposit banks – the Crédit Lyonnais, Société Générale, Banque Nationale pour le Commerce et l'Industrie, Comptoir National d'Escompte – was transferred to the State, whilst government commissioners were installed at the major merchant banks;
- a Conseil National du Crédit was created, chaired by the Minister of Finance with the governor of the Banque de France as vice-chairman, composed of representatives of the principal economic forces, national social and occupational organisations, major administrative bodies and credit institutions, and given a consultative role over the direction of monetary policy and a decision-making role for all aspects of banking regulation.

These decisions indicated the wish of the authorities, and in a general way of all those who inspired them, to limit the powers of financial circles. The nationalisation of the banks, and of the Banque de France, the integration of the latter into a structure where it was not in sole charge of monetary and credit policy, revealed clearly the hierarchy of values: it was economic considerations that must prevail over financial and monetary ones. The spirit of the reforms logically prolonged the rejection of monetary contraction. It is easy to criticise *ex post* this orientation, which can be connected with the chronic tendency towards excessive inflation and financial laxity which characterised the next 15 years; but in this country ravaged by war and the sequence of internal struggles, frustrated by the consciousness of its decline and, in spite of all, longing once more to become a great economic power, would another more 'orthodox' policy have been possible?

NOTES TO CHAPTER 8

1. 600 000 deaths due to the war, against 1 350 000 between 1914 and 1918, and a shortfall in births assessed at 530 000 against 1 500 000 during the First World War. Mention should also be made of the departure of 300 000 foreigners between 1939 and 1945.
2. As the American government only recognised the provisional government of the French Republic in October, it could not officially take action until this date over the order for new banknotes which it had been given. The first deliveries were made at the beginning of 1945.
3. It should be noted, however, that at this time the Banque de France reintegrated into the fiduciary circulation substantial amounts of banknotes which had been evacuated to Britain in 1940 (amounting to nearly FFr7 billion) or withdrawn by the Resistance (FFr4.2 billion) and the retreating Germans (FFr5 billion). In each of these cases the counterpart of these operations was recorded as a debit of the Treasury.
4. Whilst one knows the economic ignorance of the majority of the people in politics at that time, one is flabbergasted by the self-confidence of the President of the Council who, in concluding a rather complex debate, settled the question definitively: 'it is a dangerous illusion which considers the excessive abundance of the means of payment as the cause of an imbalance of which, on the contrary, it is only a symptom'.
5. 'Undoubtedly the Liberation loan by withdrawing liquidity narrowly averted the catastrophe which would have been provoked by the sudden entry of this mass of liquid funds into markets which were three-quarters empty . . . but however salutary was the expedient, something quite different is now necessary' (De Gaulle, 1954–59, vol. 3).
6. The operation was in reality more complex. Initially the old notes were exchanged for notes printed in the United States and at De La Rue in London, but the quality of the engraving was so bad as to give rise to fears of counterfeiting. The Banque de France rapidly made efforts to replace them by its own banknotes which were in the process of being manufactured; this was completed in the fourth quarter of 1946.
7. By a simple accounting mechanism, the contraction of the liabilities of the Banque de France resulting from the non-presentation of banknotes for exchange had its counterpart in a contraction by the same amount in its assets, in this instance the net claims on the Treasury.
8. Wide movements were observed: during the second half of May credit balances in bank accounts increased by 60 per cent in the provinces and 35 per cent in Paris; at the Banque de France the balance of sight deposits rose from FFr36 billion on 24 May to FFr106 billion on 2 June. The fiduciary circulation thus diminished by FFr116 billion (20 per cent) in less than two months, and had to be speedily reconstituted.

9. Taking into account a withdrawal of gold to the value of FFr9.44 billion destined for the repayment to the Banque Nationale de Belgique of the gold which the latter had entrusted to France at the time of the invasion and which the Germans had confiscated.
10. Agreements of 22 March and 16 November 1945 with Switzerland, and of 27 March 1945 with Britain; convention of 26 December 1945 with the Export-Import Bank.
11. The situation was to become even more complicated in succeeding years: CFA and CFP (Colonies françaises du Pacifique) francs did not follow, or followed only partially, the further devaluations of the metropolitan franc. Furthermore, from March 1948, to take account of the particular situation of Djibouti (a free port) a Djibouti franc linked to the dollar was created.
12. The shareholders received negotiable bonds whose nominal value was based on the liquidation value subject to a ceiling of the average price of the share on the market between 1 September 1944 and 31 August 1945. In fact the shareholders received FFr28 029 per share while the liquidation value was FFr44 500: 'the difference between the two sums exceeds by about 10% the tax on the distribution of reserves which could normally have been charged to the shareholders' (Koch, 1983). The shareholders considered themselves injured parties.

9 1946–51: Reconstruction at the Expense of the Currency

The years 1945 to 1951, often called the period of reconstruction, were obviously very difficult. The French economy had to add the handicaps which it knew before the war, industrial decay and malthusianism, to those which the ordeals of the conflict had brought. But the 'muted sadness at the bottom of the national consciousness'[1] acted as a spur; and those in charge of the economy were not going to commit the errors which their predecessors had made in the aftermath of the First World War. From the beginning there was no question of seeking a rapid return to the mechanisms of liberalism; this would be criticised *ex post* by economists analysing the facts in isolation 30 years later, but it avoided wide conjunctural fluctuations; moreover, priority was given to capital equipment rather than to consumption. The planners imposed an orientation in this direction which was not obvious at the time.

In addition, although the indices of production and the figures published in the national accounts were not so flattering in comparison with the performances of the American and even the British economies, there was no doubt that the French economy was recovering.

This recovery was closely linked to the financial structures which resulted from the choices of economic policy, and which it is necessary to describe before presenting the monetary chronicle of this period.

A BREAK IN FINANCIAL BEHAVIOUR

The war and the occupation favoured financial behaviour which, while conforming to the traditions of 'deep France', nonetheless exhibited a break by comparison with that of before the war. The instinct of 'saving' remained lively but the forms of this saving had changed radically: investments in negotiable securities had been abandoned in favour of liquid assets. The insufficient monetary

TABLE 9.1 *Major annual statistics 1945–51*

	1945	*1946*	*1947*	*1948*	*1949*	*1950*	*1951*
National income (% change)	−8	+53.7	+8.4	+6.7	+13.5	+8.3	+5.9
GNP (% change)						+7.5	+6.2
Industrial production (% change)	+31.6	+68	+17.9	+14.1	+8	+4.9	+11.7
Balance of payments (FFr million):							
Trade account	−301.4	−534.5	−508.1	−499.9	−163.7	−27.4	−269.6
Services	−88.9	−78.7	−21.5	−35.6	−25.1	−12.8	−69.9
Capital flows	+292.9	+332.2	+458	+206.9	−11.2	+7.9	−8.4
FFr/$	49.63	111.11	111.11	214.39	350	3.50	3.50
	111.11			264			
	(Dec.)			(Oct.)			
Prices (% changes)							
Wholesale (100 in 1938/100 in 1949)	+41.3	+72.4	+52.1	+72.4	+11.6	+8.3	+27.8
Retail[1]	+48.5	+52.6	+49.2	+58.7	+13.2	+10	+16.2
Balance of the State budget (FFr billion)	−311	−338	−308	−554	−642	−565	−399
M2 (% change)	+21.1	+32.9	+24.3	+29.3	+25.6	+16	+18.4

SOURCE INSEE (1966).

1. Price index for the department of the Seine until 1949; national index after that.

contraction implemented at the end of the war (see above, chapter 8) had not reversed this tendency; it had merely reduced the share of banknotes in liquid assets, which was of some importance fiscally but had hardly any impact monetarily.

In the following years the decay of the capital market and its marginal role in the financing of the economy persisted. The principles of economic policy of the authorities accentuated it, whether consciously or not, while ignoring the constraint of financing or at least considering it secondary. This was one of the great weaknesses of the first plan for modernisation and equipment, in which financial and monetary orientations occupied a very modest place.

The principles of the financing of the economy

The search for the methods of financing necessary for expansion

The problem was that of how to guarantee the resources necessary for the financing of a budget deficit, which was still considerable at the beginning of the period, and of private sector investment.

As far as covering public deficits was concerned only one limit retained any significance: that of the fiduciary circulation,[2] to which the public, excusably, but also the authorities, assimilated the creation of money. Beyond this concept there hardly existed any constraint. Those in authority at this time were haunted by the memory of the 'wall of money' and the difficulties which prewar governments, generally of the left, had experienced in obtaining resources during Treasury crises. They therefore searched for a way of setting up a system which would guarantee them disposable funds in all circumstances. The advances of the Banque de France being limited and the raising of the ceiling on them being subject to a sensitive parliamentary vote, they rapidly set up what was later called the 'circuit', that is to say a collection of mechanisms which were more or less coercive; this led numerous financial institutions, and by no means the smallest of them, to deposit with the Treasury a part, even the whole, of the resources they collected. The important links in this circuit were of two types:

- first, the Caisse des Dépôts and the savings banks, the Crédit Agricole, the major specialised organisations (Crédit National, Crédit Foncier de France), all institutions which would provide the State with financing that was considered non-monetary because it originated either from bond issues or from deposits in savings banks (although available at sight, these deposits were in fact particularly stable and their classification as outside the bounds of money was not unjustified);

• secondly, also helping to feed the circuit, postal chequing accounts, personal funds deposited with the Treasury, and the banks which were obliged by virtue of the regulation known as the 'government securities floor'[3] to devote a predetermined proportion of their employable funds to subscriptions to Treasury bills, issued on tap by the authorities at regulated rates. Now these latter resources, although less blatant than the fiduciary circulation, are just as much monetary. It was only from the 1950s, however, that the circuit was used to its full potential.

The absence of financial constraint and the search for a 'guarantee of resources' also inspired the methods of financing in both the private and the nationalised sectors, with the setting up of the mechanism for medium-term refinanceable credit. This procedure was an attempt to reconcile the requirements of the French economy for the financing of its investments, that is, medium- or long-term loans, with the essentially monetary nature of French people's financial investments. Refinanceable medium-term credit associated together the credit institutions, the banks and the financial establishments, which distributed it; the major specialised organisations, the Crédit National, Caisse des Dépôts, Crédit Foncier, Caisse Nationale de Crédit Agricole, which after studying the file on a proposed credit conferred a label of quality on it and agreed eventually to take over its financing from the banks; and lastly the Banque de France, whose approval reinforced that of the specialised organisations and endowed the credit with a 'rediscount agreement' which constituted a guarantee of refinancing. This therefore made official the 'transformation' by which it was accepted that long-term lending (five years, later seven) could be financed by the banks or by the Banque de France, and thus by the creation of money.[4]

The very rapid development of medium-term credit was in fact very largely financed during these years by the Banque de France, the banks only retaining a small fraction in their portfolios and the specialised organisations in practice only playing the role of transmitting the files.

The system was extended to the financing of public housing when the Banque de France accepted in June 1950, not without reluctance, that it would give its rediscount agreement to the fraction at less than five years of the 'special loans for construction' distributed by the

Sous-Comptoir des Entrepreneurs; the Caisse des Dépôts and the Crédit Foncier also undertaking to participate in the financing. In fact the contribution of the Caisse des Dépôts, an essential link in the Treasury circuit to which it gradually came to lend the greater part of its liquid assets, rapidly decreased to nothing. The Banque de France thus had to hold, in particular during the 1950s (see the following chapter), a considerable portfolio of special loans; it therefore became an auxiliary of the circuit.

Cheap Money

The availability of funds was to go hand in hand with their modest cost. In the context of a rate of inflation which reached more than 50 per cent per annum from 1946 to 1948, any notion of a real rate of interest was deprived of meaning. The rates at the time appeared no less derisory: until December 1946 the discount rate of the Banque de France was 1 5/8 per cent and the rate of return on bonds oscillated between 3.6 per cent and 4.6 per cent which obviously hardly encouraged purchases; to attract savers the issuers and in particular the State provided specific advantages with their borrowings – indexations, tax exemptions, lotteries – or practised forced borrowing (1948). A slight rise occurred in January 1947 (to 1 3/4 per cent for the discount rate),[5] not without the reluctance of the Léon Blum government, which embarked upon a struggle against inflation but did not want to pay the whole price. On this occasion disagreement, which became permanent, manifested itself between on the one hand the Board of Directors of the Treasury, who were anxious both to guarantee in any circumstances the financing of the economy at moderate rates and to contain the rising burden on the public debt; and on the other hand the Banque de France which was more inclined to rigour.

In October 1947 the minimum discount rate went to 2 1/2 per cent, the rate of return on bonds reaching at this time nearly 7 per cent. A new increase of the discount rate in October 1948 (to 3.5 per cent) was partly reversed (to 3 per cent) some days later. In 1950, with the slackening of inflation, the discount rate was brought back to 2.5 per cent; the rate of return on bonds was then 6.6 per cent.

The most surprising thing is that these modest rises, passed on in the cost of credit within limits strictly fixed by the Conseil National du Crédit, had some impact on the demand for financing.

Selectivity

The authorities, however, tried hard to recognise the right to credit only in return for compliance with precise criteria, by establishing the foundation of a selective credit policy intended to channel funds towards the uses judged to be of most benefit to the economy.

This selectivity was essentially founded on a prior agreement of the Banque de France, indispensable for the allotment of any credit over a certain amount, and on its agreement to rediscount; these agreements required the usual guarantees concerning the stability of the financial situation of the borrower company, but endeavoured also to take into account the economic priorities defined by the Plan. Speculative stockbuilding operations were also strictly limited. In its discounting activities the Banque de France would in addition accord preferential rates for certain operations (see above).

The financing of the economy and the structure of investments of economic agents

As shown in Table 9.7, the supply of financing was particularly important, being 25 per cent of GNP in 1946, more than 12 per cent until 1948, and then more than 8 per cent. This corresponded closely with the options of the government's economic policy; but above all this financing was only weakly consolidated in stable saving, for holdings of monetary assets represented nearly 90 per cent of financial wealth (in 1946 and 1947, however, this percentage was appreciably decreased). By comparison with the interwar period the contrast was very marked. In 1928 the supply of financing was less than 7 per cent of national income and the building up of monetary assets was entirely marginal. In 1937 the supply of financing, now become more important at 10 per cent of national income, was consolidated in the form of acquisitions of bonds for two thirds of its amount.

This abundant 'lubricant' of the economy was supplied in a significant proportion, that decreased only at the end of the period, by the budget deficit, which was 58 per cent of the total in 1946, 67 per cent in 1950 and 38 per cent in 1952.

However, it was certainly the variations in the total supply of financing, whether it had its origin in the public sector or was provided by the lending of the credit establishments to the private sector, and above all the proportion of this financing retained in monetary form, which set the pace for economic activity, the external deficit and prices, as we shall see in the chronological developments which follow.

MONETARY AND FINANCIAL NARRATIVE

Three periods can in fact be distinguished:

- the first two years, 1946 and 1947, were marked by the abundance and the almost total lack of consolidation of financing, a net recovery of industrial production, brisk inflation, and a large deficit on external trade;
- a movement in the opposite direction occurred from 1948 up to the middle of 1950: monetary policy was much more rigorous and both inflation and the external deficit were appreciably reduced, but the pace of activity slackened;
- a revival of inflation was observable during the later months of 1950; its origins were international, but the relaxation of constraints in domestic policy made a major contribution to it.

1946–47: Hyperinflation and the flight from money

During these two years a still substantial budget deficit, but above all a wages policy lacking in rigour and the almost total absence of monetary constraint, all fed a demand which was out of proportion to the productive capacity of the country. In these conditions the rise in prices persisted at a very high level – 52.5 per cent in 1946, 49.2 per cent in 1947 – and the external deficit (6.8 per cent of GNP in 1946, 3.9 per cent in 1947) led to a rapid draining away of France's reserves.

The budget deficit remained important; it reached 12.4 per cent of GNP in 1946 and was still 6.9 per cent in 1947. However, this was not on the same scale as the 1945 situation (25 per cent of GNP), even if the apparent improvement had to be qualified insofar as, from 1946, it was due in part to reparations under the heading of war damages and the decrease in military expenditure. A worrying sign, however, was that it was not spending on capital goods that deepened the deficit; not until 1948 (see below) did substantial amounts under this heading figure in public expenditure.

But it was above all the lack of rigour in wages policy which contributed to the imbalance. The famous conference at the Palais Royal (4 July 1946), which the government had counted upon to

TABLE 9.2 *Contributions to increase of M2 (FFr billion)*

	1946	*1947*
Gold and foreign exchange	−35	−30
Claims on the Treasury	+165	+176
Credits to the economy and miscellaneous	+203	+185

neutralise the (*a priori* contradictory) demands of the social partners, ended in fact in a wages rise of a minimum of 25 per cent; at the same time the farmers obtained a virtual doubling of the price of wheat, which spread to the prices of basic food products.

It is difficult to characterise the monetary policy of these two years; to qualify it as lax corresponds no doubt to a correct view of things, but one which is from too great a distance. In fact the Banque de France had no alternative but to go along with the orientations of the time.

The growth of 'net domestic credit' (claims on the Treasury plus bank credits to the economy) was 41 per cent in 1946 and a further 29 per cent in 1947; on the other hand, in accordance with a classic interdependence, the development of the 'gold and foreign exchange' counterpart revealed a destruction of money (Table 9.2).

An important sign, reflecting the re-establishment of activity, but also putting into perspective the responsibility of the public finances for the monetary excesses, was the very important increase in claims on the private sector which henceforth exceeded, in the structure of the counterparts of M2, those on the Treasury. (It is necessary to go back to the 1920s to find a similar situation.)

The financing of the Treasury was first of all ensured by using the advances from the central bank (the margin for which was reconstituted thanks to the loan of 1945)[6]; however, it was because of the reluctance of the banks to subscribe to Treasury bills that the Banque de France extended its refinancing to the acceptances of the Crédit National (drafts drawn by the State on the Crédit National in payment for services provided by companies), admitting their discounts with two signatures and including them in the type of paper which it was ready to buy on the money market. The refinancing of guaranteed bonds was also used.

The years of 1946 and 1947 were the start-up years for refinanceable medium-term lending; the institutions which collected savings (the Caisse des Dépôts and the Crédit National) contributed very little to its financing, which from this time was to be very largely of a monetary nature and mainly provided by the Banque de France.

The interest rate constraint was also weak (see above). The outlines were already visible of what was to be, almost until the beginning of the 1980s, a constant in the economic policy of the authorities: not only that interest rates should be low, but that their fluctuations should remain limited.

The money stock grew by 33 per cent in 1946 and by slightly over 24 per cent in 1947. The liquidity ratio (M2/GDP) decreased by no less because of this, since during these two years GDP, assessed at current prices, grew by 132 per cent and by 61 per cent; but this was obviously the sign not of some pressure exerted by monetary policy but of the triggering of hyperinflation and a flight from money.

In order to finance its trading deficit, France practically exhausted the rest of its reserves of gold (about 500 tonnes) and foreign exchange. In conjunction with the requisitioning of private assets in foreign exchange and in foreign negotiable securities, permitted by the devaluation law of 26 December 1945, this allowed about half of the deficit to be financed; the rest was financed by loans contracted mainly with the American Treasury but also with the governments of Canada and even New Zealand and finally with the international organisations, the International Monetary Fund and the World Bank,[7] for a total representing nearly 7 per cent of French GNP.

Stabilisation: 1948–50

These three years were marked in many fields by spectacular reorientations in favour of the laws of the market economy:

- the prices of basic products – coal, steel, electricity, railway kilometres – without being freed were fixed at much more realistic levels, almost double the previous ones;
- wages were freed;
- the prices of the majority of industrial products were freed[8];
- economic subsidies were substantially reduced;
- a fiscal amnesty was granted to previously exported capital (the holders of which could put themselves right by the payment of a tax of 25 per cent[9]; it was even envisaged that the payment of imports by clandestine capital should be authorised);
- finally the gold market was reopened, with anonymity of transactions and the non-intervention (in theory, it is true) of the Banque de France.

Some of these measures, particularly the last ones, may seem 'immoral', but they contributed to the re-establishment of confidence.

This policy was accompanied by an undeniable return to equilibrium in major matters: the rise in retail prices fell from 58 per cent in 1948 to 10 per cent in 1950; the external deficit fell from 3.7 per cent of GDP in 1948 to 1.9 per cent in 1949 and to a very small amount in 1950. On the other hand the expansion of activity, while continuing, slowed down, the increase in industrial production falling from 14.1 per cent in 1948 to 7.9 per cent in 1949 and 4.9 per cent in 1950.

These results were due to a number of factors and accompanying measures, without which even a moderate return to liberalism would undoubtedly have led to disaster: the turn in public opinion, the adjustment in the parity of the franc, American aid, and finally the bringing into operation of a policy of controlling the growth of credit.

• Psychologically, first of all, the government held some strong cards: after the failure of the great strike of November and December 1947 the trade unions were obviously demoralised; energetic measures (particularly in respect of prices) could then be taken by competent Finance Ministers – René Mayer until July 1948, and then Maurice Petsche.

• On the other hand the authorities proceeded by stages to a readjustment of the parity of the franc, which restored a realistic rate of exchange.

At the beginning of 1948 a first devaluation took the dollar rate to FFr214.39, instead of FFr119.10. In fact the operation was more complex, because a system of multiple parities against the dollar was put into operation and the official rate of FFr214.39 applied to hardly any transactions; on the other hand a free market was created for dollar purchases for financial transactions and tourist expenditure: the law of supply and demand in this market carried the dollar rate to nearly FFr310. Finally an intermediate rate between the official and the free market rates, that is FFr264, was established for commercial transactions. This operation was badly received by the IMF and by France's trading partners, particularly the United Kingdom, whose currency was not involved in this variable-geometry regime, but only in the single official rate.

On 17 October 1948 a second operation did something to unify the regimes by aligning all the currencies on the parity resulting from the 'cross rate' with the 'average rate' for the dollar (FFr264).

Finally on 20 September 1949 a new devaluation put an end to multiple rates and fixed the franc/dollar parity at FFr350. This readjustment was made necessary by the devaluation of the pound, which occurred at the close of the annual assembly of the IMF and which surprised everybody by its magnitude: the rate went from $4.04 to $2.80 to the pound, whilst on the free markets the rate which emerged was $3.20.

These successive adjustments together with the progressive recovery of industry[10] made possible a brisk growth of exports.

• Another favourable factor was the introduction of Marshall Aid, to the extent of $820 million in 1948, $1070 million in 1949 and $530 million in 1950. This aid had two consequences. It made it possible to finance the external deficit and even, from 1949, to reconstruct the foreign exchange reserves: the 'gold and foreign exchange' counterpart of the money stock went from FFr65 billion in December 1948 to FFr443 billion in December 1950. And it provided, by the equivalent in francs of this foreign exchange, the means of financing the part of the budget deficit henceforth devoted to the growth of investment. The government set up the Fonds de Modernisation et d'Equipement, the ancestor of the Fonds de Développement Economique et Social, the resources of which were budgetary (it was a special account of the Treasury). Marshall Aid made possible the financing, obviously monetary, of the early years of operation of this fund.

• Finally, and here lies one of the essential points, the authorities accompanied their arrangements with the putting into operation of a coherent and markedly restrictive monetary policy. This policy had two aspects. One, pursuing the attempts made at the Liberation, consisted of drawing off liquid funds by the more or less authoritarian measures taken at the beginning of 1948: a forced loan subscribed by companies[11] which brought in FFr120 billion, and the withdrawal and temporary freezing of FFr5000 notes (29 January 1948), a surprise measure with which the government accompanied the somewhat anti-social arrangements (see above) made at the same time. The second aspect was more concerned with the future. The preceding measures had only temporarily slowed the pace of monetary creation: in the third quarter of 1948 it accelerated again (43 per cent per year, against 26 per cent in the second quarter and 19 per cent in the first).

The weapons of monetary policy were too weak to control this excess of liquid funds: they were in fact limited to the obligation on the banks to submit to advance examination by the Banque de France credits of a certain size, with the exception, however, of discounted commercial and government bills. Did the monetary authorities really wish to put a brake on the expansion of the money stock? Their steps may seem ambiguous, for according to the report of the Conseil National du Crédit for 1949 'the money stock, in spite of a substantial increase in the course of the year, undoubtedly remains insufficient with respect to the requirements for liquid funds experienced by the economy'. But this same report, like that of the previous year, underlined the dangers of an excessive development of credit; without this being precisely explained, the idea, which can be found formalised some years later, is that the money stock ought not to develop under the exclusive pressure of 'domestic credit' (this phrase is obviously not used), that is to say, claims on the Treasury and credits to the economy, since the inevitable result would be a leak of foreign exchange. On the contrary a limitation of the growth of domestic credit, by contributing to a return to external equilibrium, gives rise to inflows of foreign exchange, which create money, admittedly, but not in an 'unhealthy' way.[12]

To control the distribution of credit the monetary authorities possessed one weapon: action on the banks' liquidity, which the circumstances of the time rendered particularly effective.

The 'factors' of bank liquidity, that is, the elements which help to restrain, or on the other hand to extend, the funds of the banks had hardly been studied before the war. Moreover, these factors had been in the main very favourable to the banks since the movement of banknotes and the growth of assets in the accounts of individuals and companies at the Banque de France either exerted a weak pressure on the liquidity of the banks or were offset by the favourable movements of gold (and, more marginally, of foreign exchange) and, especially during the second half of the 1930s, by the direct lending of the Banque de France to the Treasury (Table 9.3).

During and after the war the fiduciary circulation experienced a rapid increase[13]; the very substantial losses suffered by the foreign exchange reserves had also weighed on the funds of the banks, in spite of the extent of the direct lending of the Banque de France to the Treasury: a net requirement for liquid funds existed henceforth, which would oblige the credit institutions to refinance themselves, for non-negligible amounts, from the Institut d'Emission: it would be said that the (money) market was 'in the (central) bank', a situation which has persisted until the present.

The Banque de France thus possessed the means, by limiting its

TABLE 9.3 *Factors affecting bank liquidity (FFr billion)*

	1933	*1939*	*1946*	*1947*
Banknotes	−82.3	−151.3	−725	−853
Cheque accounts at Banque de France	−13.2	−14.2	−4	−12
Gold and foreign exchange	+81.2	+98.3	+92	+61
Treasury	+6.8	+58.2	+554	+716
Direct credits from Banque de France to economy and miscellaneous	+3.8	+4	n.s.	n.s.
Balance	−3.7	−5	−83	−83

A positive sign (+) indicates a movement which increases the funds of the banks.
A negative sign (–) indicates a movement which reduces the funds of the banks.

refinancing, of putting a brake on the dynamic growth of the credit institutions.

The banks obtained this refinancing essentially in two ways: by encashing their very large portfolios of Treasury (government) bills and by rediscounting credits to the economy. These two ways would henceforth be limited. On 29 September 'floors (minimum holdings) of government securities' were brought into effect and 'rediscount ceilings' were made more general. The banks had on the one hand to keep in their portfolios a reserve of government bills equal to at least 95 per cent of the sum held on 20 September, and on the other hand to reemploy at least 20 per cent of the annual increase in their deposits in taking up government bills. This arrangement had the double effect of limiting the ability of the banks to encash their assets at the Institut d'Emission and of ensuring for the Treasury an inflow of resources less in the public eye than direct lending from the Banque de France, which remained the focus of public opinion.

As for the introduction of rediscount ceilings, it consisted of extending to the whole of the banking sector an arrangement initially reserved for the smallest banks and intended, when it was introduced, to preserve some institutions from excessive indebtedness.[14]

Although very badly received by the banking profession, these measures had a certain effectiveness: from the end of 1948 the recourse of the Treasury to advances from the Banque de France was appreciably moderated; in 1949 their growth was less than a quarter of the amount reached in 1947 and this was succeeded by a decrease in 1950. As for credits to the economy, their growth fell from 73 per

TABLE 9.4 *Contributions to increase of M2 (FFr billion)*

	1948	*1949*	*1950*
Gold and foreign exchange	—	+89	+289
Claims on the Treasury	+167	+124	−21
Claims on the economy and miscellaneous	+300	+346	+171

cent in 1948 to 40 per cent in 1949 and 14 per cent in 1950, a trend closely followed by the refinancing of the Banque de France.

The structure of the counterparts of M2 reflected the improvement both of the economic situation and of the external balance (Table 9.4).

The relapse of 1951

The indices for 1950 continued to paint a rosy picture: foreign trade was in balance and the rise in retail prices was 11.8 per cent over the four quarters.

However, inflation and trade imbalance were virtually restarted by a certain number of measures which affected the economy at the same time as the renewal of the rise in world prices of primary products:

- On 22 August the government of M. Pleven, which had to fix the level of the guaranteed minimum wage (the SMIG), the principle of which had been adopted by the law of 11 February, set it more than 8 per cent higher although retail prices had gone down during the first half of 1950.
- The restrictive nature of monetary policy was further weakened: the marked slowing down in the rise of the index of industrial production during the early months of the year gave rise to fears of a recession, fears strongly encouraged by the complaints of wholesalers and retailers.

In these conditions the Conseil National du Crédit judged it right to relax the limits on credit, the more so because it considered the size of the money stock 'relatively small compared with the requirements for liquid funds experienced by companies' (as a percentage of GDP, however, the money stock was twice as large as it was in Germany).

The rediscount ceilings, which had already been raised from FFr175 billion to nearly FFr200 billion in the course of 1949, were also raised by 25 per cent during the first half of 1950.

The discount rate was lowered from 3 to 2.5 per cent in January; other arrangements, particularly the raising of the threshold for prior authorisations and the setting-up of the system of special loans for construction (the medium-term fraction of which could be discounted at the Institut d'Emission), completed this change of direction.[15]

All these measures, which would certainly have been opportune if the conjuncture had been characterised by a recession, were already questionable in a context of demand which was going to remain unsatisfied for many years. With the Korean war then about to encourage a considerable rise in demand and in international prices, these measures contributed strongly to the return of the imbalances.

These imbalances – the renewal of the trade deficit, which represented 1.3 per cent of GDP in 1951, and the resumption of the rise in prices (10 per cent during the second half of 1950 alone, 16.2 per cent in 1951) – were reflected in the development of the money stock and above all of its counterparts.

Gold and foreign exchange assets (including the counterpart of American aid) went down by FFr198 billion in 1951 (they had grown by FFr289 billion in 1950),[16] and the total of claims on the Treasury, claims on the economy and 'miscellaneous' rose by 28 per cent (against 6 per cent in 1950); from the last months of 1950, the growth of claims on the economy accelerated considerably, and the annual rate of increase of the money stock rose from 15 per cent to 20 per cent (in spite of the contractionary effect exerted by the outflow of foreign exchange).

In the autumn of 1951 the monetary authorities decided upon a tightening-up of their policy; these measures were very badly received by public opinion, which had difficulty in understanding the extent to which the French economy had gone off course. The discount rate was raised from 2.5 per cent to 3 per cent on 11 October, then to 4 per cent on 8 November. The arrangements for limits on rediscounting were reconsidered: the elements of flexibility which the credit institutions enjoyed and which allowed them to exceed the ceiling during the course of a month were abolished, the banks being able in exceptional circumstances to obtain a temporary discount in excess of their ceiling (up to a limit of 10 per cent) at a cost higher than the discount rate (this expensive facility was later nicknamed 'hell'). However, to take into account the 'acquired rights' conferred by the elements of flexibility that had been tolerated up to then, a general raising of the ceilings was decided upon. These measures as a whole nevertheless had a restrictive impact on the

TABLE 9.5 *Summary of monetary and financial data 1946–51 (end-period totals, averages for interest rates)* (*FFr billion*)

	1946	*1947*	*1948*	*1949*	*1950*	*1951*
M2	1363	1694	2191	2750	3189	3775
Net assets in gold and foreign exchange	92	61	53	151	443[1]	245
Claims on the Treasury	940	1116	1283	1407	1386	1570
	(+21.3%)	(+18.7%)	(+15%)	(+9.7%)	(–1.5%)	(+13.3%)
Claims on the economy	312	491	851	1189	1356	1906
	(+154%)	(+57.4%)	(+73.3%)	(+39.7%)	(+14%)	(+40.6%)
Deposits in savings banks	292.1	308.5	398	487.5	617.8	692.8
(for reference, ceiling on deposits in francs)	100 000	100 000	200 000	200 000	300 000	300 000
	(8.4)		(17.3)		(27.5)	
Discount rate	1.62	1.91	2.71	3	2.72	2.79
Yield on bonds (issued)	4.36	4.98	5.86	6.84	7.01	7.02
New issues of negotiable securities:						
shares	26.2	31.2	40.7	41	31	43.6
bonds (gross)	64.4	33.6	156.5	327	93.7	51.5
(of which government bonds)	(28.7)	—	(108)	(297)	(30.8)	—
National income	1935	3395	5582	6728	7640	9200
GNP	—	—	—	8660	10 020	12 290
Income velocity (national income/M2)	1.62	2.18	2.93	2.73	2.60	262
GNP/M2	—	—	—	3.50	3.41	3.50

1. Taking into account the revaluation of the Banque's gold reserve, consequent upon the devaluations of 1948 and 1949, which produced a capital gain of FFr126.2 billion. Out of this capital gain FFr77 billion was allocated to the redemption of Treasury bills held by the Banque de France as counterpart of the gold transferred to the Fonds de Stabilisation des Changes, FFr26 billion to the repayment of an American loan, and the balance to the repayment of Treasury bills held by foreign banks.

TABLE 9.6 *The financing of the economy 1946–51 (FFr billion)*

	1946	*1947*	*1948*	*1949*	*1950*	*1951*	
Sources of financing							
Balance of State budget[1]	338	308	414	360	323	340	
(of which loans for public sector housing and investment)	(13)	(27)	(187)	(362)	(389)	(295)	
Credits							
* Bank	189	179	360	339	167	550	
* Non-bank[2]	84	45	48	56	68	111	
External	−187	−181	−4	90	292	−198	
For reference: American aid			140	243	181	309	
							Investments
	59	3	156	136	113	54	Bonds subscriptions
	−13	−30	131	−14	147	82	Net subscriptions of Treasury bills
	23	17	89	89	129	74	Deposits in savings banks
	337	331	497	559	439	586	ΔM2
	(156)	(191)	(74)	(310)	(290)	(301)	* (of which banknotes)
	18	17	−55	75	22	7	Miscellaneous and residual[3]

SOURCES Statistiques et Etudes financières; reports of the Conseil National du Crédit.

1. A surplus reduces the supply of financing (– sign); a deficit increases it (+ sign). Including loans from the FME; balance after taking American aid into account.
2. Including net issues of bonds by non-financial companies.
3. Various uses of funds by financial institutions and deposits not included in the aggregates (deposits of Treasury correspondents, deposits at the Caisse des Dépôts et Consignations, and so on); the residual also takes into account the fact that subscriptions of bonds are in gross terms.

TABLE 9.7 *Factors affecting bank liquidity 1946–51 (FFr billion)*

	Situation at end 1945	*Changes in*						*Situation at end 1951*
		1946	*1947*	*1948*	*1949*	*1950*	*1951*	
A) Notes in circulation	−573	−152	−128	−68	−290	−282	−323	−1885
B) Gold and foreign exchange net	+128	−36	−31	−8	+98	+292	−198	+245
C) Direct claims of the Banque de France on the Treasury	+445	+109	+162	+12	+8	−82	+17	+669
D) Miscellaneous[1]	−68	+3	−14	−89	+25	−14	+43	−112
A + B + C + D = balance of autonomous factors affecting bank liquidity	−67	−76	−81	−153	−159	−86	−461	−1083
E) Portfolio of the Banque de France	+67	+76	+81	+153	+159	+86	+461	+1083

1. Bills in course of payment, accounts of financial and non-financial agents at the Banque de France, miscellaneous items of the balance sheet of the Banque de France (own funds, fixed assets, and so on) and, in certain years for important amounts, operations of the Fonds de Stabilisation des Changes.

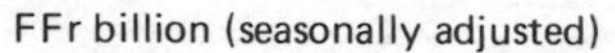

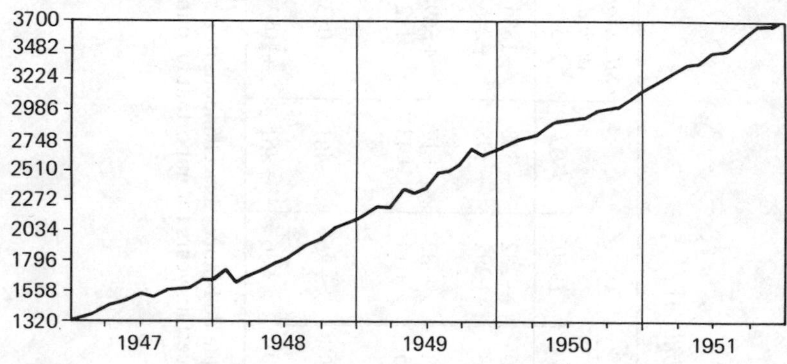

FIGURE 9.1 *Money stock 1947–51*

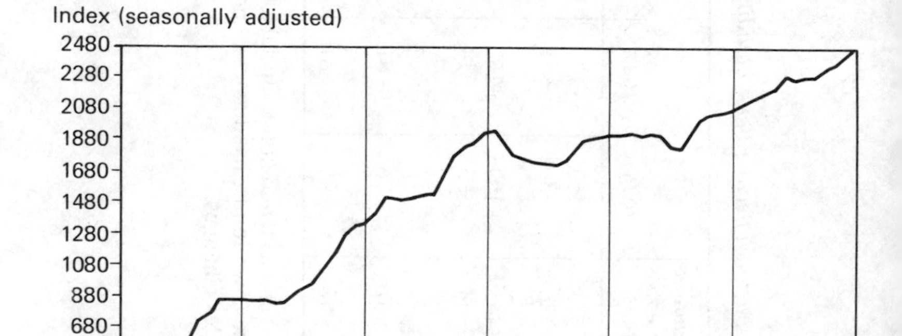

FIGURE 9.2 *Consumption prices 1946–51*

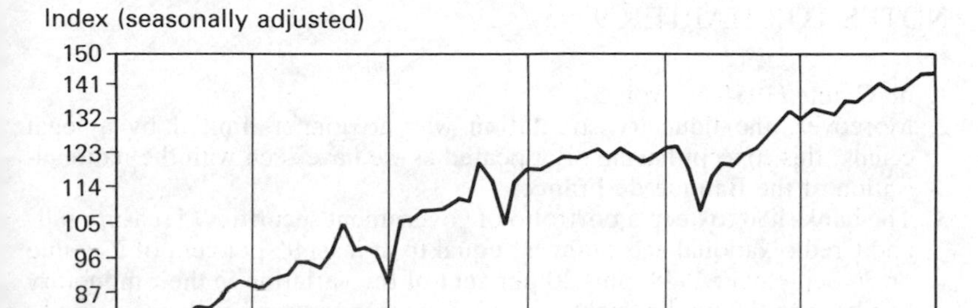

FIGURE 9.3 *Industrial production 1946–51*

distribution of credit, the growth of which fell from an annual rate of 46 per cent in the second half of 1951 to 21 per cent in the first half of 1952.

BANK LIQUIDITY

During the war bank liquidity remained at a high level: the growth of the fiduciary circulation had been offset by the massive lending from the Banque de France to the State; moreover, foreign exchange assets showed little variation.

In the postwar period there was a profound deterioration of the cash position of the banks. Whereas banknotes continued to be widely used in France – they were 54 per cent of M2 in 1946, and still 50 per cent in 1950 – the withdrawals brought about by the outflows of foreign exchange were not compensated by the operations of the Banque de France with the Treasury, which, as they started at a very high level, were bound to be reduced in relative terms.

The French banks thus became permanently 'in the bank', a situation which was all the more marked since, in view of the absence of negotiable securities in their portfolios, they had no other means of ensuring their liquidity than the refinancing of private sector credits with the Banque de France.

NOTES TO CHAPTER 9

1. de Gaulle (1954–59, vol. 3).
2. Moreover, the fiduciary circulation was no longer limited by a legal ceiling, this concept having disappeared as we have seen with the nationalisation of the Banque de France.
3. The banks had to keep a portfolio of government securities (Treasury bills and Crédit National acceptances) equal to at least 95 per cent of its value on 30 September 1948, plus 20 per cent of the variation in their monetary liabilities to the public (sight deposits, quasi-money, miscellaneous creditors).
4. Order of the General Council of the Banque de France, 11 May 1944, by which the Institut d'Emission accepted into its portfolio loans with a term of five years, whereas its original statutes limited to three months the maximum term for the credits which it could hold.
5. Two rates were then instituted, the minimum rate (for export credits, cereal stock credits and Treasury bills) and the maximum (for financial credits and medium-term refinanceable credits). This system was abolished in September 1948.
6. The facilities for lending by the Banque de France were, however, substantially increased:
   - the permanent loan was raised from FFr10 billion to FFr50 billion on 24 March 1947;
   - the temporary advances which had served during the war essentially for the financing of the occupation charges and which had been entirely repaid thanks to the funds produced by the Liberation loan of November 1944 and to the capital gain from the revaluation of the gold reserve on 26 December 1945, were increased from FFr100 billion to FFr200 billion in three stages (24 July 1947, 25 September 1947 and 12 November 1947).

   In total the margin of borrowings permitted by the permanent loan and the temporary advances represented 36 per cent of budgetary expenditure in 1947, against 17 per cent in 1946.
7. Two credits of $650 million, at 15 and 20 years, agreed on 4 December 1945 and 16 July 1946 by the Export-Import Bank; a credit of $235 million, at 20 years, agreed by the Canadian government on 9 April 1946; $125 million from the IMF in 1947; and in the same year $250 million from the IBRD without specific allocation, which was not in accordance with the regulations of that institution. A certain number of bilateral agreements were also concluded with France's European partners.
8. A measure which was not welcomed by the representatives of French employers, who thus became entirely responsible for future rises.
9. However, this rate increased by 1 per cent per month.
10. The derestriction of industrial prices had allowed the restoration of the margins and of the profitability of the sectors which were the driving forces of industry; the 'scissors' between agricultural prices, which up to then had been very high, and the particularly low industrial prices had been partly closed.

11. The option was that of either paying a tax on profits or on a percentage of turnover, or of subscribing to a loan.
12. Since June 1949, when a reform of the methods of operation of the Fonds de Stabilisation des Changes (FSC) was introduced, the movements of gold and foreign exchange have effectively exerted, according to their direction, a fully expansionary or contractionary impact on the money stock; the balance sheet diagrams below summarise the effect of the two methods of managing the Fund.

(a) up to June 1949
Banque de France

Assets		Liabilities	
Foreign Exchange	−100	FSC account	+ 100 − 100
Advances to the Treasury	+ 100	Banks' accounts Treasury account	− 100 + 100

(b) since June 1949
Banque de France

Assets		Liabilities	
Foreign exchange	− 100	FSC account	+ 100 − 100
Advances to FSC	+ 100 − 100	Banks' accounts	− 100

(a) Up to 1949, the Banque transferred a part of its stock of gold and foreign exchange to the Treasury, which paid for it in francs by using its facilities for advances from the Institut d'Emission. The Treasury transferred these reserves of foreign exchange to the FSC, which did not pay for them and sold them against francs to importers. It then paid back these francs to the Treasury's account at the Banque de France. The Treasury could pay off its advance or pay for new expenditure; the deflationary effect of outflows of foreign exchange was cancelled.
(b) From June 1949, the Banque transfers gold and foreign exchange to the FSC; the latter has to pay for them in francs and to use for this purpose an advance granted to it by the Banque; it transfers the reserves of foreign exchange to importers against francs, and uses these francs, no longer to credit the account of the Treasury, but to repay the advance which the Institut d'Emission has granted to it; outflows of foreign exchange exert a full deflationary effect.

13. When the banks created FFr100 of money, they suffered a 'leak' of banknotes of FFr57; before the war this 'leak' was less than FFr40 (except after the Munich crisis).
14. The individual ceilings thus determined were originally fixed at a total of FFr175 billion, that is, about 30 per cent of bank credits. Bills for medium-term discountable credits were considered as outside the ceiling.
15. In addition the maximum term for export credits which refinanced claims arising from deliveries made to customers abroad was raised from two to

five years; the rapid expansion of this type of credit was thereby considerably strengthened.

16. They continued to increase during the early months of 1951; in view of these results and the conversion of dollars into gold which the government was effecting (thus well before General de Gaulle!), the American government was wondering about the appropriateness of continuing with Marshall Aid.

10 1952–55: The Return of Stability

The years from 1952 to 1955 can be considered in economic terms as the most prosperous of the Fourth Republic. After a clear check to inflation in 1952, obtained by very conventional methods and accompanied by a stabilisation of output, activity picked up strongly from the later months of 1953 and maintained a rapid growth in 1954 and 1955, without any acceleration of the rise in prices; at the same time the external balance made a remarkable recovery and the foreign exchange reserves were built up again.

These almost miraculous results should obviously be located in a favourable context. First, it should not be forgotten that from 1953 the United States took over almost the whole of France's military expenditure in Indo-China. In addition the international environment was relatively supportive and the French economy remained protected because the authorities freed the exchanges very grudgingly and in 1954 carried out a disguised devaluation.

This period was, however, only a parenthesis, for the imbalances reappeared from 1956 and lasted until 1959. Although the expenditures connected with the war in Algeria were partly responsible, it is arguable that the financial policy pursued between 1953 and 1955 was fraught with inflationary possibilities. These possibilities did not manifest themselves during this period since, and this was the greatest merit of those in power at that time, a climate of confidence had been created.

FINANCIAL POLICY: THE TIME OF THE 'CIRCUIT'

Although monetary growth, which was clearly much slower than during the preceding period, may be regarded as tight, financial policy was much less so, if output and the foreign exchanges are taken into account.

A remarkable characteristic of the period was in fact the reversal of the relative growth rates of output and of the financial resources of the economy. Until 1951 the rate of increase of the money stock, although very high, was always less than that of GNP; from 1952,

TABLE 10.1 *Major annual statistics 1952–55*

	1952	*1953*	*1954*	*1955*
National income (% change)	+2.7	+3.1	+5.1	+6.2
GNP (% change)	+2.6	+2.9	+4.8	+5.8
Industrial production (% change)	+2.6	+2.9	+1.8	+5.8
Balance of payments (FFr million):				
Trade account	−216.5	−118.5	−62.8	+30.3
Current payments	−206.9	−41	+91.7	+210.8
Capital flows	+35.8	+0.3	−77.9	−63.7
FFr/$	350	350	350	350
Prices (% change)				
Wholesale	+4.7	−4.5	−7.8	−0.1
Retail	+11.9	−1.7	+0.4	+0.9
Balance of the State budget (FFr billion)	−768.8	−697.8	−346.5	−495
M2 (% change)	+13.6	+11.8	+14	+12.9

although its pace had slackened, it was clearly the greater and it remained so until 1955, without any surge in prices resulting.

The liquidity ratio of the economy, M2/GNP, which was 29.5 per cent in 1950, 28.3 per cent in 1951 and 28 per cent in 1952, rose to 30 per cent in 1953, 32.2 per cent in 1954 and 34 per cent in 1955.

Should we then conclude that financial policy was guilty of being too lax? In fact various elements contributed to making this lack of financial rigour beneficial:

- Internal prices remained controlled, and the movement of the prices of imported primary products moderated the overall rise of prices: from the end of 1951 to the end of 1955 the Reuter index fell accordingly by 17.5 per cent. 'Disinflation' was general throughout the world.
- After a period of stagnation, output picked up vigorously and responded to demand: it was mainly stimulated by a tax incentive to investment (the halving of the production tax on investments, decided upon on 30 September 1953[1]) and the boost given to the building of public housing by the involvement of the Banque de France, which had hitherto been extremely reluctant, in the refinancing of special loans for building, in application of the law of 21 July 1950.
- Finally the restoration of confidence had the consequence that the

behaviour of economic agents took the form of the 'reconstitution of their cash reserves' rather than a spurt of demand.

The financial resources at the disposal of the economy were abundant, as Table 10.6 shows, but a growing share of these flows was invested in precautionary savings. This was demonstrated by the spectacular gain, from 11.6 per cent of the increase in M3 in 1951 to nearly 25 per cent in 1955, in the market share of the savings banks in the collection of financial savings; there was an equally favourable development in the subscriptions for Treasury bills.

This reorientation of financial flows was particularly advantageous to the Treasury. Edgar Faure was overjoyed to discover in 1953 the virtues of the 'circuit', the mechanism described in the previous chapter, which was an important aspect of the financial flows of this period.

Having been set up in a rather piecemeal fashion and without a real overall 'plan', the circuit was capable at the beginning of the 1950s of being remarkably effective if savers were sufficiently confident to direct their savings on a massive scale towards public channels. As a senior official said at the time, 'The whole of the outgoings ought normally to translate itself into a comparable movement of inflows. Everything which happens to escape should normally return. As long as the circuit is working, everything runs smoothly. But as soon as the circuit gets jammed, for one reason or another, everything you do collapses . . .' Having understood perfectly the mechanism which 'even Paul Reynaud refused to assimilate'[2] the President of the Council decided to exploit the potentialities of the system and no longer to let himself be impressed by the mandarins of the Ministry of Finance and the Banque de France,[3] the eternal killjoys who knew very well that this method of financing was only a disguised resort to the creation of money, in which the equilibrium is preserved only if the expectations of economic agents are properly directed.

Thus a large budget deficit of 7.1 per cent of GNP in 1952 and 6.3 per cent in 1955 (although account must be taken of the fact that the United States were from then onward funding the war in Indo-China) could be financed without an excessive appeal to the bond market (except in 1952) and without recourse to the creation of money, the State even succeeding in reducing its indebtedness to the Banque de France (Table 10.2).

This apparently splendid situation must be qualified; the authorities had in fact pushed the potentialities of the 'circuit' to their extreme limit in making the Banque de France participate in it by

TABLE 10.2 *Financing of the budget deficit 1952, 1955 (current FFr billion)*

	1952	*1955*	
Budget deficit	706	626	
Bond borrowings	215	80	
Treasury bills *sur formules*	71***	149***	
Deposits of non-monetary financial correspondents	204*	391*	
Treasury bills and acceptances of the Crédit National taken up by the banks	63**	42**	}
Postal chequing accounts, special funds accounts, coin	40*	94*	} monetary resources (counterpart of M2)
Lending by the Banque de France	113	−130	}

* Circuit of correspondents.
** Circuit which reflects the obligations on uses of funds (public securities floor).
*** Circuit encouraged by a tax privilege.

refinancing on a massive scale the special building loans provided by the Sous-Comptoir des Entrepreneurs. Within the framework of the arrangements set up by the law of 21 July 1950, the Caisse des Dépôts should normally have been the first and principal rediscounter of the medium-term part of these loans, but it did not fulfil this task and refinanced the loans immediately through the Institut d'Emission, in order to be able to increase its advances to the Treasury without reducing its loans to its traditional customers (local authorities, public housing, nationalised corporations). A hidden transfer (of FFr1.12 billion in 1952) also reduced the 'claims on the Treasury' counterpart of the money stock, to the benefit of the 'credits to the economy' counterpart (refinancing of medium-term loans by the Banque de France). This distortion of the circuit earned France a severe reprimand from the IMF in 1957.

TABLE 10.3 *Monetary Growth 1952–55*

	1951	*1952*	*1953*	*1954*	*1955*
External (gold and foreign exchange)	−198	−43	−11	+169	+301
Domestic credit	+784	+555	+518	+502	+403
(% change)	(+28.9)	(+15.9)	(+12.8)	(+11.0)	(+8.0)
M2	+586	+512	+507	+671	+704
(% change)	(+18.4)	(+13.6)	(+11.8)	(+14.0)	(+12.9)

MONETARY AND FINANCIAL NARRATIVE

Table 10.3, which traces the contribution of the two principal counterparts – external and domestic – to the growth of the money stock, shows two periods:

- The first covers the two years 1952 and 1953; it is marked by a deflationary effect from the balance of payments and a brisk growth of domestic credit; however, it is clear that in 1953 the situation was changing rapidly.
- On the other hand the years 1954 and 1955 were characterised by a very moderate increase in domestic credit whilst the monetary effects of external operations were more and more expansionary.

These are the two periods which we shall distinguish: first, that of a deflation which progressively eliminated the effects of the imbalances of 1951, and secondly, that of 'expansion with stability', the slogan of the time which in fact corresponded to the reality.

1952–53: deflation and the stagnation of output

It may seem paradoxical to qualify as deflationary a policy which allowed the money stock to rise by nearly 14 per cent (in 1952) and domestic credit by nearly 16 per cent: nevertheless, the break with the preceding period is very marked.

1952 began with considerable difficulties: a substantial external deficit (during the first quarter, it was almost the same as that for the whole of 1951); rapidly rising prices, up 2.1 per cent in January and 1.8 per cent in February; and a growing budget deficit. For the first three months of the year the annual rate of growth of M2 was 21 per cent.

Expectations were particularly unfavourable and the government did little to moderate them; in the last quarter of 1951 there was a new rise of 15 per cent on average in the SMIG, family allowances, and the salaries of civil servants.

In these conditions the rises in the discount rate from 2.2 per cent to 3 per cent in October 1951 and from 3 per cent to 4 per cent in November had no effect.

After a short-lived government under Edgar Faure (January and February 1952) which tried vainly to impose a supplementary tax to reduce demand and suggested to the Governor of the Banque de France that he should send it a severe warning letter in order to impress the parliament, Antoine Pinay was sworn in at the beginning of March.

His monetary policy was restrictive, but by persuasion rather than constraint. The tightening of the rediscount ceilings decided upon in the last quarter of 1951 was not questioned; the discount rate remained unchanged. On the other hand the government reduced demand by stimulating saving. A large issue of bonds was made in May 1952; the bonds carried a number of exceptional advantages including indexation based on the napoléon and exemption from professional tax (as with all state borrowings), progressive surtax and death duties. The issue brought in FFr430 billion, less FFr230 billion resulting from the transfer of other securities; FFr15 billion was subscribed in gold repatriated from abroad (a law giving a fiscal amnesty to repatriated capital was associated with the loan). Another incentive to saving was provided by a substantial raising (from FFr300 000 to FFr400 000) of the ceiling on savings bank deposit accounts.

In these conditions monetary growth weakened considerably in the second quarter.

To this contractionary factor Antoine Pinay added some psychological measures: the lowering of the prices of coal and steel, the cancelling of the expected rise in the price of electricity; the stabilisation of the price of wheat, and budgetary economies (unfortunately on investment programmes).

Finally a last, and particularly favourable, circumstance was a clear accentuation of the downward trend of international prices which had begun in 1951: the Reuter index for primary products fell by 15 per cent in 1952.

The result was a spectacular reversal of price movements. From February the wholesale price index flattened out, and it declined by 8 per cent over 1952 as a whole and again by 2 per cent in 1953. The retail price index began to fall back in March and returned in July to the level of the previous December; it then went up gradually but over 1952 as a whole it remained stable, and in 1953 retail prices fell by 2 per cent.

The transmission mechanism between government action (helped by the international environment) and disinflation was the massive rundown of stocks undertaken by companies whose expectations had now been profoundly modified. On the economic level there was a marked slowing down of output: industrial production declined from the second quarter of 1952 and in the autumn of 1953 it was 5 per cent below the level reached two years before. The rise achieved at the beginning of 1952 made possible a growth in GNP of 2.6 per cent over the whole of the year (against 6.5 per cent in 1951); good harvests and the rise in services allowed it to reach 2.9 per cent in 1953.

This development permitted an improvement in the external balance which did not really show itself until 1953; in 1952 the deficit was still FFr144 billion and the government considerably restricted the freedom of the foreign exchanges, with a very strict programme for imports from the OEEC area (forerunner of the OECD); this deficit could be covered only to the extent of one quarter by France's reserves (which were practically exhausted by this, the remainder being supplied by borrowing and by American aid).

On the other hand the budget deficit, which went from FFr400 billion in 1951 to FFr706 billion in 1952, remained at the high level of FFr648 billion in 1963; the poor economic growth was largely responsible for this.

1954–55

In fact this period commences in the middle of 1953, when the government of Joseph Laniel came into office, with Edgar Faure as Finance Minister.

Its operations began under the very worst auspices with an interminable strike of civil servants, but the authorities held firm and conceded only a uniform bonus for the low-paid. This resistance reinforced the climate of favourable expectations which had been created from 1952.

The essential objective of the government and its finance minister was to stimulate production: to do this it proceeded with a relaxation of monetary policy, an incomes policy which was relatively generous but not excessively so, at least until the middle of 1955, and action to stimulate investment.

This group of measures could have been accompanied by a resurgence of inflation and an increase in the trade deficit, but this did not happen because there was general confidence in monetary stability, and the external risks were limited by a very restricted opening up of the exchanges and a disguised devaluation.

In monetary matters, the monetary authorities carried out a general easing of credit conditions: the discount rate was brought back from 4 per cent to 3.5 per cent on 17 September 1953, then to 3.25 per cent on 4 February 1954, and to 3 per cent on 2 December 1954; other conditions for borrowers, concerning medium-term credits for capital goods, export credits and agricultural credits, were similarly eased.[4]

A regulation of consumer credit (involving a limit on lending equal to ten times the own funds of the credit-granting institutions themselves, a maximum term of 18 months, and a personal contribution of at least 20 per cent) allowed this type of lending to start up and develop within an appropriate framework.

Another very important development was the stimulus given to the growth of special building loans granted by the Sous-Comptoir des Entrepreneurs and the Crédit Foncier, and above all to their refinancing, for terms of less than five years, by the Banque de France. This had been possible since 1950 but it was only from 1953–54 that it really took off, accompanying an ambitious housing programme but also allowing the Caisse des Dépôts, which should normally have been the main rediscounting organisation, to devote more resources to its loans to the Treasury.

The corruption of the system had no doubt less to do with the monetary financing of property investments (which were at that time so insufficient that an enormous effort was required) than with the distortion and impenetrability of the financing circuits which resulted from it.

In the field of wages, the government managed to some extent to detach the SMIG from other earnings: the minimum wage rose by 21.5 per cent in 1954 and wages as a whole by only 10 per cent. In 1955 the total wage bill increased by 8.5 per cent. Edgar Faure had the merit of not giving way to demagogy and of making an effort also as regards high salaries, the receivers of which, whether one likes it or not, play a key role in determining economic activity (the tax deduction for professional expenses was increased).

To stimulate investment the authorities used a variety of fiscal measures: the production tax on capital goods was halved and re-deployment funds were created, the best-known of which – the Fonds national d'aménagement du territoire – provided financial incentives for investment in the regions.

In the field of external relations Edgar Faure remained extremely prudent. He fulfilled the obligations which France had entered into over the liberation of the exchanges only after some delay: the proportion of external flows which was decontrolled was no more than 8 per cent at the end of 1953 and the promise to raise it to 75 per cent by the end of 1954 was not fulfilled until the middle of 1955. Moreover, the government imposed a temporary import tax at differential rates, varying from 0 to 15 per cent according to the product. As there had been since the beginning of 1952 financial assistance for exports which could also go up to 15 per cent (justified by the repayment of social security contributions and taxes) it was certainly a *de facto* devaluation, or rather a regime of multiple exchange rates (in formal contravention of GATT rules) which had been introduced. This financial assistance was in fact progressively reduced: at the end of 1955 there remained only a few products subject to a tax of 7 per cent and the repayments to exporters had been reduced.

The results of these measures were outstanding, but fragile, and from the second half of 1955 signs of trouble appeared.

From the last quarter of 1953 output improved strongly; GNP rose by 4.8 per cent in 1954, and 5.8 per cent in 1955. Price rises remained moderate, at 0.6 per cent and 1 per cent for retail prices. The external balance corrected itself and produced large surpluses.

Foreign exchange resources became abundant because France was benefiting in other respects from exceptional receipts: the expenses for the stationing of American troops, aid for the war in Indo-China, and the remaining Marshall aid; she was accordingly able to repay some loans.[5]

These very satisfactory results were due as far as prices were concerned to the behaviour of economic agents among whom expectations of inflation had disappeared: this is borne out by the fact that the demand for credit was very moderate, the principal sources of monetary growth being lending to the Treasury (via the refinancing of special loans by the Banque de France) and inflows of foreign currency. But it is clear that the substantial increase in the liquidity of the economy constituted a danger for the future.

In economic terms the results need to be qualified: investment increased but more in the areas of housing and central and local government than in the company sector.

Finally, France's trade surpluses relied on factors that gave little encouragement: whilst benefiting from a high level of activity abroad, France was mainly selling primary products, agricultural and semi-finished products, containing little value added.

The later months of 1955 were characterised by the beginning of a slide: incomes policy was markedly relaxed,[6] the demand for credit revived, at a rate of 19 per cent per year during the last five months of 1955 as against 13 per cent before, and by the fourth quarter the ongoing rate of inflation had reached an annual rate of 5 per cent.

TABLE 10.4 *Summary of monetary and financial data 1952–55 (end-period totals, averages for interest rates) (FFr billion)*

	1952	*1953*	*1954*	*1955*
M2	4287	4794	5465	6169
Net assets in gold and foreign exchange	214	204	380	680
Claims on the Treasury	1795	2055	2222	2228
	(+14.3%)	(+14.5%)	(+8.1%)	(+0.3%)
Claims on the economy	2272	2519	2860	3299
	(+19.2%)	(+10.9%)	(+13.5%)	(+15.3%)
Deposits in savings banks	839	1028	1229	1514
(for reference, ceiling on type A passbooks, in francs)	(400 000)	(500 000)		(750 000)
	7.52	2.53		4.55
Discount rate	4%	3.8%	3.3%	3%
Yield on bonds	7.05%	6.92%	6.63%	5.80%
New issues of negotiable securities				
shares	71	63	88	148
bonds	515	181	312	300
(of which government bonds)	(463)	(46)	(107)	(85)
National income	10 690	11 180	11 930	12 960
Income velocity (national income/M2)	2.64	2.47	2.35	2.18

TABLE 10.5 *Factors affecting bank liquidity 1952–55 (FFr billion)*

	situation at end 1951	*changes in*				*situation at end 1955*
		1952	*1953*	*1954*	*1955*	
(A) Notes in circulation	−1885	−236	−185	−245	−296	−2847
(B) Gold and foreign exchange net	+245	−31	−10	+176	+300	+680
(C) Direct claims of the Banque de France on the Treasury	+669	−6	+239	−82	−55	+765
(D) Miscellaneous	−112	−10	+11	−3	−5	−119
A + B + C + D = balance of autonomous factors affecting bank liquidity	−1083	−283	+55	−154	−56	−1521
(E) Portfolio of the Banque de France	+1083	+283	−55	+154	+56	+1521

1. Bills in course of payment, accounts of financial and non-financial agents at the Banque de France, miscellaneous items of the balance sheet of the Banque de France (own funds, fixed assets, and so on).

TABLE 10.6 *The financing of the economy 1952–55 (FFr billion)*

	1952	*1953*	*1954*	*1955*	
Sources of financing					
Balance of State budget[1]	706	648	571	626	
Credits					
*Bank	332	217	334	439	
*Non-bank[2]	60	237	411	505	
External	−43	−11	169	301	
					Investments
	283	174	301	271	Bond subscriptions
	71	92	166	149	Net subscriptions of Treasury bills
	124	186	219	285	Deposits in savings banks
	512	507	671	714	ΔM2
	241	187	240	302	*(of which banknotes)
	65	132	128	452	Miscellaneous and residual[3]

SOURCES Statistiques et Etudes financières; reports of the Conseil National du Crédit.

1. A surplus reduces the supply of financing (− sign); a deficit increases it (+ sign). Including loans from the FME, then from FDES; balance after taking American aid into account.
2. Including net issues of bonds by non-financial companies.
3. Various uses of funds by financial institutions and investments not included in the aggregates (amortisation of borrowings, deposits of Treasury correspondents, deposits at the Caisse des Dépôts et Consignations, investments in insurance companies).

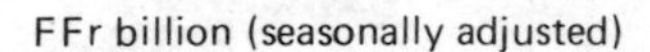

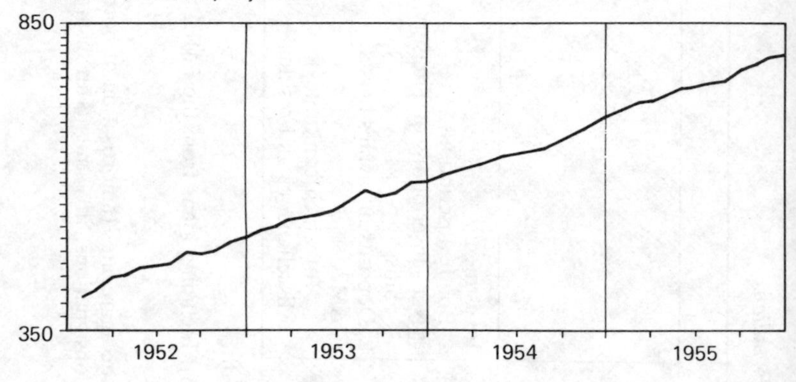

FIGURE 10.1 *Money stock 1952–55*

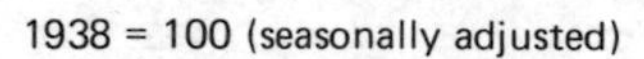

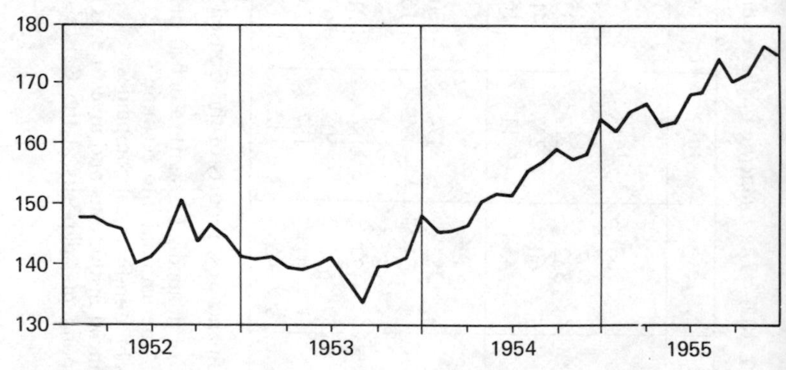

FIGURE 10.2 *Industrial production 1952–55*

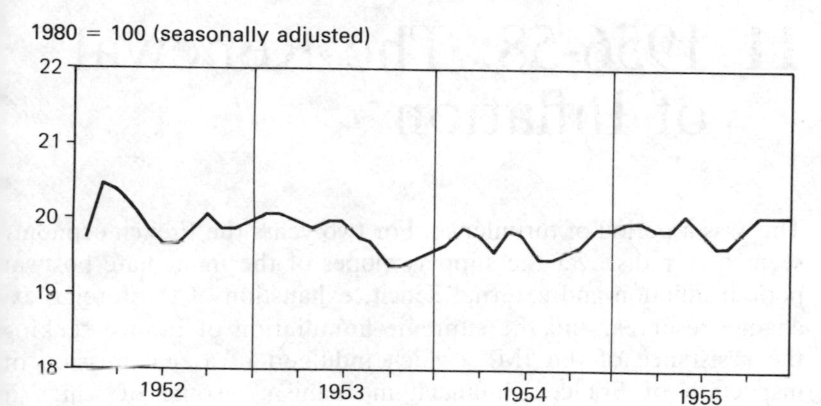

FIGURE 10.3 *Consumption prices 1952–55*

NOTES TO CHAPTER 10

1. Partly offset by an increase from 36 per cent to 38 per cent in corporation tax.
2. A mechanism which was nevertheless typical of the art of management of the public finances, and which is excellently explained in Bloch-Lainé and de Vogüé (1960).
3. See Faure (1982).
4. Generally by the reduction or abolition of the commission charged by the primary rediscounting institutions, the Crédit National and the Caisse des Dépôts.
5. In particular a part of the drawing on the IMF made in 1947 and the drawings on the European Payments Union.
6. In the dispute in the naval shipyards of Saint-Nazaire, the government resorted to an arbitrator who imposed considerable increases in earnings (17 per cent, later 22 per cent).

11 1956-58: The Renewal of Inflation

This was a period of turbulence. For two years the French economy seemed to rediscover the slippery slopes of the immediate postwar period: inflation and external deficit, exhaustion of the foreign exchange reserves, and the supreme humiliation of France seeking the assistance of the IMF, which indulged in a real mission of inspection of France's financial mechanisms, some of which it firmly denounced.

In monetary terms the period was important, at least during the second part; we can in fact distinguish approximately two subperiods of equal length, the turning point being in the spring of 1957 when the government of Maurice Bourgès-Maunory with Félix Gaillard as its finance minister succeeded the Guy Mollet-Paul Ramadier team. In 1956 and the early months of 1957 the authorities rushed headlong down the road of irresponsibility and monetary policy was non-existent; the government's most obvious action consisted in fact of trying to delay the statistical manifestation of the economic imbalances. From the spring of 1957 on the other hand a firm and coherent policy was implemented, the fruits of which were harvested not by those then in office but by the last government of the Fourth Republic led by General de Gaulle with Antoine Pinay as finance minister: the measures introduced included for the first time a particularly severe policy of limiting the growth of money and credit, which can be considered as the first experience in France of the *encadrement du crédit* system of credit controls.

Finally, it was from this period that France committed itself irreversibly to the fresh air of international competition, by signing at Rome, on 25 March 1957, the treaty which brought about the creation of the Common Market, the nucleus of the European Economic Community.

FINANCIAL DEVELOPMENTS

An observer who limited himself solely to the examination of the growth of the money stock would not see in 1956 and 1957 any sign of a striking imbalance: during these two years M2 grew less rapidly than in the previous period, but the structure of the counterparts was transformed and the growth of internal credit rose from 8 per cent in 1955 to more than 17 per cent in 1956 and 1957, whilst the external balance which in 1955 had been in surplus with an expansionary effect on liquidity went deeply into deficit and acquired a sharply contractionary effect on money (Table 11.2).

The effects of the policy introduced in 1957 were clearly visible in 1958, and the structure of the counterparts reverted to what it had been before the crisis.

The two components of domestic credit contributed equally to its excessive growth.

As far as lending was concerned the resumption dated in fact from the previous period with the sharp raising of wages in the naval shipyards in July 1955 which then spread elsewhere; this resumed growth of lending was then obviously amplified by the measures taken in 1956 to stimulate demand.

The budget deficit rose from FFr630 billion in 1955 (3.7 per cent of GNP) to FFr938 billion in 1956 and FFr1019 billion in 1957, that is, nearly 5 per cent of GNP; it returned in 1958 to the 1955 level (Table 11.3).

In spite of substantial calls on the bond market at the beginning and end of the period, the financing of this deficit was largely monetary, but there again reference merely to the 'claims on the Treasury' counterpart of M2 is deceptive, for it conceals the refinancing of medium-term credits by the Banque de France (see below), that is, FFr234 billion in 1956, FFr159 billion in 1957, and FFr40 billion in 1958, which released similar amounts of resources which the Caisse des Dépôts could make available to the Treasury.

The liquidity ratio of the economy M2/GNP ceased to rise, as in the earlier period of the immediately postwar inflation: it fell from 34 per cent in 1955 to 33.9 per cent in 1957. This was once more the start of a flight from money and liquid savings. The rate of growth of deposits in savings banks fell from 23 per cent in 1955 to 14 per cent in 1956 and 10 per cent in 1957, but rose again to 16 per cent in 1958.

MONETARY AND FINANCIAL NARRATIVE

The errors of January 1956 to June 1957

The government under Guy Mollet had to face difficult circumstances: the expansion of military operations in Algeria, an excep-

TABLE 11.1 *Major annual statistics 1956–58*

	1956	*1957*	*1958*
GNP (% change)	+5	+6	+2.6
Industrial production (% change)	9.3	+8.5	+4.4
Balance of payments (FFr billion):			
Trade account	−283.1	−323.3	−103.4
Current payments	−293.4	−421.3	−120.1
Capital flows	−34.8	+120.6	+62.9
FFr/$	3.50	3.50	4.19 (3rd quarter) 4.31 (4th quarter)
Prices (% change)			
Wholesale	+4.3	+5.7	+11.5
Retail	+4.2	+3%	+15
Balance of the State budget (FFr billion)	−770	−655.1	−262.8
M2 (% change)	+10.5	+10.5	+5.2

TABLE 11.2 *Money Stock and Counterparts 1956–58 (Changes in FFr billion)*

	1956	*1957*	*1958*
External (gold and foreign exchange)	−307	−404	+24
Domestic credit	+995	1 122	368
(% change)	(+17.4)	(+17.4)	(+4.9)
M2	+648	+718	392
(% change)	(+10.5)	(+10.5)	(+5.2)

TABLE 11.3 *Financing of the Budget Deficit 1956–58 (FFr billion)*

	1956	*1957*	*1958*
Total	938	1 019	690
Bond borrowings	383	84	294
Treasury bills *sur formules*	74	110	114
Deposits of non-financial correspondents	295	226	185
Treasury bills and acceptances of the Crédit National taken up by the banks	52	39	− 5
Postal chequing accounts, special funds accounts, coin	125	78	107
Lending by the Banque de France	9	482	− 5
(of which advances)	(−71)	(452)	(4)

tionally cold winter, then at the end of the year the blocking of the Suez Canal and fuel shortages, each a substantial cause of disequilibrium between overall demand and the supply of goods and services; the mistake of the authorities was to consider them all as transitory. In addition there were the social policy measures taken on the accesssion to office of the new government: the extension of paid holidays to three weeks, and the minimum old people's allowance.

In spite of an incomes policy rather firmer than that pursued by the preceding government and of an additional fiscal tightening (introduction of the car tax disc and an increase in death duties) demand revived strongly, particularly consumption, which at constant prices grew at an annual rate of 11 per cent in the second half of 1956, whilst during the same time the rate of growth of productive capacity was only 7 per cent. In line with this development the growth of credit established itself at an annual growth rate of over 20 per cent.

Prices as tracked by the indices did not react to these disturbances, for the government, caught in the trap of the link established by its predecessors between the passing of a certain threshold of prices and the revaluation of the SMIG, engaged in all sorts of manoeuvres to avoid crossing the fateful barrier: the lowering of value added tax on current consumption products (including cinema seats!), a reduction of 20 per cent on the price of gas, crash imports of foodstuffs. These measures were very costly; others, consisting of more direct interventions in the indices, left behind a very poor impression. But at least the thermometer was held steady for a certain time: the index of consumer prices, which had started to jump in the fourth quarter of 1955 (when it grew by 1.2 per cent) rose by only 2 per cent between December 1955 and March 1957.

The effect on external trade on the other hand was more rapid: at constant prices imports rose by 18 per cent in 1956, against less than 9 per cent in 1955, and the ratio of exports to imports (c.i.f./f.o.b.) went from 98 in the fourth quarter of 1955 to 77 at the end of 1956, and 82 in the second quarter.

In truth the government had no monetary policy. It refused until April 1957 to follow the discreet recommendation of the Banque de France for a rise in the discount rate, which until then remained therefore at 3 per cent; it was raised to 4 per cent from 11 April, while the 'hell' and 'superhell' rates were fixed at 6 per cent and 10 per cent. In 1956 and during the early months of 1957, the only actions by the authorities to moderate the tensions on demand consisted of a slight modification of the conditions for loans to finance hire-purchase sales,[1] and the launching of several government loans, the most important of which, the so-called 'Ramadier' loan, also had considerable advantages attached to it: exemption from progressive surtax and above all indexation on the average price of shares on the Paris Bourse. Issued in September, this last loan brought about a 1 per cent decrease in the money stock in October, but its effect on demand was only weak since it mainly drew off idle balances.

In the spring of 1957 the government seemed to have retreated from the illusions it had held at the beginning over the short duration and limited nature of the surge in demand ('One must believe in Father Christmas', Paul Ramadier used to say), and it fell when it proposed to parliament a rise in taxes; by this time the foreign exchange reserves included in the balance sheet of the Banque de France had fallen in 18 months by FFr380 billion.

The stabilisation measures

Entering into office in June 1957 when the public finances were undergoing a major crisis, the Bourgès-Maunory government had to start its life by asking for an extension of the advances of the Banque de France. It rapidly erased this unfortunate impresssion, for which it was, moreover, hardly responsible, by an energetic adjustment policy aimed at reducing overall demand, returning to true prices, and adapting the exchange rate to reality. These changes of direction put it in a better position when it was obliged to solicit the assistance of the International Monetary Fund and the European Payments Union in the autumn of 1957.

The action on demand was based on an effort at rigorous budgetary control and above all on a strict monetary policy.

The forecast deficit for 1958 was brought down to FFr600 billion, essentially by a draconian reduction of the tax allowances and subsidies which the previous government had introduced in order to 'hold prices'.

In the monetary area the measures were extremely harsh:

• the discount rate, which had already been raised to 4 per cent in April 1957, was put up to 5 per cent in August whilst the 'hell' and 'superhell' rates went up to 7 per cent and 10 per cent. In April 1958 these rates were raised to 8 per cent and 12 per cent;

• above all, at the beginning of 1958 it was decided to set a general ceiling on bank lending. This first experience of the *encadrement du crédit*, adopted on 7 February 1958, consisted of limiting bank lending for the year 1958 to below an amount determined by the arithmetic mean of the figures obtained for each bank at 30 September 1957 and 31 December 1957; the system was strengthened in April 1958 by the threat of a sanction (consisting of a lowering of its rediscount ceiling) on any bank that exceeded the norm.

Obviously there was nothing in the principle of this rationing to arouse enthusiasm, particularly in view of the fact that it was the example for other later experiences of much greater duration; but in the present context this temporary measure (a relaxation of 2 per cent was granted in July 1958 and the system was repealed entirely in February 1959) proved beneficial.

The authorities took other measures to limit monetary growth; in line with the deeply-held views of the Banque de France and the recommendations of the IMF they decided gradually to phase out the refinancing of special loans by the Institut d'Emission. For this purpose an office for the consolidation of medium-term credits was set up. At the beginning of its existence its resources were essentially budgetary, which, in a situation of deficit in the public finances, qualified the idea of consolidation somewhat; but at least the principle was established.

Finally, with the laudable aim of directing saving towards the most productive uses (the stock exchange was then going through a period of intense speculation triggered off by discoveries of oil in Algeria) the government took the decision, which was questionable in principle, to reinforce the check that already existed (in the form of prior authorisation) on the issue of negotiable securities.

Truth in prices

With regard to prices, the government speedily took measures which reversed those of its predecessor, abolishing the subsidies and tax allowances the purpose of which had been to block the rise in the index, and of course ceasing to manipulate it.[2]

A rapid rise in prices was therefore bound to follow the almost surrealistic constancy of prices which had characterised 1956 and the beginning of 1957: prices rose by 8.6 per cent in the second half of 1957 and 7.6 per cent in the first half of 1958.

Foreign exchange market policy

The maintenance of a large trade deficit (FFr5 billion in 1957 and an equally pessimistic prospect for the following year) necessitated an immediate restoration of the competitivity of France's products and the acquisition of financial resources which would make it possible to wait for the effects to be realised.

Having abandoned the idea of freeing the foreign exchanges in June 1957, the government proceeded with a devaluation in several stages:

• the unification in June 1957 at a rate of 15 per cent of all import taxes, taxes which had been created by Edgar Faure but the rates of which had been considerably lowered;

• the replacement on 10 August 1957 of import taxes and all the existing assistance to exports by a payment of 20 per cent, charged on the majority of imports and credited to exporters. Thus an importer would pay for each dollar FFr350 plus a payment of FFr70; and an exporter handing over his dollars would receive for each dollar

FFr350 plus a payment from the Treasury of FFr70. These measures, presented as a harmonisation of existing arrangements, were in fact a devaluation, but one which did not need to be declared to the IMF.[3] On 26 October the tax and the payment were extended generally to all operations. Expectations of devaluation were obviously fostered by these measures; and as soon as he came to power General de Gaulle made it official by raising the exchange rate against the dollar from FFr3.50 to FFr4.20.

While it was taking these measures the government was negotiating several external loans, the major one being obtained through the IMF and the European Payments Union. This assistance and the more than total utilisation of France's foreign exchange reserves (the Banque de France's balance sheet item 'net gold and foreign exchange' was negative during the first half of 1958) made it possible to hold out until the first signs of recovery.

The results of this policy were astonishingly rapid, but not sufficiently so, however, in view of the rate of turnover of governments, for those in charge to reap the rewards they deserved.

As far as intermediate objectives were concerned the rate of growth of bank lending fell from 25 per cent per annum in the first quarter of 1957 successively to 16 per cent, 9 per cent, 6 per cent and 1.5 per cent in the course of the following quarters. For claims on the Treasury the decline was less immediate; during 1957 they increased by 25 per cent but from the first half of 1958 they grew at an annual rate of no more than 4 per cent.

Demand slackened from the fourth quarter of 1957: household consumption, which had been rising at a rate of 7 per cent, more or less flattened out until the autumn of 1958; investment was unfortunately also affected; but all the same positive growth was maintained, at 4.5 per cent in 1958 as against 8.5 per cent in 1957.

From the second half of 1958 external trade was once more balanced; the net assets in gold and foreign exchange of the Banque de France increased by FFr1 billion. Finally the rise in prices was appreciably moderated: from an annual rate of more than 25 per cent in the first quarter of 1958 it fell to 6 per cent in the second and to less than 1.5 per cent during the later months of the year.

This recovery, completed by the measures of the de Gaulle government (see below), was the starting point for the expansion with stability which marked the ten succeeding years.

TABLE 11.4 *Summary of monetary and financial data 1956–58 (end-period totals, averages for interest rates) (FFr billion)*

	1956	*1957*	*1958*
M2	6817	7535	7927
Net assets in gold and foreign exchange	373	−31	−7
Claims on the Treasury	2414	3013	3075
Claims on the economy	4024	4577	4809
	(+22%)	(+13.7%)	(+5.1%)
Deposits in savings banks	1746	1922	2225
(for reference, ceiling on deposits, in francs)	(750 000)	(750 000)	(1 000 000)
			(3.58)
Discount rate	3%	4.1%	4.9%
Yield on bonds	5.98%	7.1%	7.2%
New issues of negotiable securities			
shares	148	280	219
bonds	654	429	673
(of which government bonds)	(423)	(108)	(319)
National income	14 380	16 080	18 510
Income velocity (national income/M2)	2.20	2.26	2.43

TABLE 11.5 *The financing of the economy 1956–58 (FFr billion)*

	1956	*1957*	*1958*	
Sources of financing				
Balance of State budget[1]	936	952	337	
Credits				
*Bank	728	553	232	
*Non-bank[2]	523	617	932	
External	−287	−404	24	
				Investments
	627	362	623	Bond subscriptions
	86	99	114	Net subscriptions of Treasury bills
	216	213	298	Deposits in savings banks
	682	718	392	ΔM2
	261	155	201	*(of which banknotes)
	279	326	98	Miscellaneous[3] and residual

SOURCES reports of the Conseil National du Crédit.

1. A surplus reduces the supply of financing (− sign); a deficit increases it (+ sign). Including loans by the Fonds de Développement Economique et Social.
2. Including net issues of bonds by non-financial companies.
3. Including in particular investments in insurance companies, deposits not counted in the monetary aggregates (especially deposits with the Treasury by correspondents and deposits at the Caisse des Dépôts et Consignations) and miscellaneous uses of funds by financial institutions; amortisation of bond borrowings, and so on.

TABLE 11.6 *Factors affecting bank liquidity 1956–58 (FFr. billion)*

	situation at end 1955	*changes in*			*situation at end 1958*
		1956	*1957*	*1958*	
(A) Notes in circulation	−2837	−250	−180	−172	−3439
(B) Gold and foreign exchange net	+680	−290	−299	−98	−7
(C) Direct claims of the Banque de France on the Treasury	+765	−145	+433	+83	+1135
(D) Miscellaneous[1]	−129	+38	−125	+13	−203
A + B + C + D = balance of autonomous factors affecting bank liquidity	−1521	−647	−171	−175	−2514
(E) Portfolio of the Banque de France	+1521	+647	+171	+175	+2514

1. Bills in course of payment, accounts of financial and non-financial agents, resident and non-resident, at the Banque de France, miscellaneous items of the balance sheet of the Banque de France (own funds, fixed assets, and so on).

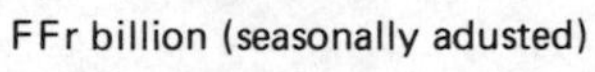

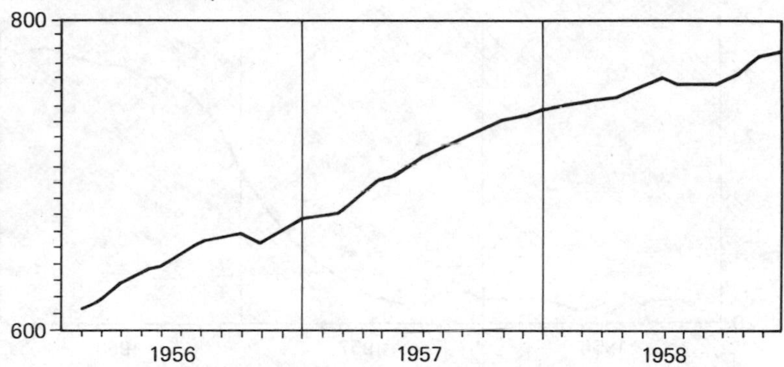

FIGURE 11.1 *Money stock 1956–58*

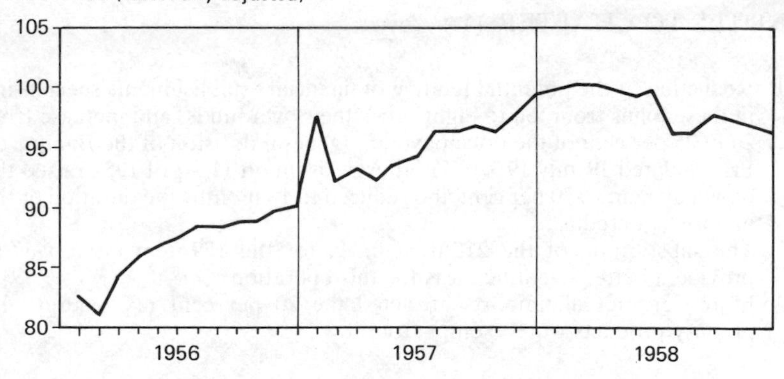

FIGURE 11.2 *Industrial production 1956–58*

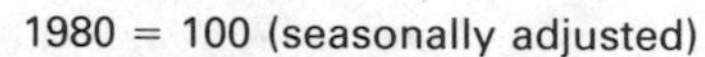

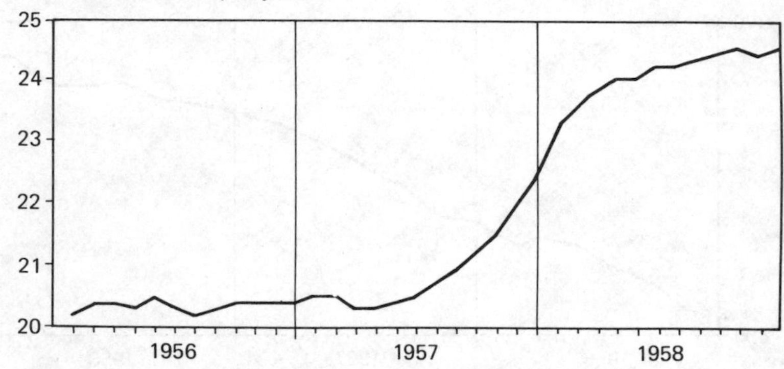

FIGURE 11.3 *Consumption prices 1956–58*

NOTES TO CHAPTER 11

1. Reduction of the potential lending of financial establishments specialising in these loans from ten to eight times their own funds, and increase from 20 to 25 per cent of the downpayment (general decision of the Banque de France dated 19 July 1956). Another decision on 11 April 1957 raised the downpayment to 30 per cent and reduced to 18 months the duration of the majority of credits.
2. The substitution of the 215-item index for the 179-item index was to provide a better scientific basis for this operation.
3. Moreover, not all imports attracted the 20 per cent tax; energy and primary products were exempt from it.

12 1959–67: The 'Grande Epoque' of the Fifth Republic

A few figures serve to characterise this long period: an average annual rate of growth of GDP of 5.5 per cent, inflation below 4 per cent, an external trade balance which was almost always positive, a sustained effort of investment in real property, and the rate of household savings an average of two points higher than in the ten previous years.

In financial matters a certain number of developments and reforms, some of which occurred at the end of the period, were to have a profound effect in shaping the structure of the economy. These transformations were to lay the foundations of the strength of the financial system and of a new start for French growth; but they carried a heavy responsibility for the reinforcement of inflationary tensions during the years 1968–73.

The outstanding results of the years 1959–67 were not without problems; after three years of stabilisation the pressure of demand was increased in 1962 and 1963 and imbalances emerged once more: very restrictive action, in which monetary policy played a major role, was then taken and was relaxed only very gradually from the second half of 1965 onwards.

FINANCIAL DEVELOPMENTS: DEBUDGETISATION AND THE POLICY OF STRENGTHENING THE BANKING SYSTEM

This period was characterised by what was later to be called the 'privatisation' of money; it was marked by the progressive withdrawal of the Treasury from the financial circuits and by a process of financial innovations in abundance, in constrast with the sclerosis of previous periods in this area. Although these innovations were introduced by the authorities, they nonetheless heralded a transformation of the financial system, the reach of which was extended by the banking reforms of 1966 and 1967. Financial behaviour also under-

TABLE 12.1 *Major annual statistics 1959–67*

	1959	*1960*	*1961*	*1962*	*1963*
GNP (% change)	+2.8	–	–	–	–
GDP (% change)	–	+7.1	+5.5	+6.7	+5.3
Industrial production (% change)	+3.3	+10	+5	+7.5	+2.2
Balance of payments (FFr billion):					
Trade account	+2.1	+0.5	+2.4	+2.3	+0.8
Current payments	+3.6	+3.1	+4.7	+4	+2.4
FFr/$	4.90	4.90	4.90	4.90	4.90
Prices (% change)					
Wholesale	+4.8	+2.6	+2.1	+2.7	+3.7
Retail	+6.1	+3.6	+3.3	+4.8	+4.9
Balance of the State budget	−6.3	−4.2	−4.4	−6.1	−9.7
M2 (% change)	+14.4	+16.6	+17.2	+18.7	+13.9

	1964	*1965*	*1966*	*1967*
GDP (1929 = 100)	+6.5	+4.8	+5.2	+4.8
Industrial production	+9	+2	+7.7	+2.7
Balance of payments (FFr billion)				
Trade account	−0.5	+1.8	−0.1	+0.8
Current payments	+0.4	+2.3	+0.2	+0.7
FFr/$	4.90	4.90	4.90	4.90
Prices (% change)				
Wholesale	+1.6	+1.5	+2.2	−0.8
Retail	+3.1	+2.8	+2.6	+2.7
Balance of the State budget	−2.4	−0.9	−2.9	−8.3
M2 (% change)	+9.9	+10.9	+10.6	+13

went a profound modification, marked by the sharp decline in the material forms of money; but this development essentially benefited liquid or short-term investments, while negotiable securities continued to occupy a very minor place in the financial assets of economic agents.

The privatisation of money

The most striking feature was the progressive withdrawal of the Treasury from the financial circuits.

This development manifested itself first in the supply of financing in the economy: the contribution of the budget deficit to the overall flow of this financing fell from more than 20 per cent in 1959 to slightly more than 10 per cent in 1967. Among the counterparts of M2, the share of claims on the Treasury fell during the same period from 37 per cent to 22.6 per cent.

This withdrawal did not concern only the central government; the financing of social security also played its part. The size of its budget in relation to GDP went from 15.9 per cent in 1959 to 20 per cent in 1967, but the increase in the costs of redistribution thus recorded was charged to the contributors and not to the budget: households participated to the extent of 12 per cent, companies by 41 per cent.

By the principle of communicating vessels, which is rarely found wanting in economics, a reversal occurred in the financial balances of the two main borrowing sectors of the economy, the public authorities and companies. Whilst between 1952 and 1957 in the capital account statistics of the national income accounts the borrowing requirements of companies and of the public authorities were divided in the ratio 40:60, the deficits of the former grew continuously between 1958 and 1967, representing on average 4 per cent of GDP, and those of the latter gradually disappeared.

Obviously such a structure is not neutral, for heavy indebtedness of companies does not help to moderate inflationary expectations. Furthermore, when the crisis came ten years later, the addition of the borrowing requirement of the authorities, which was now rising, to an indebtedness of companies which had become structural, was to create a formidable imbalance for the French economy.

The reduction of the budget deficit and even, in some years, its disappearance, is due first to the regular pattern of economic growth which ensured a continuous increase in fiscal receipts, nearly 60 per cent of which were collected by that excellent tax, Value Added Tax, introduced during the previous period. But expenditure and especially expenditure on intervening in the economy decreased appreciably; this development was accentuated after 1965, with 'debudgetisation', an operation by which the state progressively handed over to the productive sector, in particular to the nationalised enterprises and to the public credit institutions, mainly the Caisse des Dépôts, the financing of a number of activities for which it had up to then been responsible (for example, public sector housing was taken over by the CDC). Thus the outstanding loans of the FDES, which represented in 1959 29 per cent of the total of credits to the economy, constituted no more than 17 per cent in 1967. The decline was even more pronounced during the subsequent period.

THE EXPANSION OF THE BANKS AND THE BEGINNING OF THE TIME OF THE 'TRANSFORMATION'

Since 1945 the banks had been locked into a set of particularly restrictive regulations, which virtually prohibited those institutions which possessed sufficient resources from dealing in anything other than short-term credits, if we except the procedure for refinanceable medium-term credit for which the central bank assumed a large share of the financing. The financing hitherto effected by the authorities could have been taken over by a further development of the role of the specialised non-bank public and semi-public credit institutions, the Caisse des Dépôts, the Crédit National, the Crédit Foncier, and the Socíetés de Développement Régional which had been created in 1955; or, alternatively, the task could have been entrusted to the banks. The first solution assumed that household savings would, more than in the past, take non-monetary forms, such as deposits in savings banks, and above all subscriptions to bonds and shares. This last direction seemed risky, since attitudes were still very much coloured by inflation; it was above all expensive since, to stabilise saving, it was necessary to reward it appropriately, which at that time appeared questionable since it was felt that the financing of investment ought to be cheap. The banking route was accordingly chosen; a more forceful intervention by the banks in the financing of investments seemed all the more logical as they diversified by reason of the modernisation of the economy and of its progressive opening up to the outside world.

Two essential reforms were therefore introduced:

- the arrangements for medium-term refinanceable credit were modified in 1965, by prolonging the term but also by putting a brake on refinancing by the Banque de France;
- the laws of 1966 and 1967 in practice put an end to the regulations on specialisation by banks which dated from 1945, in such a way as to permit the banks, whatever the nature of their resources, to grant credits of any term.

In terms of general economic equilibrium the financing by monetary creation of investments, the contribution of which to the supply of goods and services is felt only with a lag, entails a risk of demand pressure which can result in persistent inflationary tendencies. In simple terms, if, in the quantity equation of $M \times V = P \times T$, M increases without the volume of goods offered (T) increasing simultaneously, there is a danger, on the assumption that V is constant, that adjustment would be brought about by a rise in P. In an open economy, an external trade deficit can be an additional consequence of such a policy.

In terms of the individual equilibrium of the banks, the process of transformation presented risks of illiquidity and of loss of profitability if the cost of monetary resources, by definition relatively volatile, came to exceed the return on employed funds.

To offset these dangers, the authorities were going to put into effect, or to encourage, a thoroughgoing mutation of the financial system.

THE MUTATION OF THE FINANCIAL SYSTEM

This consisted of two elements: measures to encourage saving and a considerable reinforcement of the power of the banks; and the introduction of new techniques of monetary policy more appropriate to the new banking structure.

The encouragement of stable saving was certainly not neglected

The returns from the bond market were improved and a number of incentives were introduced: in particular tax credits on income from shares and exemptions on income from bonds.

The results were disappointing. From the preparatory work for the Fifth Plan, moreover, that is to say in the years 1964–65, the debate on the transformation was resolved: the risk would have to be taken,

TABLE 12.2 *Shares in the money stock M2 (%)*

	1959	*1965*	*1967*
Banknotes	37.5	30.6	26.8
Sight deposits	53.2	54.3	49.8
Quasi-money	8.3	14.1	22.4

but it had to be lessened, even eliminated, by developing the resources of the banks, and above all by increasing the share of those resources which took the form of short-term savings instruments (which started to be called 'quasi-money') to the detriment of deposits which were immediately encashable by cheques or transfers. To put in another way, to compensate for the over-rapid development of one of the first two terms of the quantity equation, M, it was appropriate to weaken the second, the velocity of circulation of money, V.

To complete these new directions and to allow banks more easily to refinance their long-term claims, two major innovations were introduced into the circuits of financing: the first, of an institutional nature, was the creation of a market in mortgage claims; the second, less spectacular but equally important, was the relaxation of the constraints which weighed upon the correspondents of the Treasury: the Caisse des Dépôts and the Crédit Agricole could in future invest freely at short term their funds which were awaiting employment, and could lend them to the banks on the money market.

The results of this policy were observable, from the end of the period, in the structure of the financial assets of economic agents. If the investments in negotiable securities kept the smallest share, monetary investments on the other hand were 'consolidated' (Table 12.2).

New monetary techniques

The bringing into operation of new techniques of monetary policy had to respond to the new directions taken by the authorities in the financing of the economy and, equally, to the development of the structure of the financial assets of economic agents.

Although the *encadrement du crédit* was used during the period (between 1963 and 1965) it was not considered as a permanent procedure of monetary policy. Action on banking liquidity, which had already, in 1948, obtained its first instruments with the discount ceilings and the Treasury bill 'floors', had to remain the weapon *sui generis* of the central bank.

A first improvement was introduced in 1960 with the liquid assets ratio; but it rapidly became clear that to base monetary policy on obligations imposed on the banks as to the use of funds was ineffective and in addition created differentiations between the situations of the various credit institutions.

The reduction in the fiduciary circulation, which at the end of the period represented only 25 per cent of the money stock, on the one hand, and the inflows of foreign exchange on the other, brought substantial relief to the cash positions of the banks, and the requirements of the latter for refinancing tended to decrease accordingly. It was becoming opportune to introduce the system of monetary policy in operation in the majority of Western countries, the instrument of simple and overall action on the liquidity of the banks constituted by obligatory levels of reserves. This was effected at the end of 1966.

MONETARY AND FINANCIAL NARRATIVE

We shall distinguish three periods:
- between 1959 and 1962 the French economy recovered remarkably quickly: inflation moderated and foreign trade improved;
- in 1963 some demand pressures appeared and the government introduced a 'stabilisation' plan in which monetary policy played a major role;
- 1966 and 1967 were two years of relaxation of the constraints and of the continued implementation of the reforms of the financial system.

1959–62: A remarkable recovery

This was founded upon:
- a new adjustment of exchange rates which made French products particularly competitive;
- a brisk expansion of the financing of the economy which translated itself into a very rapid increase in the money stock. This expansion of liquidity did not immediately provoke pressure on prices and on foreign trade, in view of the conjunction of a favourable international environment and the restored confidence of economic agents. From 1961, however, the excessive liquidity of the economy led to a strengthening of demand, with which productive capacity was less and less able to cope; the situation deteriorated further in 1962.

A new parity for the franc

The devaluation of June 1958 made official the *de facto* readjustment already put into effect in 1957 with 'operation 20 per cent'. Its results did not appear to be sufficient and the monetary authorities themselves thought a new devaluation imperative.

Between a very large depreciation and a minimum depreciation, which calculations of the gap in wholesale prices and in wage costs with France's principal trading partners assessed at about 10 per cent, the government chose a middle course: a devaluation of 17.5 per cent against the US dollar, which had the additional advantage of establishing a ratio in round figures with gold (FFr1 = 1.8 milligrams of fine gold).

This readjustment was accompanied by several measures appropriate to bringing the French economy out of the cocoon in which it had been kept until then:

- an almost complete freeing of the exchanges: 90 per cent of transactions were deregulated compared to 0 per cent at the beginning of 1958[1];
- an initial lowering of customs barriers (by 10 per cent) *vis-à-vis* France's partners in the Treaty of Rome;
- the abolition of many subsidies to public undertakings, and the prohibition of index-linking, particularly in the field of public borrowing and agricultural prices.[2]

Finally, to give this package a stronger psychological impact, the monetary unit was 'made heavier': a new franc was created, equal to 100 times the old franc; the French currency was now of an equivalent order of magnitude to the German mark (FFr1 = DM1) or the Dutch guilder.[3]

The expansion of financing and liquidity

From the beginning of 1959, the *encadrement du crédit* system was withdrawn; in July the regulations on hire purchase sales were significantly relaxed.[4] The discount rate was reduced from 4.5 per cent to 4.25 per cent in February, then to 4 per cent in April. Hire-purchase regulations were further relaxed in June 1960.

As a result there was a lively growth in the financing of the economy, principally fed by credit; this financing, which had been markedly restricted in 1957 and 1958, falling from the equivalent of 10 per cent of GDP to 6.2 per cent, rose to 8.5 per cent from 1959, and in 1962 reached 10 per cent once more.

In financial investments the preference for liquidity was over-

TABLE 12.3 *Money stock and counterparts 1959–62 (changes in FFr billion)*

	1959	*1960*	*1961*	*1962*
External[1]	7.2	3.4	4.9	4.8
Domestic credit	3.2	11.7	14.8	18.5
(% change)	(+4.-%)	(+14.-%)	(+15.6%)	(+17.1%)
M2	10.4	15.1	19.7	23.3
(% change)	(+14.2%)	(+16.6%)	(+17.2%)	(+8.7%)

1. Net gold and foreign exchange.

whelming, and the share of investments in negotiable securities declined continuously – 17 per cent in 1959, 14 per cent in 1962 – while that of purely monetary assets (M2) went from 50 per cent to 62 per cent . The rise in the rate of household saving (from 13.1 per cent to 16.7 per cent) was reflected essentially in the rebuilding of liquid reserves; it was above all from the end of the third quarter of 1959 that the growth of the money stock accelerated to reach an annual rate of more than 18 per cent in 1962. The liquidity ratio M2/GDP thus went in four years from 31.7 per cent to 37.6 per cent.

At first the monetary authorities saw nothing sinister in this: the restoration of liquidity was regarded as tangible proof that confidence had returned. Moreover, among the counterparts of M2 the recovery in foreign trade brought a lively growth of net assets in gold and foreign exchange, the contribution of which to the creation of money was not negligible, and domestic credit expanded by less than M2 (Table 12.3).

As will be seen, this situation held less and less true through the years and in 1962 the expansion of domestic credit was almost the same as that of the money stock, which reflected the dwindling of the external surplus.

The expansion of domestic credit was above all due to that of bank credits to the private sector; budget deficits continued to be financed by the creation of money, but fell consistently in relative terms. By contrast the granting of credit increased rapidly. From the second quarter of 1959 it reached an annual rate of more than 18 per cent, which did not slacken in the following years but even reached 20 per cent in 1962.

Economically the results were outstanding. From the fourth quarter of 1959 production was again stimulated by domestic demand: the index of industrial production rose by 7 per cent in 1960 and 5 per cent in 1961, and GDP at constant prices grew by 7.2 per cent and 5.5 per cent respectively.

The rise in prices, which was very moderate in 1959, was practically nil in 1960; but during the latter months of 1961 significant jumps in the price index started to cause the authorities anxiety.

The latter had been in possession for some months of a new instrument of monetary control: the liquid assets ratio. Brought into force from 3 January 1961, this ratio constrained the banks to maintain among their assets an amount equal to at least 30 per cent of their deposits in the form of Treasury bills and refinanceable medium-term credits. The underlying purpose of the liquid assets ratio was no longer to finance the budget deficit, for the Treasury bill 'floor' which remained within the newly-created ratio was in effect lowered from 25 per cent to 17.5 per cent; but to curtail the facilities for refinancing available to the banks from the central bank, and particularly the rights to refinancing 'outside the ceiling' which refinanceable medium-term credits conferred on the banks.

The hopes placed in this ratio as an instrument for the regulation of the money stock proved to be exaggerated, since the major banks had in their assets extensive access to liquidity and, for the most part, were well within the limits set for them by their discount ceilings; although raised to 32 per cent in February 1962 the liquid assets ratio did not produce any slowdown of the pace of monetary expansion.

1963–65: the stabilisation plan

This subperiod was marked by a very restrictive monetary and financial policy, the effects of which on economic activity and prices are still today a subject of controversy.

Several reforms designed to modernise the money market and to encourage the investment of savings on the capital market were also introduced.

Restrictive action

As we have seen, the rate of inflation rose in 1962, a year when it exceeded 4 per cent: it accelerated markedly in the first half of 1963 (to an annual rate of 6.9 per cent) under the influence of the pressure on demand of more than a million new consumers arriving from Algeria. The return of the expatriates had encouraged the worst fears, but in the field of employment rather than inflation: there was a dread of unemployment. But in the event this new influx, to whom the first compensation payments were distributed, initially stimulated demand and production: the index of industrial production, which had increased by a little over 4 per cent in 1962, rose at an annual rate of 10 per cent in the first six months of 1963. Suddenly, and according to a process which was classical but incomprehensible to many (even today!), the demographic growth, far from causing unemployment, was at first reflected in a shortage of manpower. The overheating was maintained by the growth of bank credit and of the money stock, by 20 per cent in 1962. Demand outstripped capacity and the external trade balance worsened.

The new arrangements

In these conditions the authorities introduced a stabilisation plan consisting of a monetary wing and a budgetary wing, the effects of which, however, only started to be felt during the second half of 1963 and above all in 1964.

The monetary wing consisted of the raising of the liquid assets ratio from 32 per cent to 35 per cent in February 1963, then to 36 per cent in May; a rise in the discount rate from 3.5 per cent to 4 per cent in November 1963; an appreciable tightening of the conditions for hire-purchase finance[5]; and above all an *encadrement du crédit* which was reinforced and prolonged in several stages: in February 1963 the banks were encouraged not to increase their credits by more than 12 per cent during the following 12 months; this rate was lowered to 10 per cent in September 1963, while the limitation was also extended until October 1964, and then until September 1965 (the banks being constrained from October 1964 to keep to monthly rather than quarterly norms.).

The budgetary wing of the plan was equally severe: the budget deficit, swollen in 1963 by the measures of assistance to the returning expatriates, reached FFr8.8 billion in that year: it was brought back down to FFr1.5 billion in 1964, and gave way to a balance in 1965 (excluding the debt amortisation charge). Expenditure, especially investment expenditure, was reduced, whilst the Treasury benefited in 1964 from the growth in tax receipts resulting from the high rate of economic expansion in 1963.[6] The reduction in expenditure largely reflected the phenomenon of 'debudgetisation', that is, the transfer by the State to the nationalised industries and the major credit institutions of the investment financing for which it had up to then been responsible. This action mainly took the form of a reduction of the loans of the FDES to nationalised enterprises, which in future had to resort more to the bond market and to the Caisse des Dépôts, and of a progressive taking over by the Caisse des Dépôts, from 1964, of the financing of public sector housing, which up till then had been provided exclusively out of public funds.

At the beginning of 1966 there was created the Caisse des prêts aux organismes d'HLM, the CPHLM, a satellite institution of the Caisse des Dépôts, which functioned, at least during its earlier years, only thanks to advances from the latter,[7] and which was entrusted with the centralisation of operations concerned with the low-rental housing sector.

The scope of debudgetisation can be appreciated through the development of the loans by the Treasury to the economy, which went down from FFr6.9 billion in 1963 to FFr4.4 billion in 1965. As can be seen, it is difficult to dissociate the budgetary wing from the monetary wing of the plan. There too the principle of communicating vessels comes into play: any reduction of the burden on the State not resulting from a genuine cut in expenditure creates a demand for financing in the productive sector which will be satisfied without additional monetary creation only if savings develop sufficiently (see below).

The effects of the stabilisation plan

The measures taken gave rise to a severe contraction of the supply of financing in the economy, which went down from 10.4 per cent of GDP in 1962 to 8.8 per cent in 1963 and 7 per cent in 1964 and 1965. Above all, this reduction was reflected almost entirely in the formation of monetary assets, the rate of growth of M2 thus going from 18.7 per cent in 1962 to 13.9 per cent in 1963, 9.9 per cent in 1964, and 10.9 per cent in 1965. The growth of net domestic credit underwent a reduction of the same magnitude.

The impact of these strongly restrictive measures was felt above all from 1964, just when the economic indices were showing that for several months the imbalances had been lessening: from the last quarter of 1963, the rate of growth of household consumption became more compatible with the growth of productive capacity, the external balance improved and the annual rate of inflation fell during the fourth quarter of 1963 to less than 3 per cent.

In fact the authorities, like public opinion, having wrongly estimated the dangers of the demographic growth due to the influx of returning expatriates, seem then to have overestimated the scope and duration of the danger of inflation caused by the pressure of demand. The newly assimilated addition to the population in fact constituted a skilled and highly adaptable labour force, the entry of which into the labour market contributed to a rapid clearing of bottlenecks.[8]

In these conditions the stabilisation plan struck heavily at the real economy: industrial production was practically stagnant in 1964 and did not get moving again until the spring of 1965. During these two years the rates of growth of GDP, which remained more than respectable (at 6.5 per cent and 4.8 per cent), were largely due to the expansion of agricultural production; an atmosphere developed which some rather excessively described as 'recessionist'.[9] The slackening of demand affected consumption, but even more investment, the rate of growth of the gross fixed capital formation of companies in volume terms falling from 11.3 per cent in 1963 to 3.2 per cent in 1965.

The improvement in foreign trade was moderate, for the ratio of exports to imports (f.o.b.-f.o.b.), which started to recover in the middle of 1964 (when it stood at 93 per cent), rose to 108 per cent at the end of 1965 (it fell again in 1966), whereas it had reached 118 in 1961. In fact the international environment worsened, the growth of the GDP of France's main trading partners falling from 6.4 per cent in 1964 to 2.8 per cent in 1967.

The modernisation of the money market, the measures to stimulate saving, and the reform of medium-term credit

(1) The creation of a market in public securities

In France there was no money market in the Anglo-Saxon meaning of the phrase, in which short-term claims were bought and sold, and which allowed credit institutions to lend their surplus funds, the Treasury to borrow, and large companies, pension funds, and so on, to invest their liquid funds.

If there was indeed an 'interbank' market in France, it should rather be considered as an outgrowth of the clearing operations, the working of which did not interfere with the financing of the economy nor with the conditions in which monetary policy was set to work.

In effect the refinancing of the banks was achieved basically by rediscounting with the Banque de France which, thanks to the 'hell' and 'superhell' mechanisms, enabled the essential requirements for borrowings of central bank money to be fulfilled; in these conditions recourse to the money market had a marginal and penalising character. The central bank intervened there, by temporarily taking in short-term claims on the private sector, when it judged that the interest rates in operation were excessive; and the use of the liquid assets ratio could complete its action: the lowering or the raising of this ratio led the banks to reduce, or on the contrary to increase, their recourse to refinancing on the money market, which relaxed or tightened the pressure on interest rates. The money market also lacked the basic instruments for intervention, unlike the Anglo-Saxon countries, where public debt instruments (Treasury bills) circulated in a range of maturities, held and bought and sold by anyone. The compartmentalisation of the French national debt and the network of correspondents had until this time exempted the Treasury from conforming to the laws of the market for its short-term indebtedness. Treasury bills were issued on tap, but at a regulated rate, and banks held them only to meet the rule of the government securities 'floor'.

Thus there was nothing in existence resembling the 'open market' as practised in the Anglo-Saxon countries, in which the central bank by buying or selling Treasury bills increases or reduces at its discretion the liquidity of the banks according to the requirements of monetary policy.

Without going so far as to want to imitate this model, which was in any case hardly appropriate to a market that permanently required significant amounts of refinancing from the central bank (a market 'in the bank'), the monetary authorities were nevertheless concerned to enlarge the Paris market to some extent. The issue to financial institutions of Treasury bills on tap and at a fixed rate was thus partially abolished: it was kept in existence only in order to allow the banks to comply with the rules of the government securities floor. Apart from this a procedure of periodic auctions was instituted by which the state issued short-term bills on market conditions; however, only the credit institutions could take up these bills, and individuals and non-financial companies continued to have the right to take up only issues at regulated fixed rates.[10]

We can see that this was far from a major market of public securities; but at least the development of government paper and trading in it between banks would provide the money market with a universal and convenient transactions instrument.

(2) The measures to stimulate saving

These came into effect mainly in 1965 and had three aspects:

• The standardisation of conditions of remuneration on liquid savings, whatever the managing institution: the fiscal privileges enjoyed by Treasury bills (exemption from tax) were therefore abolished; and all income from liquid investments, with the exception of those on savings bank pass-books of type A[11] were made subject to income tax, with the opportunity for beneficiaries to opt for a flat rate levy of 25 per cent.

• The encouragement of long-term saving: for shares the system of a tax credit of 50 per cent to the advantage of the bearer (by the finance law of 1966) significantly lightened the double tax liability borne by dividends; for bonds the authorities made a variety of fiscal changes: exemption to a limit of FFr500 for income from bonds, and beyond this the opportunity of opting for the lump sum levy of 25 per cent. This was not enough to develop markets in negotiable securities; certainly the return was attractive – 6.3 per cent for income from public sector bonds, that is 4.7 per cent after tax, a rate higher than the rise in prices (3 per cent) – but issues remained rationed under the protection of the 'timetable' operated by the authorities.

• Finally a new short-term savings instrument was created, the housing savings account (2 December 1965), the holders of which could, by making a minimum savings commitment, claim the benefit of a property credit of from two to ten years at a reduced rate (together with a premium paid by the Treasury).

The results of this policy were ambiguous: the rate of household saving increased, but because of property investment; as for financial savings, they continued to be invested largely in a liquid form.

(3) The reform of medium-term refinanceable credit

The need to stimulate investments, the pace of expansion of which did not conform to the recommendations of the Fifth Plan, and the putting into practice of the first reflections on the necessity of 'transformation' were to lead the monetary authorities to take the first step towards the enlargement of the capacity of the banks to undertake medium-term and long-term financing.

The life of medium-term refinanceable credits was increased from five years to seven years whilst the facilities for rediscount with the central bank were limited to the first three maturities[12] (decision of 23 September 1965 of the General Council of the Banque de France, which came into force in 1966). The participation of the Institut d'Emission in the financing of these medium-term credits, which was already declining after the introduction of the liquid assets ratio, was rapidly reduced still further.

The relaxation of constraints and the flagging economic recovery (1966, 1967)

During these two years in which the monetary authorities did away with all the constraints of the stabilisation plan, economic development was disappointing; paradoxically it was also during this period that the authorities gave full scope to the reforms of the financial system, reforms which were going to bring radical changes in the operating conditions of the credit institutions and which carried the seeds of great dangers of uncontrolled monetary expansion.

The end of the stabilisation plan

The *encadrement du crédit* had already been lifted in June 1965, but the recommendation had been made to the banks to moderate the expansion of their outstanding credit, excessively expansionary behaviour being liable to the sanction of reductions in the discount ceilings.

At the beginning of 1967 the last credit growth recommendations were not renewed. In fact the rate of increase of bank credits rose moderately in 1966 (by 14.4 per cent against 12.5 per cent in 1965) and the money stock rose by only 10.5 per cent.

Industrial production recovered vigorously during the first six months, stabilised and even declined slightly at the end of 1966, and stagnated during the first three quarters of 1967. This downturn was due chiefly to external demand, for West Germany was passing through a serious recession as a consequence of a particularly energetic anti-inflation plan. The number of those seeking work went from 142 500 in June 1966 to 185 100 a year later and 222 500 at the end of 1967. This was enough for warnings of recession to be sounded in all social and occupational circles (GDP increased all the same by 5.2 per cent in 1966 and by 4.8 per cent in 1967!). As prices remained remarkably stable, the authorities decided to introduce a fiscal stimulus: the deficit went from FFr2.9 billion in 1966 to FFr8.3 billion in 1967. 1967 also saw a particularly sharp expansion of the sources of financing in the economy, which reached nearly 10 per cent of GDP against 7.9 per cent in 1966.

Production went ahead strongly during the later months of 1967, by reason of a renewal of external demand and of the expansion of company investments. This revival was spontaneous: the measures of stimulus had in fact scarcely had time to take effect, instead they contributed to the appearance of imbalances in 1968, just as the government had to put into action a package of reforms which gave considerable power to the financial system.

The reforms of the financial system

These reforms were inspired by three objectives: the strengthening of the power of the banks, the widening of the capital markets and the modernisation of the instruments of monetary policy.

(1) The reinforcement of the power of the banks

This was a matter of the development of the process of transformation and of the mainly quasi-monetary resources of the banks. The decrees of 25 January 1966, 26 December 1966 and 1 September 1967 practically put an end to the distinction which had existed between deposit banks and merchant banks: the former could now give credits of any term and saw their ability to take on equity participations enlarged, while the latter could now collect sight deposits.

A notice of the Crédit Foncier of 23 September 1966 set out the organisation of the mortgage market on which the institutions that granted long-term loans for housing, essentially the banks and financial institutions, could discount their claims, together with the mortgage attached to the operation, with organisations which had savings resources available, such as pension funds and the Caisse des Dépôts.

On 20 January 1967 the Conseil National du Crédit decided to make completely free the opening of bank branches, which had been subject since 1945 to prior authorisation.

The law of 2 July 1966 made arrangements for leasing, a technique by which capital goods were hired out, with the promise of sale, that was already well developed in the Anglo-Saxon countries, while reserving exclusivity in these operations to the institutions registered on the lists of the Conseil National du Crédit, in effect the banks and financial establishments.

The expansion of quasi-money was to be stimulated in future by the prohibition of interest payments on sight deposits as from July 1967, the abolition of ceilings on pass-books, and the end of restrictions on interest payments on time deposits with a term of more than two years or of an amount of at least FFr250 000.

Finally, to encourage competition among the banks, the system of minimum conditions for credit which dated from 1945 was abolished. Credit institutions (other than specialised public and semi-public organisations) were henceforth free to fix the interest rates on the credits which they granted.

This burst of reforms was bound to affect other areas, in particular the techniques of credit, with the setting up of the Crédit de mobilisation des créances commerciales, CMCC, by which a company could discount, by combining them in the same package, a group of claims with similar maturities. This innovation, in the mind of those who devised it, should have gradually replaced the discounting of bills of exchange which they wished to see disappear, because it was considered an anachronism and expensive to manage; but the results were disappointing.

(2) The widening of the capital markets

The most significant step was the abolition of exchange control (by the law of 28 December 1966 and regulatory documents of 27 January 1967). Freedom of exchange was henceforth the rule for all transfers of funds; only direct investments intended to secure control of a company, whether effected by non-residents in France or by residents abroad, had to be reported to the Banque de France. Borrowings of significant amount issued by non-bank agents were made subject to prior authorisation.

The authorities took further steps in opening up the money market. The opportunity for depositors under certain conditions to obtain an unrestricted return on their term accounts had already partly opened up the market to non-financial agents. The admission of pension funds, insurance companies and holding companies was to mark a new stage in this widening.

All the same the market remained a closed 'club', the participants in which were limited to those registered on a list drawn up by the Banque de France; short-term borrowing and lending operations between non-financial agents were not possible; the channels of communication with the bond market were weak since, on the one hand, the principal operators in the money market had little business in the bond market, and, on the other hand, there was no 'paper' of all maturities circulating in the two markets (of the type of US Treasury bonds).

(3) The modernisation of the instruments of monetary policy

To exert an influence in limiting or extending credit and liquidity, the monetary authorities used two types of intervention:
• the possibility of varying the cost of refinancing by the banks, by manipulating the discount rate, indeed by operations on the money market;
• the reduction of the refinancing facilities open to the banks, by discount ceilings and the liquid assets ratio.

The second type of instrument was not very efficient, and especially as far as the liquid assets ratio was concerned, interfered with the management of the banks and created situations of inequality between them.[13]

In other countries the system of mandatory reserves had existed for many years, which constrained banks to hold assets in accounts with the central bank in relation to certain categories of their liabilities, essentially sight and time deposits.

By this procedure, the central bank adds an additional factor in its pressure on bank liquidity, the importance of which depends only on its own decisions, which does not interfere in the management of the banks, and which bears equally on all credit institutions.

Since the war the factors of bank liquidity had been very unfavourable to the banks (the importance of the fiduciary circulation, disequilibrium of the balance of payments) and the need for such an instrument had thus not made itself felt.

At a time of modernising reforms of the financial system, and when the factors of bank liquidity had been for some years very favourable to the banking system (the important inflows of foreign exchange in particular) it appeared opportune to initiate the system of mandatory reserves (by the decree of 9 January 1967). The liquid assets ratio was abolished and replaced by the retention ratio (or minimum portfolio) of securities representing medium-term refinanceable credits.

BANK LIQUIDITY

For the first time since the war, the bank liquidity situation seemed to change.

The fiduciary circulation decreased appreciably; it was 42 per cent of M2 at the end of 1958 and 30.5 per cent at the end of 1965. Gold and foreign exchange movements were favourable practically throughout the period. These two factors largely compensated for the considerable reduction in the lending given by the Banque de France to the Treasury. The refinancing of the banks by the Institut d'Emission declined continuously and became marginal, at 14 per cent of the credits granted at the end of 1965, against 35 per cent at the end of 1958.

This development was one of the reasons which encouraged the monetary authorities to put into effect a system of mandatory reserves, a form of monetary policy which the majority of countries had known for many years.

TABLE 12.4 *Summary of monetary and financial data 1959–65 (end-period totals, averages for interest rates) (FFr billion)*

	1959	*1960*	*1961*	*1962*	*1963*	*1964*	*1965*
M2	90.7	105.8	124	147.2	167.7	184.3	204.4
Net assets in gold and foreign exchange	7.2	10.5	15.3	20.1	24.2	28	31.4
Claims on the Treasury	33.4	34	38.3	42.3	47.2	47.8	49.8
Claims on the economy	53.3	61.9	73.5	88	99.6	111.6	125.5
Deposits in savings banks	25.3	28.7	32.5	37.7	43.1	51.5	58.4
(for reference, ceiling on deposits, in francs)	10 000	10 000	10 000	10 000	15 000 (11–63)	15 000	15 000
Discount rate	4	3.5	3.5	3.5	3.8	4	3.5
Yield on bonds	5.9	5.5	5.6	5.3	5.4	5.5	5.8
New issues of negotiable securities	7.7	7	8.8	9.9	14.2	14.4	15.4
shares	3.2	2.4	3.2	4	4.2	5	5
bonds	4.5	4.6	5.6	5.9	10	9.4	10.4
(of which government bonds)	—	—	—	—	(3)	(1.5)	(1)
National income	241.2	269	293.2	328.6	368.4	409.2	440.1
Income velocity (national income/M2)	2.7	2.5	2.4	2.2	2.2	2.2	2.2

TABLE 12.5 *The financing of the economy 1959–67 (FFr billion)*

	1959	*1960*	*1961*	*1962*	*1963*	*1964*	*1965*	*1966*	*1967*	
Sources of financing										
Balance of State budget[1]	6.3	4.2	4.4	6.1	9.7	2.4	0.9	2.9	8.3	
Credits										
*Bank	5.9	8.2	11.2	12.6	11.3	11.8	14	18.4	32.2	
*Non-bank[2]	6.5	8.4	8.8	8.2	10.2	12.7	14.4	14.3	13.5	
External	7.2	3.3	4.8	4.8	4.2	3.8	3.4	1.6	−0.6	
										Investments
	4	4.5	5.5	5.4	9.6	9.2	10.1	11.5	15.2	Bonds subscriptions
	3.7	3.6	3.9	3.6	2	0.6	—	−1	0.4	Net subscriptions of Treasury bills
	3.8	3.3	3.7	5.2	5.6	8.6	7.1	9	9.2	Deposits in savings banks
	11.3	15.1	18.2	23.2	20.5	16.6	20.1	21.6	29.6	ΔM2
										*(of which banknotes)
	3.1	2.4	−2.1	3.3	−2.3	−4.3	−4.6	−2.9	1	Miscellaneous and residual[3]

SOURCES reports of the Conseil National du Crédit.

1. A surplus reduces the supply of financing (− sign); a deficit increases it (+ sign). Including loans by the Fonds de Développement économique et social.
2. Including net issues of bonds by non-financial companies.
3. Miscellaneous uses of funds by financial institutions; deposits not counted in the monetary aggregates (deposits with the Treasury by correspondents and deposits at the Caisse des Dépôts et Consignations), investments in insurance companies, amortisation of bond borrowings.

TABLE 12.6 *Factors affecting bank liquidity 1959–65 (FFr billion)*

	Situation at end 1958	*changes in* 1959	1960	1961	1962	1963	1964	*situation at end 1965*
(A) Notes in circulation	−34.39	−0.56	−4.37	−5.03	−5.73	−5.70	−3.76	−59.54
(B) Gold and foreign exchange net	−0.07	+8.57	+3.25	+6.53	+4.73	+4.14	+2.47	+29.62
(C) Direct claims of the Banque de France on the Treasury*	+20.22	−4.70	−3.11	+0.34	+0.93	+1.17	+0.31	−14.94
(D) Miscellaneous[1]	−2.25	−0.15	+0.08	+0.06	−0.28	+0.01	+0.13	−2.18
A + B + C + D = balance of autonomous factors affecting bank liquidity								
(E) Portfolio of the Banque de France	+16.49	−3.16	+4.15	−1.90	+0.35	+0.38	−0.25	+16.06

1. Bills in course of payment, accounts of financial and non-financial agents at the Banque de France, miscellaneous items of the balance sheet of the Banque de France (own funds, fixed assets, and so on), direct lending by the Banque de France to non-financial agents.

* Including the refinancing of special loans at the Caisse des Dépôts et Consignations.

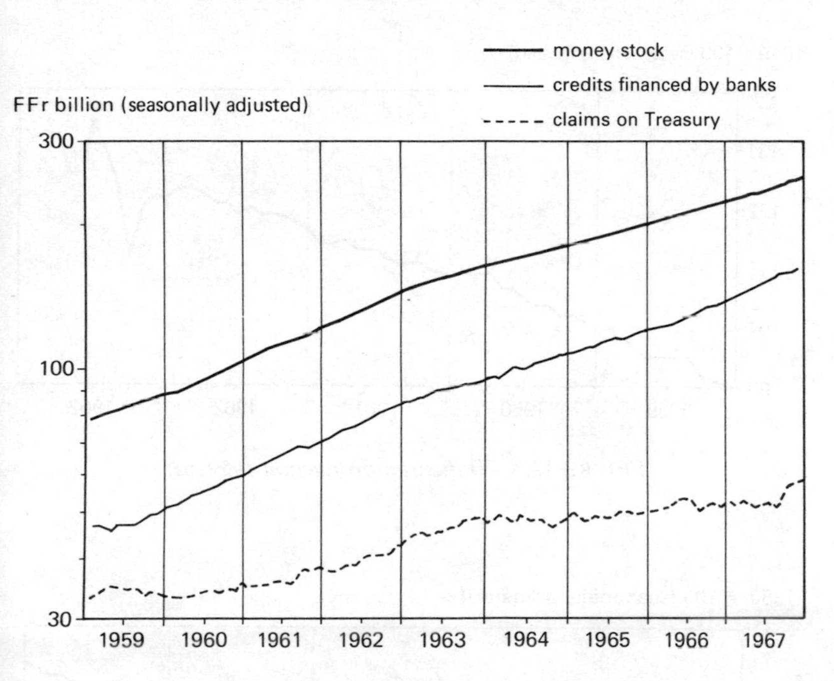

FIGURE 12.1 *Money stock and counterparts 1959–67*

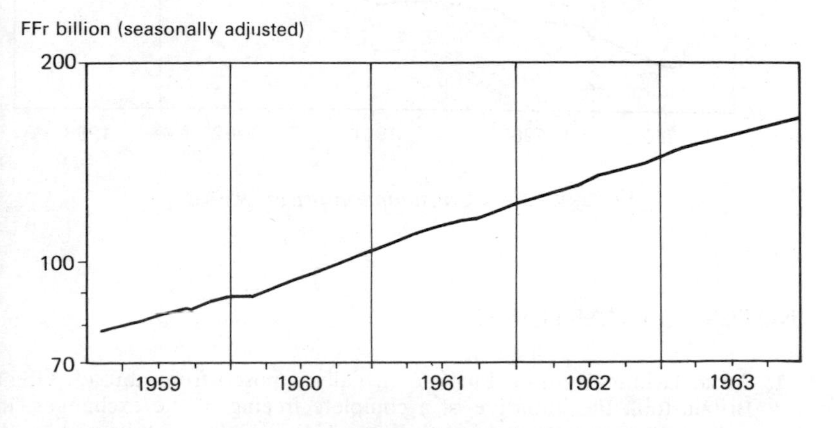

FIGURE 12.2 *Money stock 1959–63*

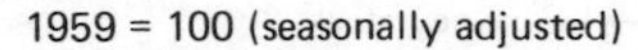

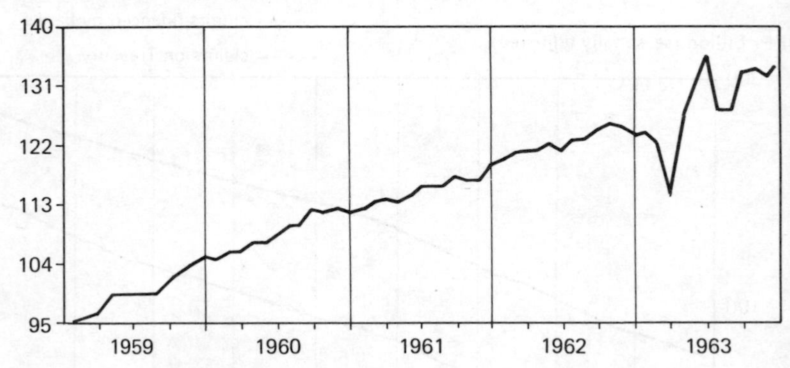

FIGURE 12.3 *Industrial production 1959–63*

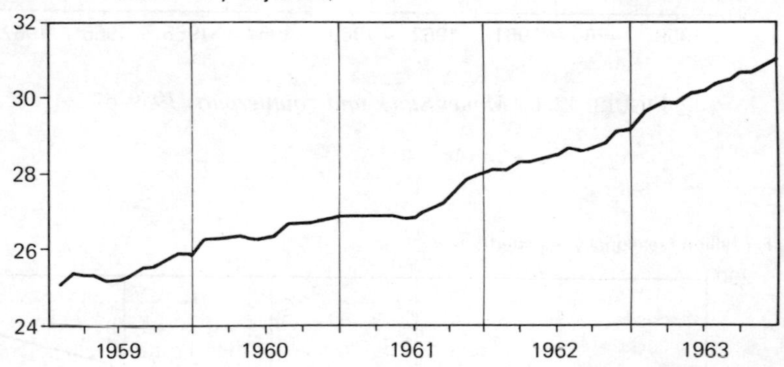

FIGURE 12.4 *Consumption prices 1959–63*

NOTES TO CHAPTER 12

1. An audacious decision, but one virtually imposed from abroad: Great Britain took the initiative of a complete freeing of the exchanges, in order to preserve the role of the pound sterling. It was followed by all France's EEC partners and by the countries which were later to associate themselves with the United Kingdom to form the European Free Trade Association (EFTA).

2. It was, however, permissible to continue to index contracts between two parties carrying on the same economic activity.
3. This monetary reform was, however, put into effect only very gradually, since the old banknotes only disappeared ten years later. A less gradual introduction of the new notes would undoubtedly have avoided the situation by which in 1985, 26 years after the measure was taken, many people still thought in terms of 'old francs'.
4. Lowering of the cash payment, extension of the maximum duration of credit to 18 months, the raising of the financing 'potential' of the credit-granting institutions to nine times their own capital. For financing the purchase of cars, the duration of the financing period could vary between 18 and 24 months according to the time of year. In June 1960 the 'potential' was raised to ten times own capital.
5. The 'potential' of credit-granting institutions was reduced again from ten times to nine times their own capital in September 1963, then to eight times in November 1964; the buyer's contribution was raised by 5 per cent; and the duration of credit was limited to 18 months (against 21) for car purchases.
6. Additional receipts were further obtained for the Treasury by the transfer to the Fonds de Stabilisation des Changes of the claims of the State on the International Monetary Fund. These operations amounted to FFr1.6 billion in 1962 (plus FFr1 billion in 1963 and FFr0.34 billion in 1964).
7. The CPHLM later had its resources increased by the repayments on loans already granted, which it received without deduction.
8. Bottlenecks in industrial production, which went from 32 per cent to 38 per cent in 1963, fell again to 22 per cent in 1964.
9. The developments in the labour market were particularly revealing: the number of those seeking work, which had gone up from a quarterly average of 98 000 to 168 000 between the second and fourth quarters of 1962, then went down rapidly to 106 000 during the earlier months of 1964, which reflected the complete integration of the returned expatriates, then rose continuously (to 148 000 at the end of 1964).
10. There were thus three categories of Treasury bills: 'liquid assets certificates' at regulated fixed rates for fulfilling the liquid assets ratio and government securities at money market rates, investment in these two categories of securities being reserved for financial institutions; and finally bills *sur formules*, at regulated fixed rates, reserved for non-financial agents.
11. A second type of savings bank book, type B, was introduced, with interest subject to tax, comparable to bank savings accounts.
12. A rather complex system of discount at a normal rate (for the next two annual instalments due) and at an increased rate (for the third instalment) was brought into force.
13. Even profits for some banks well provided with assets in the form of medium-term refinanceable credits.

13 1968–73: Expansion with Inflation

This period began with the social and cultural turbulence of May 1968, no clear and objective explanation of which has even yet emerged; it continued with the most brilliant years of expansion France has ever known, but in a context of inflation that was at first muted and then more and more robust. The crisis which followed the fourth Arab-Israeli war of October 1973 seemed to bring this happy period to a close and, for many, from this date onward 'the world had changed'.

In fact it seems that the change had been coming into operation for many years already, and that the sharp rise in oil prices merely uncovered an existing situation.

This change had taken three forms: the greater and greater openness of frontiers or the 'growing interconnectedness of economies'; the emergence of the developing countries as industrial partners; and finally what has been called the 'crisis of the international monetary system', especially the problem of the dollar and the growth of the Eurocurrency markets.

The French economy seemed to sail remarkably easily through this period of turbulence on the international scene. It benefited from the momentum given to it by a flexible incomes policy and an unprecedented growth of credit and money.

THE CONTEXT

The changing world

(1) The opening of frontiers and the interconnectedness of economies

The Common Market, the Treaty for which was signed on 25 March 1957 and which came into force on 1 January 1958, was from that moment a living reality. By 1968 customs 'disarmament' could be considered as total and a common external tariff was in existence. The Common Market extended to agriculture, very largely through

TABLE 13.1 *Major annual statistics 1968–73*

	1968	*1969*	*1970*	*1971*	*1972*	*1973*
GDP (1929 = 100) (% change)	4.1	7.5	6.1	5.4	5.9	5.4
Industrial production (% change)	5.1	10.3	6.7	5.4	6.9	6.8
Balance of payments (FFr billion):						
Trade account	−1.5	−6.4	−4.7	−1.5	−1.5	−2.2
Current payments	−6.8	−10.4	−5.0	−0.3	−0.8	−3.8
Capital flows	−9.1	−1.1	6.1	8.2	−0.4	1.1
FFr/$ (end of year)	4.94	5.55	5.55	5.16	5.08	4.58
Prices (% change):						
Wholesale	3.3	7.1	6.2	5.3	5.3	7.3
Retail	5.2	6.4	5.2	6.0	6.9	8.5
Balance of the State budget (FFr billion)	−14.0	−1.9	+0.6	−1.8	+1.8	+4.8
M2 (% change)	18.0	5.3	15.3	18	18.8	14.6

SOURCES GDP – up to 1970, domestic production; 1971–73, gross domestic product on base of 1970 – and industrial production (including construction): national income accounts; Budget: Les Notes bleues; M2: Conseil National du Crédit; prices – wholesale = production prices for 29 sectors, retail = up to 1970 259 articles, from 1970 295 items – national income accounts.

French pressure: thus the Common Agricultural Policy (CAP) came into being, involving in particular freedom of trade in goods and a common policy of relatively high prices, which stimulated agricultural modernisation.

Certainly progress remained to be achieved, in the matters of harmonisation of incomes policies, of making headway against regional disparities, and of fiscal policy (though the member states reached agreement in 1967 on the principle of the general application of VAT).

The Common Market, soon called the European Economic Community, came rapidly to be the focal point of the Western world. It could not avoid agreements of association with other countries: with Britain first, whose entry to the system was to be fiercely opposed by France but which reaped several agreements to lower customs duties by the intermediacy of the European Free Trade Association, which it wanted for a while to make into a rival grouping to the EEC. Agreements were also signed with other European countries, Austria, Greece and Turkey, and with the countries of the franc zone; finally the Kennedy Round in 1967 brought about a general compromise on the lowering of customs tariffs.

For the French economy the results of these developments were absolutely remarkable: from being relatively closed, it became one of the most open; mainly oriented until the middle 1960s towards its former empire, it became once more deeply involved in intra-European trade. The share of exports in GDP was only 12 per cent in 1960; it rose to 15 per cent of market sector GDP in 1969, and to nearly 20 per cent in 1973. In 1960 37 per cent of France's exports were destined for the countries of the 'Union Française' and 22 per cent for the Common Market; the respective proportions were 13 per cent and 43 per cent in 1968, and 5 per cent (including exports to Algeria) and 48 per cent in 1973.

(2) The emergence of developing countries as industrial partners

Although a certain number of geographical regions, in particular in Africa and to a lesser degree in Latin America, remained plunged in destitution and underdevelopment, which were accentuated after a brief bright interval (the 'green revolution'), some islands of power came into being and developed: Brazil, South Korea, Taiwan, and so forth, which already competed more and more effectively with the Western countries in the production of consumer and capital goods of ever greater sophistication. This rise in power was responsible, at least as much as the energy crisis, for the 'crisis of the West' which began in the middle of the 1970s.

(3) Finally the crisis in the international monetary system supported a climate of latent inflation

The role of gold, as an international settlement and reserve asset, weakened in proportion as its market value increased, under the effect of anxieties aroused by the world conjuncture and American monetary policy.

The deficit in the American balance of payments, which had long been limited to tourist expenditure and movements of capital (notably for the acquisition of participations in European industry) widened considerably with the war in Vietnam. Paradoxically, the weakness of the dollar and the rise in the price of gold reinforced the former as a reserve currency, the second no longer being usable in practice. Whatever one's opinion of the regime of the gold standard, it is certain that the total disappearance of the constraint which had been given weight by the use of gold in international settlements put a premium on lax behaviour by the countries issuing reserve currencies.

The situation was to take on another dimension with the development of Eurocurrencies and, especially, Eurodollars.

Originally a Eurodollar was a dollar which had left United States territory because of the US balance of payments deficit, and which its holder wanted to keep in a bank not 'resident' in the US, or Eurobank. The latter could lend the dollars thus deposited to those carrying on international trade; in practice, and in a more and more assertive way, it appeared that a Eurobank lent dollars, or another currency, which it did not possess and thus created money in accordance with the most classical mechanism. Of course, a Eurobank could have liquidity problems and requirements for 'central' money arising from its customers' transfers to other banks, or by the conversion of the Eurodollars it had created into other currencies, or again by the return of these Eurodollars into the domestic monetary circuit of the United States. This central money consists of the dollar assets of Eurobanks with American banks and above all of the lines of credit at their disposal with American banks.

But Eurocurrencies were nonetheless a powerful factor in the development of international liquidity, of which there was at one time a fear of a shortage (which justified the creation of Special Drawing Rights in 1969)! This was an element which contributed significantly to the speculative movements which were to affect the dollar, the major European currencies and the Japanese yen in 1968, 1970 and 1971.

The domestic context: the search for an economic expansion up to the limits of productive capacity and the boom in the transformation process and the creation of money

(1) A generous wages policy which contributed to the unbalancing of company finances

The years 1963–68 had been characterised by a relatively strict incomes policy, which some people have identified as one of the origins of the social upheaval of May 1968. This rigour was, however, quite relative, for the expansion permitted an increase in the real cost of labour at an average annual rate of 3.5 per cent. After 1968 a significant leap was apparent, to 5.6 per cent, and after a short period of restriction in 1969 which accompanied the devaluation, the years 1970 to 1973 saw annual gains of nearly 6 per cent on average. The rise in household disposable income was quite remarkable, at an average of 12.6 per cent between 1969 and 1973 against 8.2 per cent between 1963 and 1968; the gain in purchasing power of one period over the other was nearly 3 points.

The impulse was given by the policy followed in the public sector but the main weight was felt by companies.

In effect the public finances, after a temporary deficit in 1968, returned over the period to a situation of equilibrium: debudgetisation continued, public capital expenditure was restrained and the high rate of economic expansion ensured regular fiscal returns.

On the other hand, the financial situation of companies was severely burdened by the weight of wages and the rise in social security contributions: the 'division of value added' became more and more unfavourable to company savings (Table 13.2).

As elsewhere, investment policy was very dynamic; the result was a rapid increase in the borrowing requirements of companies, in contrast with the virtual balance in the situation of the public authorities (Table 13.3).

But this situation did not provoke an external imbalance since the supply of finance was adjusted to the requirement for it thanks to a

TABLE 13.2 *Distribution of value added of companies (%) (Incorporated and Unincorporated Enterprises)*

	1967	*1973*
Wages and salaries	35.6	39.3
Social security contributions	11.1	12.2
Taxes	10.5	8.2
Interest payments	3.2	4.9
Other	4	4.1
Gross disposable income	35.6	31.3

TABLE 13.3 *Borrowing requirements or surpluses as % of market sector GDP*

	1967	*1973*
Companies	−3.8	−5.7
Public authorities	—	+1
Households	+3.4	+3.9
Other[1]	+0.3	+0.5
Total domestic	−0.1	−0.3

1. Including credit institutions.

strong expansion of credit and liquidity. The result was a gradually strengthening inflation which did not, however, have an unfavourable impact on the balance of payments since on the one hand France's principal trading partners were hardly better off than she was, and on the other the devaluation of August 1969 (see below) had given the French economy a competitive edge.

Monetary and financial policy had in effect a fundamental impact on the conditions of economic equilibrium during this period.

(2) The Monetary and Financial Context

At the end of the preceding period the reforms of 1966–67 and the restructuring carried out in the financial sector had given the credit institutions and particularly the banks a solid basis for their future expansion. The full extent of this expansion was achieved between 1970 and 1973; it is true that an *encadrement du crédit* was imposed once more between the end of 1968 and the autumn of 1970, but its lifting was followed by an extraordinary development of credit and liquidity, that monetary policy could control only with difficulty. In effect the system of mandatory reserves on credits, brought into operation after the lifting of the *encadrement du crédit* (see below) was shown to be ineffectual in an environment where very low interest rates had to be maintained in order to limit movements of capital provoked by the lack of confidence in the dollar.

This was the period when the use of banks became much more widespread in the French economy: the bank account achieved much increased importance; it became the most used form of money and came to consist more and more of short-term savings deposits and bills (quasi-money), which conformed, moreover, to the wishes of the monetary authorities (Table 13.4).

This was also the period when the process of transformation achieved its full extent, with the financing of investment (gross capital formation) more and more secured by the creation of money (Table 13.5).

The banks diversified the uses of their funds in two ways:

- as far as maturities were concerned, since short-term credits, which had been in the majority at the beginning of the 1960s, represented in 1973 less than 50 per cent of outstanding loans, to the gain of medium- and long-term credits; among the latter the share of re-financeable medium-term credits diminished. This latter development bore witness to the change in the behaviour of the senior management of the banks, who were now confident of the stability of their resources and no longer hesitated to commit themselves without the guarantee of refinancing by the Banque de France;
- as regards the types of credit and of debtor: in 1965 almost all short-term credits were granted to companies, with the exception of modest amounts of specialised credits for hire-purchase finance; moreover, the banks took little interest in credits for property except through the mechanism of refinanceable medium-term credit. From 1970 short-term bank lending to households developed rapidly in the form of advances on accounts and above all of personal loans. This type of facility, taken over from the American example, which was easy to explain and required no justification other than the production of a wages slip, enjoyed a great success. In the field of property financing, credits eligible for the mortgage market competed effectively with the various forms of medium-term credits which existed before 1966.

TABLE 13.4 *Components of the money stock M2*

	1968		*1973*	
	FFr. billion	%	*FFr. billion*	%
Notes and coin	73.3	25.2	89.5	15.8
Sight deposits	138.8	48	242.7	42.8
Quasi-money	75.9	26.5	235.5	41.4
M2	287		567.7	

TABLE 13.5 *Financing of the gross capital formation* of companies (%)*

	1969	*1973*	*1974*
Saving of companies (internal finance)	65.4	56	45
Recourse to long-term saving of other economic agents	19.6	14	14.8
Monetary financing	15	30	40.2

*Including stockbuilding

The result was a significant gain in the market share of the banks in the granting of credit, whilst the role of the major specialist organisations, which had been dominant at the beginning of the 1960s, was reduced to 40 per cent in 1973.

This unprecedentedly relaxed financing position (the supply of new finance reached 13.5 per cent of GDP in 1972) had its results. The expansion of production was particularly striking (5.4 per cent in volume in 1971, 5.9 per cent in 1972 and 5.4 per cent in 1973) and the French economy became one of the very foremost in the world, clearly overtaking Britain from 1970.

The macrofinancial linkages can be stated simply as follows:

- Acquisitions of stable savings assets, represented by shares and bonds, were very limited; in fact as an average over the period they scarcely covered more than a third of the demand for finance.
- Households, to which higher incomes were rapidly becoming available, were encouraged by the economic context to consume and invest even beyond the limit of their incomes: they went into debt the more readily as credit became cheaper and more easily available (in personal loans and mortgage loans).

• Stimulated by the growth of demand and by a general strategy of extending productive capacity (of which the massive steel complex at FOS was an example) company investments increased apace; they were largely financed by bank credit, which created purchasing power, without a simultaneous increase in the supply of goods and services.

The pressure of demand encouraged by consumption and investment was reflected in the development of prices and, in consequence, of wages, the indexation mechanisms being particularly efficient. There followed an even more massive increase in credit to finance the requirements of companies for increased working capital, even for speculative stockholding. On the other hand households were holding higher reserves, which inflation and the level of interest rates hardly encouraged them to convert into stable savings: these higher reserves could be considered as a sort of inflation tax. The rate of household saving was thus one of the highest in Western countries (it bordered on 17 per cent between 1970 and 1973), but this saving consisted largely of investments in housing, and the balance (what is known as financial saving) was almost entirely in a monetary form.

Thus, at the end of the development, production and incomes were *ex post* much higher, but with a reinforced rise in prices. This very tense equilibrium, at the limit of productive capacity, was maintained without external deficit, because the international context was itself inflationary and supportive; but it obviously would not withstand a reversal of this context, which developed from 1974.

MONETARY AND FINANCIAL NARRATIVE

Three phases can be distinguished:

• In 1968, the extent of the shock of May surprised the authorities; the very expansionary monetary policy allowed the productive apparatus to stand up to the repercussions of strikes and wage rises, but it also fed the outflows of capital which started in the spring crisis.

• In 1969 and 1970, the authorities resigned themselves to a devaluation of the franc and a return to austerity; the *encadrement du crédit* was re-established.

• In 1971, 1972 and 1973 the economy enjoyed a remarkable growth whilst, simultaneously, credit and liquidity grew at an accelerated rate; a new *encadrement du crédit*, brought into operation in a more sophisticated form from the end of 1972, still did not succeed in moderating these developments in 1973.

1968

The year 1967 finished with a brisk recovery in production, partly stimulated by fiscal measures and sustained monetary expansion.

This resulted in a slight deficit on the balance of payments between the end of December and the end of March. A decrease of about FFr300 million was recorded in the Banque de France's net assets in gold and foreign exchange. The situation had, however, appeared sufficiently normal for exchange controls to have been entirely lifted some months before.

Public opinion took hardly any account of these improvements and there was general gloom. On the domestic financial plane, the consequences of the May events were of two kinds: the public finances suffered the repercussions of the delays in recovering taxes and social contributions, while companies, deprived of income by the interruption of production and of sales, had to bear the burden of large wage rises (between 10 and 15 per cent according to the sector and the social and occupational category concerned).

The parity of the franc could therefore be called in question, in view of the loss of competitiveness that the economy was theoretically going to suffer; it was not obvious, nevertheless, that the reserves of productivity were insufficient to deaden the impact. But expectations were very soon to become unfavourable; from May capital outflows were observed, though these were moderate since the net assets in gold and foreign exchange fell from FFr34.1 billion at the end of April to FFr32.6 billion a month later. A relatively mild form of exchange controls was introduced.

It is easy, 25 years later, to pronounce on what action should have been taken: credit and the money stock should have been held firm so as not to encourage outflows of foreign exchange by an excessive expansion of domestic credit.

Such a policy was hardly practicable in the climate of the time; the first concern was to restart production and to make up for the wealth lost during a month and a half of virtually total stoppage of activity.[1] Monetary policy had at the same time to supply resources to the Treasury and to allow companies to get through this difficult spell.

Claims on the Treasury, which for several years had experienced a very moderate increase, rose by more than FFr10 billion between the end of May and the end of August.

A system of exceptional cash-flow advances to small and medium-sized companies (later called Operation Ginger) was set up; it supplied about FFr3 billion of cheap credit. At the same time the banks were temporarily freed from the obligation to constitute reserves and their discount ceilings were raised.

The discount rate was increased to 5 per cent in July, a rise of one and a half points, but a large proportion of credits (for exports, medium-term capital goods, exceptional cash-flow advances) escaped this price increase.

Domestic credit went on rising at a sustained pace until the autumn. The outflow of foreign exchange increased in June (to FFr7.2 billion) because of the reversal of leads and lags: importers were hurrying to pay their debts and exporters were delaying the repatriation of their receipts.[2] The drain on the foreign exchange reserves continued at an average rate of FFr2 billion a month, rising somewhat in November after rumours of the introduction of a wealth tax.

In the autumn, however, economic and monetary policy was drastically modified. The government refused to devalue the franc under speculative pressure and much stricter exchange controls were set up, involving the banning of forward cover operations in particular, the requirement for exporters to repatriate their receipts within a short period and the re-establishment of the 'investment currency' system. Above all, the *encadrement du crédit* was reintroduced, with particularly strict norms: short-, medium- or long-term bank lending, which was not discountable at the Banque de France and not eligible for the mortgage market, denominated in francs or in foreign currency and granted to residents, had to be kept to the level of 107 at the end of December 1969 relative to the base of 100 in September 1968.

In all, however, although the money supply rosc less than in 1967, by reason of the external outflow, it found its sources in very different operations (Table 13.6).

1969–70

During these two years monetary policy was tightened appreciably. This action, combined with a very rapid return to a balanced budget, had only a limited effect on inflation but contributed to the recovery of the external balance, with the help, it is true, on the one hand of a

TABLE 13.6 *M2 and its counterparts 1967–68 (FFr billion)*

	1967	*1968*
Gold and foreign currency	+1.2	−15.7
Claims on the Treasury	+5.2	+3.3
Credits to the economy	+25	+36
M2 (%)	+13.1%	+11.6%

more and more inflationary world situation, and on the other of a devaluation of the franc in August and a revaluation of the German mark in October 1969.

The credit restrictions to a large extent spared the financing of investment; economic growth was therefore rapid.

After the introduction of the *encadrement du crédit* at the end of 1968, the reaffirmation, in November, of the maintenance of the parity of the franc was followed by a short period of calm on the foreign exchange markets. From February 1969, however, capital movements took an unfavourable direction, and in July the net assets in gold and foreign exchange fell to less than FFr6.5 billion, more than FFr12 billion below their level at the end of the preceding December.

The monetary authorities consequently reinforced the controls on credit, principally by limiting more strictly the growth of the various bank assets not so far included in the scope of the *encadrement* and also by trying to moderate the expansion of refinanceable medium-term credits and credits eligible for the mortgage market: these two types of lending (with the exception of export credits) were thenceforward subject to a specific norm.[3] The regulations for hire-purchase credit were also tightened (in September 1969) by a reduction of the lending potential of the credit institutions concerned, and by a reduction of the proportion of credit allowed and the maximum duration of the finance.

In a world environment itself characterised by an appreciable rise in interest rates, the defence of the franc required an increase of the discount rate from 6 per cent to 8 per cent between June and October. The result was that credit became significantly more expensive; the most favourable commercial discount rate went from 6.1 per cent at the beginning of 1969 to 8.5 per cent at the end of the year.

All these measures contributed to a very sharp slowing down of the expansion of money and of credit: the growth of the money stock M2

TABLE 13.7 *M2 and its counterparts 1969–70 (FFr billion)*

	First half 1969	*Second half 1969*	*First half 1970*
Gold and foreign currency	−11.4	+2.1	+8.8
Claims on the Treasury (s.a.)	+5.1	−1.5	−5.3
Claims on the economy (Bank-type credits, s.a.)	+18.4	+10	+16.1
M2 (s.a.)	+11.9	+4.8	+15.4

eased from December 1968; for 1969 it was 5.9 per cent, that is about half of the 1968 level. For bank credits[4] ('bank type credits') the rate of growth fell from 18.4 per cent to 12 per cent. This rate of 12 per cent although down on that for 1968 was obviously far from the 2.9 per cent permitted by the *encadrement* for the credits subject to it. It was an example of the flaw, which was to worsen, that any regime that allows dispensation (in this case for refinanceable medium-term capital goods credits and mortgage credits, the special norm for which was higher than the general norm) introduces into the effectiveness of a quantitative control.

The counterpart structure, which was again very unfavourable in 1969, nevertheless improved from the later months of the year (Table 13.7).

The slowing down in the accumulation of monetary assets was accompanied by a strong rise in investments in negotiable securities, encouraged by the rises in yields: FFr20.2 billion were invested in bonds against FFr15 billion in 1968, FFr3.4 billion in shares against FFr1.6 billion; conditions in the market, however, remained very tight.

These developments reflected the improvement in the external balance, monetary policy having provided effective support to the devaluation of the franc in August 1969 (from 180 milligrams of fine gold to 160). A revaluation of the mark in October further stimulated France's exports. The ratio of exports to imports improved from 86.4 per cent in 1969 to 93.8 per cent in 1970 (c.i.f./f.o.b.).

As concerns prices, the results were much less convincing: the consumer price index went up by 5.9 per cent in 1969 against 5.3 per cent in 1968, and slowed down slightly in 1970 (to 5.3 per cent). However, these rises were hardly bigger than those seen abroad, except, it is true, in West Germany.

The years 1969–70 give a rather rare example of a strongly restrictive monetary policy which had practically no deflationary influence on production. It is true that it only had a very partial effect on credits for investment and that, for their part, wages continued to rise sharply; household disposable income thus rose by 13.5 per cent in 1969 (against 9.7 per cent in 1968) and by another 13 per cent in 1970. GDP also recorded a growth of nearly 8 per cent in 1969 and of 6.1 per cent in 1970, and the growth of investment reached 8.8 per cent and 6.8 per cent.

Observing the improvement of France's external trade and the restored stability of the franc, the authorities quickly relaxed the constraints. From the first half of 1970, the special norms applied to medium-term refinanceable credits and to credits eligible for the mortgage market were considerably increased and the hire-purchase regulations were made more flexible. The relaxation of interest rates abroad had repercussions on the level of the money market rate and also on the discount rate, which returned to 7 per cent in October.

From the first half of 1970 the growth of credit and of the money stock increased sharply.

At the same time, it is true, to compensate for the supply of liquidity which the reversal of capital movements was providing for the banks, the Banque de France increased the rate of mandatory reserves. In addition, the authorities sought to encourage those monetary investments which showed the greatest stability: they created housing savings plans and authorised savings banks (brought together in the Groupements Régionaux d'Epargne et de Prévoyance) to issue five-year bonds. For long-term investments tax exemption on bond income was widened.

The culmination of the liberalisation measures was the lifting of the *encadrement du crédit* from October 1970.

Although the authorities accompanied this cancellation with the usual recommendations to credit institutions and took various measures intended to prepare for the operation of new methods of bank refinancing (lowering of discount ceilings and reduction of the facility for the refinancing of medium-term credits) there followed a particularly rapid acceleration of credit and liquidity.

This growth was amplified by the fact that the banks were now reintegrating into their lending figures what were known as 'face to face' operations, which had developed widely during the *encadrement*. A 'face to face' operation consisted of the bringing together of one customer seeking credit and another with unemployed funds at his disposal, the bank playing no role other than that of a broker, or even a guarantor.[5]

Thus 'bank type credits', which had grown by 9.8 per cent (s.a.) during the first nine months of 1970, increased by an almost equivalent rate during the last quarter, and the money stock, the rate of increase of which had been 8.6 per cent (s.a.) until September, grew by 15 per cent over the whole year.

1971–73

These three years were characterised by practically uninterrupted international monetary tension. The lack of confidence in the dollar gave rise to large-scale speculative movements which were fed mainly by the stock of Eurodollars in circulation.

On 20 August 1971 the American authorities decided upon the inconvertibility of the dollar into gold and placed a surtax of 10 per cent on imports into the US.

The objective weakening of the dollar in fact reinforced its place within the international monetary system and gold was mentioned less and less.

In December 1971 an agreement was arrived at between the ten major industrial countries on a devaluation of the order of 8 per cent of the American currency, which would, however, operate through an adjustment of the exchange rate of the other currencies, principally the mark, the yen and the Swiss franc. The French franc-dollar parity on the other hand remained unchanged. At the same time a decision by the IMF doubled, to 4.5 per cent, the margins of permissible fluctuations around the official parities.

From January 1972 the dollar, which from that time was floating, started to fall again in the principal European markets and this trend of lack of confidence lasted practically until the end of the year. The member countries of the EEC, with which Britain and Ireland were now associated, set up in April an intervention mechanism limiting to 2.25 per cent the maximum instantaneous gap between the strongest and the weakest of their currencies. As this reduced margin fell within the 4.5 per cent margin permitted by the IMF, the European agreement was called the 'snake in the tunnel'.

Soon the pound sterling, itself much weakened, was detached from this mechanism and floated freely.

The European agreement was completed at the end of 1972 by the creation of the European Monetary Co-operation Fund, set up to support the interventions which the central banks had to make in order to observe the reduced margins of fluctuation. At the same time the governments of the European countries decided to commit themselves simultaneously to a programme to fight inflation, involving in particular a reduction in the rate of increase of the money stock.

After a lull of several weeks at the end of 1972, due in particular to the prospect of peace in Vietnam, speculation against the dollar redoubled in intensity.

On 12 February the American government devalued the dollar by 10 per cent: this decision led to the withdrawal of Italy from the European snake, and the decision of the European governments no longer to observe the 4.5 per cent margin of fluctuation against the dollar. The floating of currencies thus became general, with the exception of those currencies taking part in the European agreement, which floated together as a bloc.

In this context the franc was, almost until the autumn of 1973 (except for a brief period at the end of 1972), the subject of speculative movements favouring its revaluation and the monetary authorities took appropriate measures from 1971 to put a brake on this movement:

- the regulation of the foreign exchange positions of the French banks (which led the latter to suspend the payment of interest on non-resident accounts that were less than three months old);
- and the creation of a dual foreign exchange market; on the first market the parity of the official franc was defended and currencies were exchanged as necessary for commercial payments, while on the second the franc floated freely.

The situation of the franc was reversed from September 1973 and the pressure on it increased continuously after the Arab-Israeli war of October 1973: the position of the United States, much less dependent on imported energy than the European states, appeared stronger, and the dollar recovered sharply; to limit this appreciation the Deutsche Bundesbank intervened energetically, which maintained the mark rate at a high level. The franc was unable to keep its place within the European snake and left it on 19 January 1974.

The international speculative context contributed to the reinforcement in France of a phase of exceptional expansion of liquidity.

Between the end of December 1970 and the end of August 1973 the net movement of foreign exchange showed on balance an inflow of FFr26.4 billion, that is, nearly 6 per cent of the money stock.

But credits to the economy also contributed significantly to the creation of money; they grew by 19 per cent in 1971 and 23.4 per cent in 1972.

The money stock increased at rates which had not been seen since the immediate postwar period and which have not been seen since: 18 per cent in 1971 and 18.4 per cent in 1972.

Monetary policy was caught in the contradiction which arises from the necessity to combat speculation and therefore to lower interest rates, and the intention to moderate the expansion of credit and liquidity; it was in fact, up to the end of 1972, powerless to achieve this second objective.

This policy was, however, the subject of an original change in its methods. Partly following the recommendations of the Wormser-Marjolin-Sadrin report, which was drawn up at the end of 1968 and which advocated an evolution towards the open market techniques employed in the Anglo-Saxon countries, the Banque de France from the beginning of 1971 brought the rate at which it intervened on the money market down below the discount rate, on a long-term basis. This decision was also motivated by the desire to provide an effective counter to the movements of foreign capital, by lowering the level of the interest rate on short-term money while keeping the terms for credit, which were still largely linked to the discount rate, relatively high on the domestic market.

The rate of the interventions of the Banque de France on the money market accordingly fell from nearly 7 per cent at the end of 1970 to 3.5 per cent in June 1972; during the same period the discount rate declined only from 6.5 per cent to 5.75 per cent.

The rise in rates which occurred from the second half of 1972 was not at variance with the new scale which had now been established. The money market rate rose to 5 per cent at the end of 1972, remained in this region during the first half of 1972 and was then raised to 11 1/6 per cent in December. During the same period the discount rate was increased, moreover, to 11 per cent on 20 September 1973.

In consequence, the main part of the refinancing of the banks by the Institut d'Emission was effected henceforth on the money market, by temporary purchases of bills representing credits[6] or of government securities.

The gradual decline of the discount mechanism and the absence of sufficient quantities of government securities among the assets of the banks meant that the 'open market' operations were carried out through the medium of bills representing credits to the private sector. Among the latter, the Banque distinguished between first category bills, endowed with a refinancing agreement, which in fact carried on the spirit of the discount agreement, and second category bills, which it would discount only exceptionally and which represented forms of lending which the monetary authorities wished to see wither gradually away (particularly commercial discount paper).

This policy did not, however, represent a true 'open market', since no market existed for short-term negotiable securities in which the banks could secure their liquidity and in which the central bank could intervene.

It was in fact a 'variable rate discount' where the central bank had no genuine freedom of action to operate on bank liquidity and had to satisfy the demand of the banks for refinancing. The money market rate rapidly became the reference point for the banks in fixing the rates on their lending to their customers, which were thus particularly advantageous until the middle of 1973.

The second important development of monetary policy was the introduction of a system of mandatory reserves on credits, the application of which became more and more sophisticated. This measure was intended to control the creation of money at source, and to subject all the institutions concerned to the same constraints, including those such as merchant banks and financial institutions which managed few or indeed no deposits.

The new instrument was brought into operation in April 1971; it was soon based not only on outstanding lending but principally on the changes in outstanding lending,[7] with rates that were more and more burdensome.

This arrangement proving ineffective, the monetary authorities introduced in December 1972 the 'supplementary reserves' system; this system bore increasingly heavily, as a function of the rate of increase of outstanding lending, on credits that grew more rapidly than a certain norm, fixed at 19 per cent between the end of March 1972 and the end of March 1973, at 17 per cent between the end of June 1972 and the end of June 1973, and at 13 per cent between the end of December 1972 and the end of December 1973.

The *encadrement du crédit* was in fact resuscitated, even if this was not the original intention.[8]

The effect of these measures was rather limited in 1973: bank type credits still went up by 18.3 per cent and the money stock by nearly 15 per cent.

It is certain that, until the later months of 1973, the state of mind of economic agents, like that of the government, was hardly in favour of deflation. The French economy was thus able to benefit from an

TABLE 13.8 *Summary of monetary and financial data 1968–73 (end-period totals, averages for interest rates) (FFr billion)*

	1968	*1969*	*1970*	*1971*	*1972*	*1973*
M2 Residents (M2R)	—	300	345.9	408.1	484.7	555.7
M2	287.9	307.2	354.3	417.2	494.6	569
External	—	5.9	13.8	25.2	26.8	29.9
Net assets in gold and foreign exchange	18.6	9.3	23	40.8	47.3	39.9
Claims on the Treasury	59.9	65.1	64	67.1	64.9	56.1
Claims on the economy	240.4	—	—	—	—	—
Claims on the economy (residents)	—	264.7	313.2	374.5	464.9	544
Deposits in savings banks	82	95	109.6	126	143.1	163.1
(for reference, ceiling on deposits, in francs)	15 000	20 000	20 000	20 000	20 000	22 500
Discount rate	5.5	8	7.1	6.6	6.6	11
Yield on bonds	7.4	8.6	8.6	8.5	8	9.5
New issues of negotiable securities	13.8	19	24.4	23.8	35.1	44.4
shares	3.6	7.5	8.7	8	9.3	10.5
bonds	10.2	11.5	15.7	21.8	25.8	34.9
(of which government bonds)	—	—	—	—	—	6.5
National income	559.7	639.3	712.4	796.7	894.6	1 014.8
GDP	614.5	700.7	782.5	872.5	981.1	1 114.2
Income velocity (national income/M2)	1.9	2.1	2.1	2	1.8	1.8
GDP/M2 or M2R	2.1	2.3	2.3	2.1	2	2

TABLE 13.9 *The financing of the economy 1968–73 (FFr billion)*

	1968	*1969*	*1970*	*1971*	*1972*	*1973*	
Sources of financing							
Balance of State budget[1]	2.8	−2	−6.9	1.8	−5.7		
Credits:							
Bank	36.5	39.8	51.2	62.2	89.5	85.2	
Non-bank[2]	21	25	27.6	33.5	37.6	43.6	
External	−15.8	−9.4	10.7	11.3	2.5	−5	
							Investments
	11.2	12.9	17.8	25.3	28.9	37.2	Bond subscriptions
							Net subscriptions of Treasury bills
	11	15.1	16.1	21.4	22.6	24.8	Deposits in savings banks
	29.6	17.4	47.2	62.9	74.7	71.4	ΔM2
	−7.3	8.4	1.5	−0.8	−2.7	−9.6	Miscellaneous and residual[3]

SOURCES reports of the Conseil National du Crédit.

1. A surplus reduces the supply of financing (− sign); a deficit increases it (+ sign). Including loans by the Fonds de Développement Economique et Social.

2. Including net issues of bonds by non-financial companies.

3. Miscellaneous uses of funds by financial institutions; deposits not counted in the monetary aggregates (deposits with the Treasury by correspondents and deposits at the Caisse des Dépôts et Consignations), investments in insurance companies, amortisation of bond borrowings.

TABLE 13.10 *Factors affecting bank liquidity 1968–73 (FFr million)*

	situation at end 1967	*changes in* 1968	1969	1970	1971	1972	1973	*situation at end 1973*
(A) Notes in circulation*	−67.52	−2.09	−1.55	−0.87	−2.39	−3.94	−5.93	−84.29
(B) Gold and foreign exchange net*	+33.41	−8.14	−15.71	+8.44	+14.15	+12.67	+1.58	+46.40
(C) Direct claims of the Banque de France on the Treasury*	+15.33	+1.71	+0.69	−1.55	−0.27	−1.35	−2.51	+12.05
(D) Miscellaneous[1]	−0.55	−0.38	−1.25	−0.26	+0.40	+0.51	−0.75	−1.29
A + B + C + D = balance of autonomous factors affecting bank liquidity*								
(R) Mandatory reserves*	−3.15	−1.95	−1.17	−2.05	−8.69	−7.32	−18.56	−42.89
(E) Portfolio of the Banque de France*	+21.38	+10.85	+18.99	−3.71	−3.19	−0.57	+26.27	+70.02

1. Bills in course of payment, accounts of financial and non-financial agents at the Banque de France, miscellaneous items of the balance sheet of the Banque de France (own funds, fixed assets, and so on).
* New accounting periods, from the 21st of each month to the 20th of the following month, instead of between two ends of months, in order to fit in with the calculations for the constitution of obligatory reserves.

opportunity for exceptional growth (5.2 per cent in 1971, 5.8 per cent in 1972 and 5.5 per cent in 1973). The rise in prices increased to 8.5 per cent in 1973, but in a particularly inflationary world context. It was not until after the first energy crisis that the potential problems and imbalances which this expansionary policy concealed were to materialise.

NOTES TO CHAPTER 13

1. Televised speech by Georges Pompidou, early June 1968.
2. This conduct was obviously facilitated by the availability and low cost of credit.
3. The Banque de France at the same time increased the severity of the penalties inflicted on the banks which did not respect the *encadrement du crédit*, by substituting for the system based on the reduction of discount ceilings the constitution of special non-interest-bearing deposits at the central bank, the amount of which would be a function of the extent to which the norm had been exceeded.
4. A statistical reform at the end of 1970 introduced the new concept of 'bank type credits' which embraced all credits granted by banks and comparable organisations (financial establishments, the Comptoir des Entrepreneurs, and so on), whether or not they were financed by the banking system.
5. The legal and organised form of 'face to face' operations is 'commercial paper', long known in the United States and introduced in France in 1986.
6. With the exception of bills representing medium-term credits for exports to countries outside the European Community, which were discountable without limit at a rate of 3 per cent.
7. A rate of 4 per cent was initially applied to the outstanding lending after the deduction of an allowance equal to 90 per cent of the figure reached on 31 March 1971; then a rate of 15 per cent was applied to the change recorded since 5 April 1972, this rate being raised to 33 per cent from November 1972.
8. The system of progressive reserves as a function of the amount by which the norm was exceeded in principle made each bank responsible for deciding either to respect the norms, or to exceed them (in order to increase its share of the market, for example) while constituting the reserves and accepting the cost. Very quickly those institutions which possessed the means to practice such a policy, and which wished to do so, were dissuaded from it by the monetary authorities.

14 Concluding Remarks

Our detailed commentaries stop at 1973, for several reasons.

- 1973 marks an important break in economic history. Although, as has been emphasised in the previous chapter, the change had begun before that date, it was the first oil crisis that made people aware of a new economic order; it was clearly from 1973 that economic, but also monetary, policies were to experience a new phase.
- This first reason would undoubtedly have been insufficient if we had been separated from the period commencing in the mid-1970s by the passage of the time necessary to make a historical judgement upon it. This condition does not appear to us to be fulfilled. We shall give the broad outline of monetary development between 1974 and 1985, in the second part of our conclusion, but we think it would be premature to draw up a critical balance sheet of the experience during this period of policy based on the control of monetary aggregates and on encouragement to savers to invest on the capital market.
- Finally, the third, more pragmatic, reason is that the reader who wants detailed statistical information on these more recent years has at his disposal a number of periodic surveys in the collections produced by the research services of the Banque de France and published under its imprint or that of the Conseil National du Crédit.[1]

Our conclusion thus comprises two parts: the first devoted to the period 1898–1973, the other to recent developments in the monetary sphere.

1898–1973

At the immediate end of the period studied, it would be presumptuous to deliver any sort of lesson from experience. Nevertheless we can try to distinguish the major tendencies which have characterised the monetary history of the French economy up to the middle of the 1970s.

It will surprise no-one that the essential feature which emerges is a chronic tendency towards the creation of money on a significant scale.

Between 1900 and 1973 the money stock M2 rose from FFr12.6 billion in old francs to FFr569 billion in *new* francs, that is, it increased 4515 times! During the same period National Income at factor cost (we use this as a reference rather than Gross Domestic Product, a recent concept which it is difficult to connect with the past) grew from FFr30.6 billion to FFr868 billion in new francs, that is, by a factor of 2837. The liquidity of the economy (M2/National Income) thus experienced a marked upward tendency, rising from 42 per cent in 1900 to 62 per cent in 1973, or, to use another criterion of analysis, the velocity of circulation of money (National Income/M2) declined appreciably, from 2.4 to 1.6.

The main source of monetary growth was generally claims on the economy, which represented 85 per cent of the counterparts in 1973, against 41 per cent in 1900. Claims on the Treasury were practically non-existent until 1913; after being greatly inflated as a consequence of the First World War, they stabilised between 1928 and 1935 at about 12 per cent of the counterparts; in 1973 they barely exceeded 9 per cent. As for gold and foreign exchange assets, their share, which had represented 59 per cent of the counterparts in 1900 (taking account of the specie in circulation), fell to 6 per cent by 1973.

These few indications obviously provide nothing in the way of a reply to the eternal question: what has been the role of money in the economy?

It is necessary as a preliminary to break down these overall developments, for they cover strongly contrasting periods. The Second World War provides a clear break, and there is a striking difference between the two periods which it separates.

Until 1939 the creation of money was moderate. The velocity of circulation recorded contrasting movements between one subperiod and another, in particular a heavy fall during the First World War followed by a brisk recovery during the immediate postwar years; but in 1938 it was at the same level as in 1913, 2.22, hardly less than that of 1900; the liquidity ratio of the economy (M2/National Income) was 0.45, against 0.44 in 1913 and 0.42 in 1900.

Everything changed after the Second World War; monetary expansion was in fact concentrated during this period and experienced only rare fluctuations in its rate.

The liquidity ratio (M2/National Income) which had risen rapidly during the years of the Occupation, reaching 1.15 in 1944, fell back to 0.34 in 1948 with the great inflation of the immediate postwar period. It then rose continuously and by 1973 had practically doubled (to 0.62).

There was the same contrast in the structure of the counterparts:

until 1939 'domestic credit' or its approximation (claims on the economy and claims on the Treasury) represented an important but not overwhelming source of monetary growth, being 41 per cent in 1900, 55 per cent in 1913 and still 52 per cent in 1936. After the last war its share went to 86 per cent and it reached 95 per cent in 1973.

The developments in the two components of domestic credit were themselves very different before and after the Second World War. Between 1920 and 1939 the respective sizes of claims on the Treasury and claims on the economy, although very variable, were not disproportionate, and no very clear trend emerged: the shares were 66 per cent for the former and 34 per cent for the latter in 1920 and 37 per cent and 63 per cent respectively in 1935.

After the Liberation a practically uninterrupted decline was apparent in the relative share of claims on the Treasury, starting, admittedly, from a very high level (75 per cent in 1946); this decline was slow at first (the share was still 51 per cent in 1950, and 40 per cent in 1959), then very rapid (to less than 10 per cent in 1973) with a short interruption in 1969.

Another notable difference between the two periods lies in the importance of issues and purchases of negotiable securities. It is striking to note that between 1900 and 1939, gross issues of bonds amounted each year to at least 5 per cent of National Income (with years of rapid expansion in the immediate postwar period, which was, however, due to the growth of government indebtedness). These issues experienced a marked fall after the Second World War, for they no longer amounted to more than 1.2 per cent of National Income; during the 1950s and until 1965–66 they did not move far from a level of around 2.5 per cent of National Income; a certain recovery appeared at the beginning of the 1970s, but in 1972, 1973 and 1974 issues, which then represented about 4 per cent of National Income, had still not reached the amounts observed before the war.

Was this contrast due to movements in interest rates? This is certainly the major explanation: during the 1900–38 period interest rates were in general higher than inflation, often much higher (in 1931–35); when this order was reversed (in 1920, 1924 and 1938) issues fell back. After the war inflation was, practically to the end of the 1960s, above interest rates, often to the extent that any idea of a 'real rate' made no sense.

The slow recovery of the bond market coincided, exactly at the end of the 1960s, with the appearance of (moderately) positive real interest rates.

The contrast between the two periods in monetary and financial conditions was accompanied by an equal contrast, of which everyone, even the least well-informed on these questions, is aware, in terms of growth and inflation.

Between 1900 and 1938, while the money stock was increasing at an average annual rate of 7.6 per cent, industrial production grew by 0.9 per cent and prices by 5.6 per cent. Between 1944 and 1973 the mean annual rate of growth of M2 was 15.6 per cent, that of industrial production 9.5 per cent and that of prices 20.2 per cent.

Let us eliminate the periods of war and the immediate postwar years, for the economic and monetary developments during these years (which are always explosive) obscure the analysis. The period before 1914 was the 'best-behaved' in monetary terms, with M2 increasing at a mean annual rate of 4.3 per cent; it was also the least inflationary, with a 1.3 per cent annual rise of prices. The increase in industrial production was not negligible, at 3.2 per cent a year. Between 1922 and 1938 the annual increase of the money stock was 6.6 per cent, that of industrial production 1 per cent and that of prices 5.2 per cent. Between 1948 and 1973 M2 rose by 14 per cent per annum, industrial production by 6 per cent and prices by 5.6 per cent.

These few figures seem to suggest that during the prewar period the fluctuations in the money stock were fairly closely linked with those of prices, whereas the link with economic activity was rather loose. On the other hand after the war the reverse phenomenon is apparent: the doubling of the mean annual rate of growth of the money stock was accompanied by a sixfold increase in the rate of growth of economic activity, whilst the rate of inflation increased only moderately in comparison with the prewar period.

Obviously the general context of the two periods was very different: before 1939, if one excepts the pre-1914 years, there were disturbances due to the unprecedented shock which the First World War provoked in the productive and social structures, then world depression; after 1945 there was a general environment of expansion, supported by reconstruction and by the rise of the middle classes and of the consumer society.

Beyond what has so far been noted, however, it was the *process* of monetary expansion, and the behaviour of economic agents in holding balances, which seem different from one period to the other: before the Second World War monetary growth was for most of the time passive and ineffective; after 1945 it was conscious and its role as a stimulus to the economy was obvious.

Monetary growth was 'passive' before the war in the sense that it was very often and to a remarkable extent the result of movements of capital in and out of the country. The 'hegemony of the exchanges' was clear, when the variations in the assets in gold and then in foreign exchange of the Banque de France were responsible for nearly 30 per cent (in 1926) and nearly 100 per cent (in 1927 and 1930) of monetary creation, or even compensated in large measure for the restrictive effect of the fall in domestic credit; thus between 1930 and 1935 domestic credit decreased by 40 per cent and M2 by only 17 per cent.

In total, between 1920 and 1935, the share in monetary growth of foreign exchange movements (apart from the effect of the revaluation of the gold reserve in 1928) reached 40 per cent. This influx of liquidity, often purely speculative, inundated the economy without irrigating it, the more so as holdings of banknotes, which were rising rapidly, bore witness to the hoarding that was general. However, between 1901 and 1913 monetary growth was supported by the development of claims on the economy; this factor, allied to reasonably positive interest rates, was accompanied by a continual increase in transactions and in activity.

On the other hand monetary growth was 'active' after the Second World War. Its sources were the claims on the Treasury which financed public expenditure, an important component of which was represented by loans for investment (through the Fonds de Modernisation et d'Equipement, then the Fonds de Développement Economique et Social), and claims on the economy; in addition interest rates were systematically negative. It is hardly controversial to claim that in these conditions the role of monetary growth as a stimulus to the economy is particularly strong. It contributes to the expansion of productive capacity and to its maximum utilisation. This role was paradoxically reinforced by the periodical applications of the brakes (rediscount ceilings in 1948, *encadrement du crédit* in 1957–58, 1963–65 and 1969), accompanied by devaluations which brought the exchange rate back to the right level and allowed the economy to be 'cooled' before a new phase of growth, and allowed 'leaks' outside the national 'circuit' to be limited. It is, moreover, an unrealistic exchange rate which explains why in 1936, during one of the prewar subperiods when the creation of money was 'active' (it was claims on the Treasury and claims on the economy which were expanding), the effect of the exchange rate on economic activity should have been slight while inflation was spectacularly corrected.

Will not the reader draw the conclusion from these rapid observations that monetary policy was intelligently managed after the Second World War and disastrous between the two great wars?

If one makes the reservations that before 1939 it would be more precise to speak of exchange rate policy than of monetary policy, and that the postwar years benefited, up to the end of the 1960s, from an extremely supportive environment by contrast with the preceding period, then one can admit that more flexible monetary action during the 1930s, with in particular less aggressively positive interest rates and a less marked cult of the exchange rate, would have spared France its worst period of economic decline. This orientation would not have been very dangerous in a country which had almost completely shut itself off from the outside world (the ratio of imports to national income had fallen to 8.5 per cent in 1935 against 17 per cent in 1913).

As for the interpretation which can be made of monetary and economic development after the war, it must no doubt be severely qualified.

An annual average rate of inflation of 5.6 per cent between 1948 and 1973 may appear respectable in the face of the brisk rise in production. It was high in an environment where the majority of countries had rapidly put a stop to the inflation arising from the war. Between 1949 and 1966 the Western world had in fact experienced a very small rise in prices: the annual average was 1.7 per cent in Germany, 1.8 per cent in the United States, 3.3 per cent in the United Kingdom, 3.4 per cent in Italy, but 5.2 per cent in France. Even between 1960 and 1967, a period which those who lived in it considered as non-inflationary, our average price rise of 3.4 per cent was above that of most of our major trading partners: 1.7 per cent for the United States, 2.6 per cent for Germany, 3.0 per cent for Britain.

The inflationary pressure in France had its origin principally in a permanent saturation of productive capacity which, whilst expanding rapidly, was insufficient in the light of the handicap suffered by an economy which was also bearing the burden of colonial wars and high military expenditures.

A priori it seems difficult to link these phenomena to the creation of money: in fact the rate of growth of M2 between 1949 and 1973 was comparable to that observed in Germany, a model country as regards price stability; but several factors must be borne in mind:

- the French economy started in 1948 with a decidedly stronger liquidity ratio, the withdrawal of money effected at the Liberation having been very limited, so that the M2/GNP ratio was 34 per cent in France in 1949 against 20 per cent in Germany;

- domestic credit increased to a greater extent in France than in Germany, by more than 15 per cent as against 12.5 per cent, which had an impact on the external balance;
- the demand for money assumed, in France more than in Germany, the form of the holding of balances which were immediately available for spending: between 1949 and 1973 M1 rose by an average of 11.5 per cent in France, but by 9.0 per cent in Germany;
- finally monetary development took a different turn from the end of the 1960s which, in view of the new international economic context was an unfavourable factor. The principal source of monetary growth became medium- and long-term credit (this was the time of the transformation) which introduced a formidable upward pressure on the total of outstanding credit: between 1969 and 1973 the rate of growth of M2 rose to nearly 17 per cent (against 13 per cent in Germany).

This shift appeared when the economy was becoming much more open: the ratio of imports to national income rose in fact from 16.4 per cent to 21 per cent during these four years, which rendered the discrepancy in inflationary pressures between France and other countries more and more intolerable.

It could thus be said that monetary expansion succeeded in appearing beneficial after the war, as long as the French economy was introverted and was able, by periodic devaluations, to get rid of the consequences of excess demand; it started to be counterproductive when the environment changed.

THE RECENT PERIOD

The year 1974 marked the beginning of a profound change in the monetary and financial sphere. The policy of restricting the volume of credit (brought into operation at the end of 1972, but still relatively relaxed in 1973) made its effects positively felt in the economy after this year. But over and above this aspect, a new context was gradually appearing, marked by the disappearance in stages, sometimes large stages, of what has been called the *économie d'endettement*.

This term, which is the rather unsatisfactory translation (though it is difficult to think of an alternative) of the English phrase 'overdraft

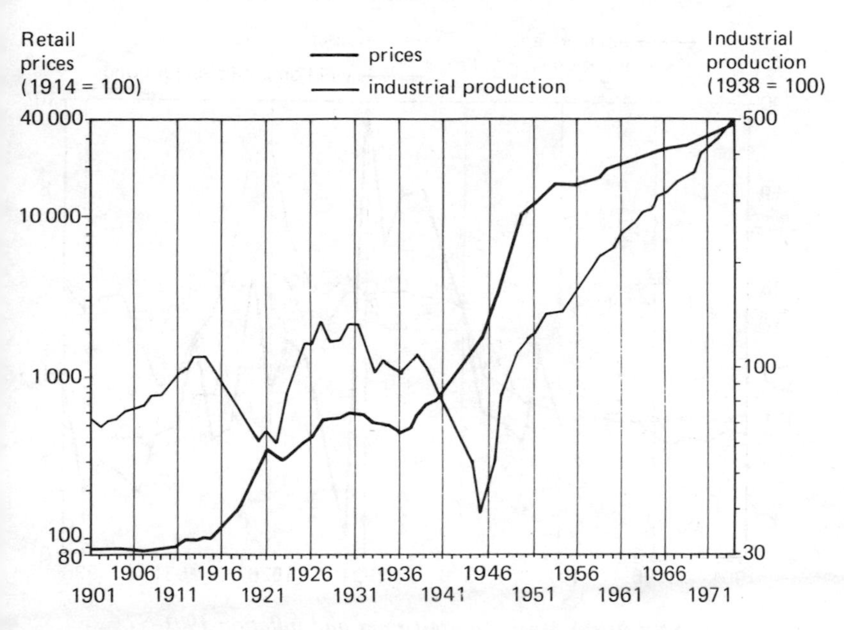

FIGURE 14.1 *Retail prices and industrial production 1901–74*

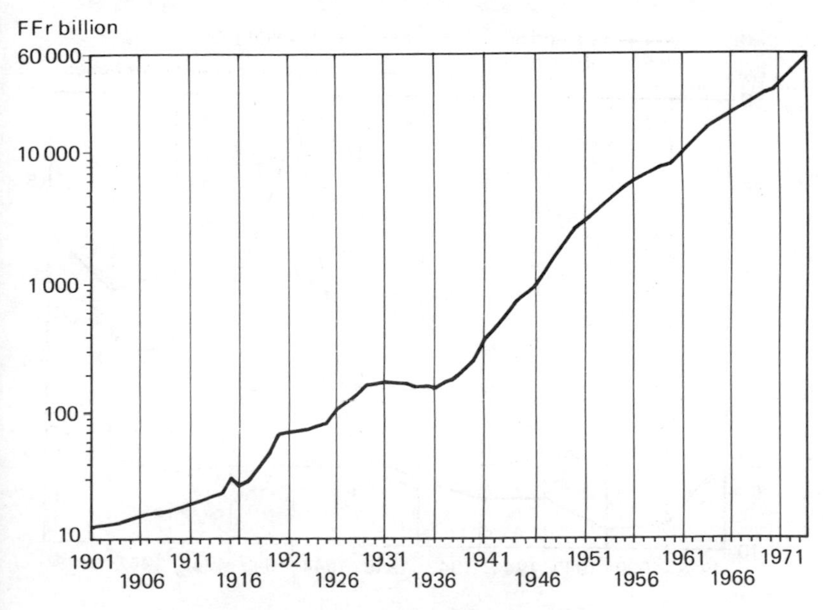

FIGURE 14.2 *Money stock 1901–74*

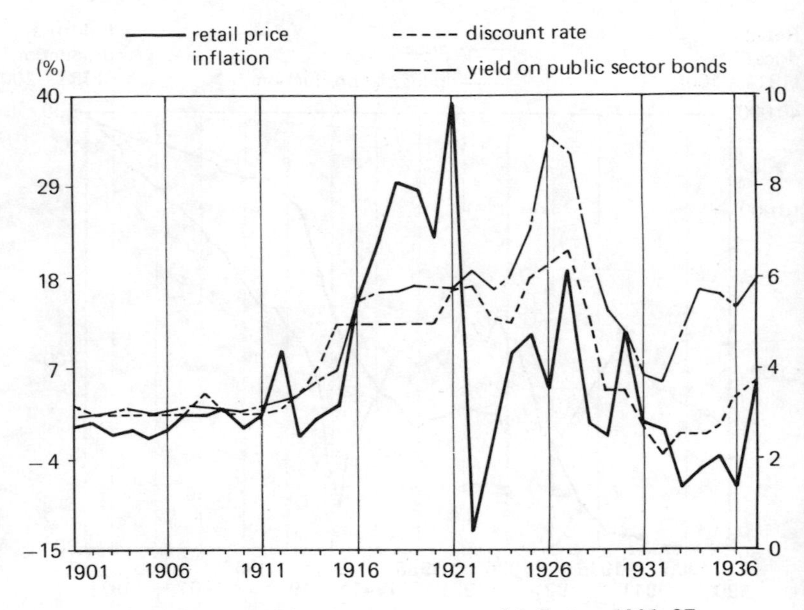

FIGURE 14.3(a) *Interest rates and inflation 1901–37*

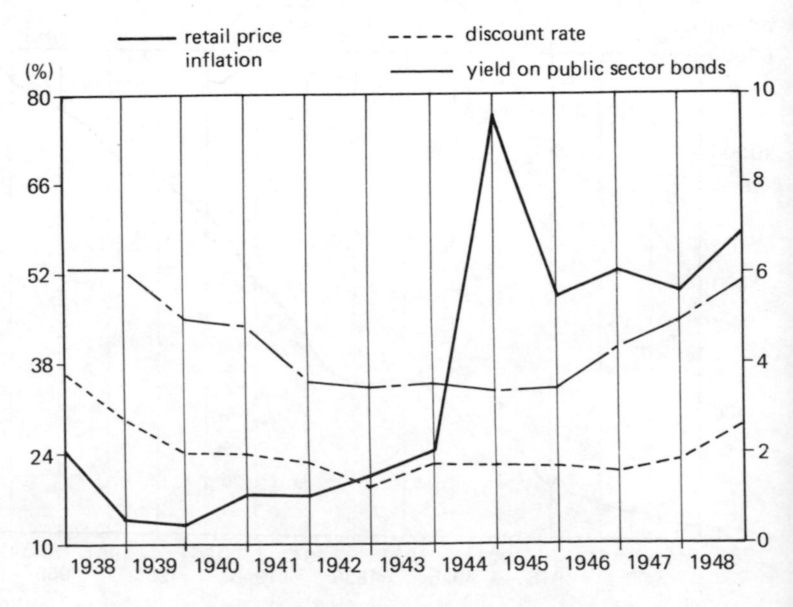

FIGURE 14.3(b) *Interest rates and inflation 1938–48*

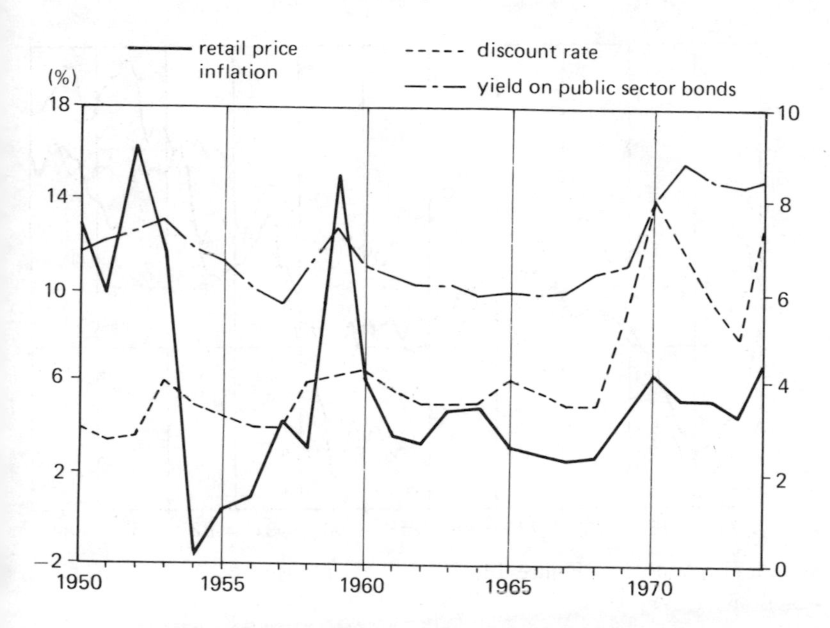

FIGURE 14.3(c) *Interest rates and inflation 1950–74*

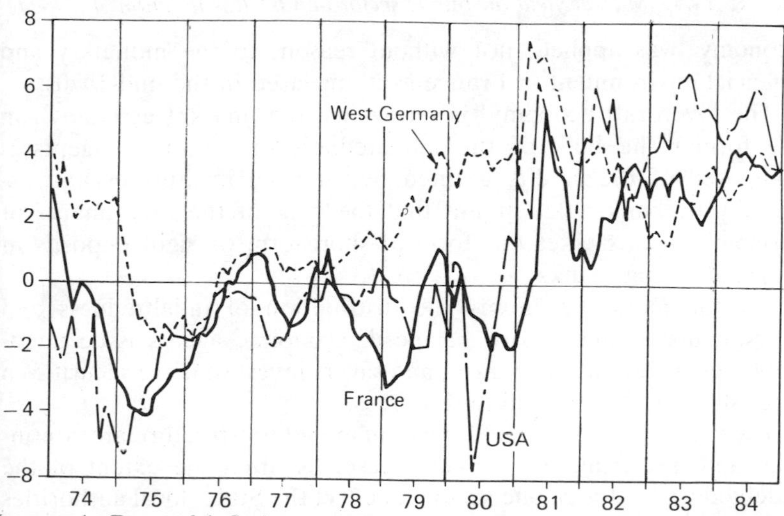

NOTES 1. Rate of inflation over last 12 months, which means that the divergence calculated for 1983 are increased as a result of the price freeze in France (11 June to 31 October 1982).

SOURCE: Banque de France

FIGURE 14.4 *Three month money market rate less inflation 1974–84*

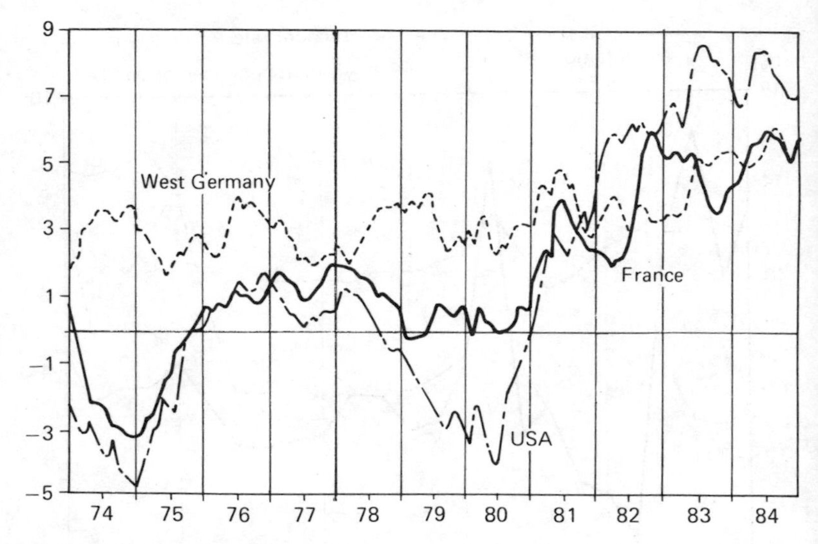

NOTES 1.See note to Figure 14.4.
*Public sector bonds

SOURCE: Banque de France

FIGURE 14.5 *Market yield on public sector bonds* less inflation*[1] *1974–84*

economy' was applied, not without reason, to the monetary and financial environment of France as it appeared in the mid-1970s.

The 'overdraft economy' is set against the 'market economy': in the former the bulk of the indebtedness of economic agents is composed of the credits granted by financial institutions and especially by banks; this means that the bulk of the investments of economic agents takes the form of short-term or sight deposits in banks or savings banks.

For the market economy the distribution of indebtedness and investments is much more balanced: economic agents issue negotiable securities on the market, and savers invest in these securities a large share of their available resources.

The reasons for these differences in monetary structure are contingent and historical: the primary reason is often the extent of the indebtedness of the public sector. In effect the State, local authorities and public enterprises incur debt preferably by issuing securities on the market; the private sector is more by intent the customer of the banks and financial institutions.

Thus the Anglo-Saxon countries, where traditionally public sector deficits remained at a high level, whilst the demands of the private sector for finance were moderate, are considered as market economies.

If we return to the case of France, we note in fact that in 1973 the French economy found itself at the end of an uninterrupted period (accelerated from 1959) of reduction in State indebtedness, and of a simultaneous growth of credits to the private sector. This element certainly contributed to the mediocre development of the financial market.

But two other essential factors also played a part: the policy of systematically low interest rates, and the privileges granted to certain types of credits and short-term investments, which have favoured the incurring of debts by firms and individuals and have encouraged savers to invest the greater part of the funds at their disposal in short-term instruments, which often enjoyed tax exemptions.

The distinction between these two types of economy is not without purpose: in concrete terms an overdraft economy is an economy in which monetary growth is extensive and, insofar as market mechanisms play little part, it is difficult for monetary policy to utilise the 'open market' mechanisms in use in Anglo-Saxon countries. It is easy to recognise here the French context, in which the money stock has grown rapidly since the war, even more so since 1969 with the increase in transformation, and in which, when the authorities wanted to slow down this growth, they had to employ for monetary policy the *encadrement du crédit* and not market mechanisms.

But all this was going to change, and sometimes very tangibly, from 1974.

The manifestations of this change can be summarised as follows: the lasting rise in budget deficits and the very appreciable slowing down of the growth of private indebtedness; higher and higher interest rates; and simultaneously, and as consequences of the two preceding phenomena, a very sharp deceleration of monetary expansion and a brisk development of the market. This development went further in the 1980s and the French economy experienced a process of 'financial innovations' which principally concerned the capital market, and tended to bring its monetary and financial environment closer to the pattern of the Anglo-Saxon countries.

Given the closed and firmly administered situation which had prevailed until the 1970s, this 'earthquake' obviously engendered numerous problems: the banks found their basic business crumbling away; the monetary authorities found their field of manoeuvre being broadened whilst traditional definitions, particularly those of money, became increasingly blurred.

All this was happening in an environment of slow growth and tenacious inflation which slowed down only at the end of the period:

some people quickly established the link between leaving the overdraft economy and the persistence of a recessionary climate.

Let us illustrate briefly the gradual departure from the overdraft economy by a few data: the budget deficit, which had been zero in 1972, grew rapidly in 1974 with the recession in 1975 followed by an ineffectual policy of reflation; contained not without difficulty during the following years, it again grew strongly at the time of the second oil price shock and the second attempt at reflation in 1981–82, to establish itself on a lasting basis at a level of at least 3 per cent of GDP.

Simultaneously, under the effect of a gloomy economic context and of the barbarous but effective grip of an *encadrement du crédit* which was continually being perfected, and also by the system of 'communicating vessels' so often observed (in 1984 the borrowing requirements of companies and quasi-corporate enterprises were for the first time less than those of the public authorities), private sector indebtedness started to slow down. Households, dissuaded from incurring debts by high interest rates and encouraged rather to put their money in financial investments (see below), reduced their investment in housing. In this way the mean annual rate of growth of (bank and non-bank) credits to the economy fell from 16.5 per cent between 1969 and 1973 to 14.2 per cent between 1973 and 1984.

This development, which was accentuated in more recent years, was particularly marked for the banks, whose outstanding loans had risen by 20 per cent annually between 1969 and 1973 and increased by no more than 14 per cent in the last ten years: even this rate of growth was supported by the development of operations with non-residents; lending to residents alone increased only by 12.6 per cent on average between 1973 and 1984, against 19.5 per cent between 1969 and 1975.

Interest rates reached levels never equalled in the past. The need to combat the speculative hysteria associated with the first oil crisis took the bank base rate to 12.4 per cent in 1974; it fell back gradually to 8.6 per cent in December 1975, then rose again to more than 13 per cent in 1980 with the second oil price shock, and to 17 per cent in May 1981 with the crisis of confidence in the franc. These developments were obviously linked to the movements of interest rates on the capital markets: the international context and in particular the increasingly erratic behaviour of the dollar, were largely responsible for them.

On the bond market the authorities in the main allowed free play to the law of supply and demand; the latter was particularly fed by the requirements of the State for finance and the borrowings of the banks which found in it a way of reducing the constraint of the *encadrement*.[2] Rates of return thus became particularly attractive; in addition the tax regime for investments on the financial market became very favourable, in comparison with that for short-term investments. Bond issues, which hardly reached 4 per cent of National Income in 1973, thus rose to 6.5 per cent in 1984.

The stock market itself experienced a far from negligible development, in spite of the cutback brought about in 1982 with the nationalisations: new issues of shares, which were less than 1 per cent of National Income in 1973, represented 1.5 per cent in 1983.

At the same time the growth of monetary investments slowed down. This was the result of a deliberate policy of the authorities, embodied from 1977 in the publication each year of a target for the growth of the money stock M2: the growth of this aggregate fell from 16.7 per cent per year between 1969 and 1973 to 12.3 per cent between 1973 and 1980, and to 10 per cent between 1980 and 1984.

These new trends were accompanied by an increasingly prolific process of 'financial innovations', that is to say of the appearance of new products on the capital market. The two main motivations were the need to 'live with' high interest rates and the desire of savers to reconcile the appeal of market investments (high income) and the principal quality of monetary assets (liquidity).

It was above all after 1980 that financial innovation developed. There was a multiplication of bonds at variable rates or at mixed rates (one part at a fixed rate, one part at a variable rate), convertible ('window') bonds, negotiable bills, renewable Treasury bonds (ORT), and above all institutions for collective investment in negotiable securities (OPCVM), SICAV and Fonds Communs de Placement, which contributed decisively to the development of the financial market.[3]

More recently the creation of certificates of deposit and the introduction of commercial paper (called *billets de trésorerie*) and of negotiable short-term Treasury bills are bringing the French capital market closer to its Anglo-Saxon counterparts.

These developments have several effects. For the banks it is their traditional business, principally directed towards the granting of credits to the private sector, which is crumbling away. This change was bound to occur with the growth of public indebtedness and the reduction of the demand of companies for finance. Financial innovation accelerates the process by the phenomenon of 'disintermediation' which results from it; but at the same time it can furnish new opportunities for the redirection of the banks' activities: commissions, guarantees, transactions in negotiable securities.

For the authorities, and in particular the central bank, the redirection is not a minor one; the frontier between money and other financial assets becomes blurred, and the traditional monetary aggregates lose their significance. In particular this is true of the money stock M2, the reference used in our monetary history, in spite of the rejuvenation effected in 1984 with the creation of an aggregate limited to the assets of residents alone (M2R).

In the same way, can monetary policy continue to be founded upon the quantitative control of credit? The *encadrement* was replaced from 1984 by a system of mandatory reserves at a progressive rate based on the total amount of credit outstanding. But it is clear that the development of market mechanisms implies a monetary policy adapted to this new context.

These monetary and financial changes are being produced in a particularly dull economic environment: the mean annual growth of GDP was only 2 per cent between 1973 and 1984, against 5.6 per cent between 1969 and 1973.

Is this slow growth linked to the break which we have seen in the rate of expansion of credit and money? Without doubt, indirectly; but its primary cause is the stronger and stronger pressure of the 'external constraint'.

The openness of the French economy is becoming comparable to that of Britain and Germany: the ratio of imports to National Income has risen from 16.4 per cent in 1969 to 21 per cent in 1973 and 31 per cent in 1983, and those imports are more and more of an irreducible kind. This situation makes devaluations ineffective and even harmful, since their effect on the price of imported products and the resulting contagion for domestic prices greatly exceeds the positive impact on exports, which has become more haphazard in a world where technical standard, quality and reliability are for many products more important criteria than the sale price; and in these areas and for a number of consumer goods French industry does not perform well.

For all these reasons the French economy had to impose on itself two disciplines:

- a (relative) stability of its exchange rate. After having left the European snake at the beginning of 1974, France rejoined it in 1975, but had to abandon it again in 1976. In March 1979 the franc was pegged firmly to the European Monetary System (EMS) and it maintained its initial parity until 1981. Three readjustments (October 1981, June 1982 and March 1983) then took place, but their total magnitude was quite limited: on the whole the experience was by no means discouraging, and the policy of monetary restrictions and high interest rates no doubt contributed to this relative success;

- a rate of economic growth always less than that of its principal trading partners (whereas the reverse had occurred up to 1973).

In this process of readjustment, monetary developments played their role: the policy of monetary targets, the control of the growth, not only of the reference aggregate, but from 1982 of its domestic counterpart (net domestic credit), the maintenance of a cost of credit well above the rate of inflation, the particularly attractive remuneration and tax treatment of investments in negotiable securities, were without question factors which weakened domestic demand.

But these measures for the first time formed part of a comprehensive policy framework which implied in particular the non-indexation of the growth of wages with respect to the rise in prices.

This action bore fruit, for the external accounts were once more balanced (in terms of current transactions) after having experienced alarming deficits: 2 per cent of GDP in 1974, 1.7 per cent in 1976, 1 per cent in 1980, 2 per cent in 1982. But the social cost was high: the number of those unsuccessfully seeking work reached 2.4 millions at the end of 1984, that is four times more than in 1973. In addition, the results in the field of prices appeared less convincing: the rate of inflation exceeded 10 per cent from 1974 and did not clearly fall below this again until 1983, a performance which was the more mediocre insofar as disinflation was from that time general in the West.

The problem of striking the correct balance is therefore posed. After the excesses of the overdraft economy the pendulum swung too far in the opposite direction. During the interwar period J. M. Keynes wrote that a 'debtors' premium' (that is to say interest rates which are low in real terms) was the obligatory ransom for growth. This assertion is undoubtedly less obviously true today, when unemployment and inflation coexist and the competitiveness of production is no longer assessed within the confines of the national market.

One cannot, however, prolong indefinitely a situation in which the real return for savers is higher by several points than the growth rate of national wealth, and in which it is much more profitable for an enterprise to make financial than productive investments.

TABLE 14.1 *Summary of monetary and financial data 1973–79 (end-period totals, averages for interest rates) (FFr billion)*

	1973	*1974*	*1975*	*1976*	*1977*	*1978*	*1979*
M2 Residents (M2R)[1]	555.7	642.6	759.8	852.2	973.5	1092.4	1245.1
M2	569	659.7	779.7	879.8	1001.9	1124.4	1286.3
External[1]	52.80	39.70	97.23	87.90	81.1	118.1	139
Net assets in gold and foreign exchange	39.9	37.4	49.7	41.3	46.3	55.7	63
Claims on the Treasury	56.1	67.6	104.1	120.3	121.3	124.8	137
Claims on the economy[2]	528.4	612.6	702.1	816.1	919.6	1026.8	1170.4
Claims on the economy (residents)	509	593.7	660.9	757.9	847.7	925.3	1048.7
Net domestic credit[1]	491	572.6	655.3	754.2	845.3	926.3	1095.4
Deposits in savings banks	176.6	209.3	263.1	315.4	368.5	432.9	497.9
(for reference, ceiling on type A passbooks, in francs)							
Discount rate	8.8	12	10.5	8.9	10.2	9.5	9.5
Money market rate	8.91	12.91	7.92	8.56	9.07	7.98	9.04
Yields on bonds	8.95	11	10.49	10.46	11	10.66	10.78
New issues of negotiable securities:							
shares	10.46	10.69	11.82	11.47	13.47	15.77	16.61
bonds	36.9	23.8	44.3	42.2	49.4	57.8	65.5
(of which government bonds)	(6.50)	—	—	(2.50)	(8)	(13.50)	(15)
National income	868	991	1122.5	1278.7	1460.8	1651.7	1872.5
GDP	1114.2	1278.3	1452.3	1678	1884.6	2141.1	2442.3
Income velocity (national income/M2R)	1.67	1.65	1.60	1.59	1.60	1.60	1.60
(GDP/M2R)	2.2	2.2	2.13	2.11	2.12	2.12	2.14

1. New aggregate used from 1984, with two new counterparts, external and net domestic credit. Cf. the methodology at the end of the appendix.
2. Bank-type credits to the economy.

TABLE 14.2 *Summary of monetary and financial data 1980–84 (end-period totals, averages for interest rates) (FFr billion)*

	1980	*1981*	*1982*	*1983*	*1984*
M2 Residents (M2R)[1]	1350.2	1490.4	1651.5	1836.9	1959
M2	1412.4	1573.6	1754.5	1961.7	2140.8
External[1]	153.9	122.4	70.6	40.3	39.8
Net assets in gold and foreign exchange	88.2	81.9	31.9	39.1	71.7
Claims on the Treasury	130.8	165.1	197.6	254.8	273.5
Claims on the economy	1372.5	1586.5	1865.8	2106.5	2342
Claims on the economy (residents)	1194.5	1371.1	1577.6	1780.5	1968.4
Net domestic credit[1]	1144.42	1310.76	1520.44	1692.50	1835.33
Deposits in savings bank	559.6	635.8	721.6	802.4	867.8
(for reference, ceiling on passbooks, in francs)					
Discount rate	9.5	9.5	9.5	9.5	9.5
Money market rate	11.84	15.30	14.87	12.54	11.74
Yields on bonds (Public Sector)	13.69	16.26	16.02	14.41	13.45
New issues of negotiable securities:					
shares	24.25	31.14	38.57	43	48.43
bonds	111.7	106.9	154.7	193.7	242.1
(of which government bonds)	(31)	(25)	(40)	(51)	(84.9)
National income	2113.1	2368.6	2679.4	2943.8	3196.3
GDP	2769.3	3110.6	3567	3935	4277.2
Income velocity (national income/M2R)	1.63	1.67	1.71	1.69	1.68
GDP/M2R)	2.19	2.21	2.27	2.29	2.29

1. New aggregate used from 1984, with two new counterparts, external and net domestic credit. Cf. the methodology in appendix.

TABLE 14.3 *Monetary targets and outturns*

	1977 *I*	*1978* *II*	*1979* *III*
Forecasts/targets			
1. Forecasts of total GDP[1] published with the monetary target	13.2% volume 4.6% price 8.1%	12.6% volume 4.5% price 7.8%	13.0% volume 3.6% price 9.1%
2. Target for money stock (M2) (December to December)	12.5%	12.0%	11.0%
3. Target for money stock residents (M2R) (between 3-month averages[3])			
Outturns			
4. M2 (December to December) deviation (outturn – target)	13.9% (+1.4 point)	12.2% (+0.2 point)	14.4% (+3.4 points)[2]
5. M2 (annual average)	12.3%	13.2%	13.4%
6. M2R (between 3-month averages[3]) deviation (outturn – target)	13.5%	12.7%	13.2%
7. M2R (annual average)	12.3%	13.2%	13.0%
8. M3 or M3R (December to December) deviation (M3 – M2 or M3R – M2R) (residents aggregates from 1984)	14.5% (+0.6 point)	13.5% (+1.3 point)	14.5% (+0.1 point)
9. Domestic credit (between 3-month averages[3])	n.d.	9.2%	12.7%
10. Total GDP[1]	12.3% volume 3.1% price 9.0%	13.6% volume 3.8% price 9.5%	14.1% volume 3.3% price 10.5%
11. Annual average liquidity ratio M2/GDP change	48.7% (+0 point)	48.5% (–0.2 point)	48.2% (–0.3 point)
12. Annual average income velocity GDP/M2R change	2.11 (+0 point)	2.12 (+0.01 point)	2.14 (+0.02 point)

NOTES 1. Total GDP = Market GDP + non-market GDP.

2. The franc entered the EMS in March 1979.

3. Change between the quarterly averages for the months of November, December and January.

4. Implicit target of 12% in 1983 and explicit target of 7% in 1984.

SOURCE Banque de France

TABLE 14.3 *Monetary targets and outturns*

1980 *IV*	*1981* *V*	*1982* *VI*	*1983* *VII*	*1984* *VIII*	*1985* *IX*
11.9% volume 2.6% price 9.1%	12.3% volume 1.6% price 10.6%	17.0% volume 3.1% price 13.4% BdF: 15.0%	11.2% volume 2.0% price 9.1%	7.7% volume 1.0% price 6.6%	7.5% volume 1.8% price 5.5%
11.0%	10% raised officially to 12% in summer 1981	12.5-13.5%	or 10% reduced to 9% in March	—	—
				5.5-6.5%[3]	4-6%
9.8% (–1.2 point)	11.4% (–0.6 point)	11.5% (–1.0 point)	10.2%[3] (+1.2 point)	— —	— —
11.6%	12.6%	12.3%	9.7%	—	—
9.4%				(+0.6 point)	
10.9%	11.4%	11.5%	9.2%	8.3%	
10.4% (+0.6% point)	11.7% (+0.3 point)	11.7% (+0.2 point)	11.2% (–0.6 point)	7.6% (–0.1% point)	
9.1	15.8%	16.2%	12.2%[4]	6.8%[4]	
13.4% volume 1.1% price 11.8%	12.4% volume 0.2% price 11.8%	14.7% volume 2.0% price 12.5%	10.9% volume 1.0% price 9.8%	9.1% volume 1.3% price 7.7%	
47.5% (–0.7 point)	47.6% (+0.1 point)	46.6% (–1.0 point)	46.1% (–0.5 point)	—	
2.19 (+0.05 point)	2.21 (+0.02 point)	2.27 (+0.06 point)	2.31 (+0.04 point)	2.32 (+0.01 point)	

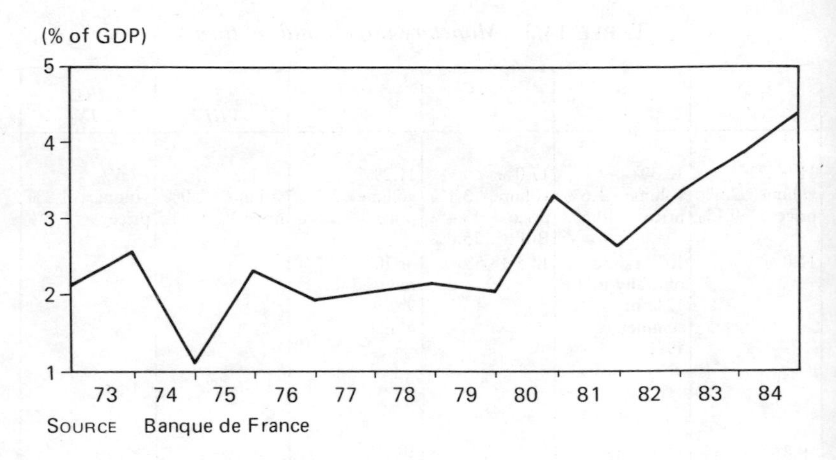

SOURCE Banque de France

FIGURE 14.6 *Net issues of bonds 1973–84*

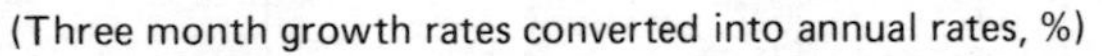

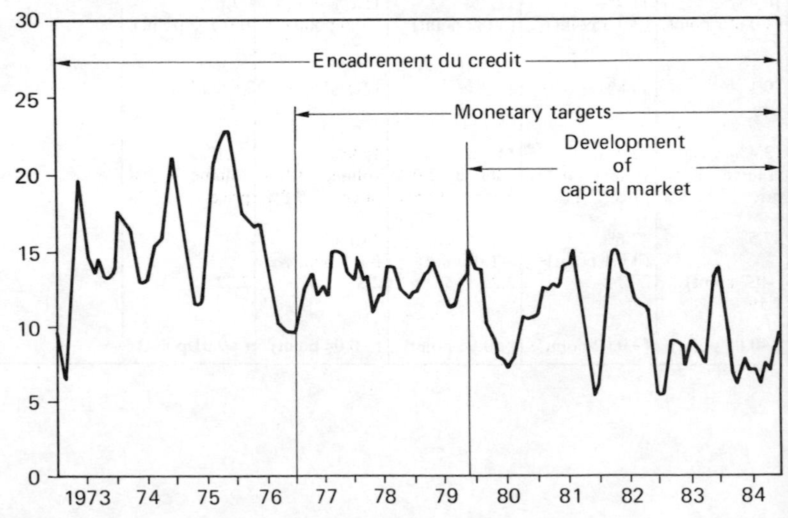

FIGURE 14.7 *Growth rate of money stock M2R 1973–84*

NOTES TO CHAPTER 14

1. The publications of the Conseil National du Crédit date from 1946 and we have used them extensively for the period commencing after the Second World War. These publications have, of course, been refined and enriched over time. From 1969 new statistical series have been available, and in particular a money stock net of the liquid resources of the banks.
2. The general principle of the *encadrement* is that it applies only to the growth of the total credit outstanding, net of that of the non-monetary resources of the banks (bonds and own capital).
3. The process of financial innovation is described in detail in the reports of the Conseil National du Crédit for the years 1982, 1983 and 1984.

Statistical Appendix

METHODOLOGY AND SOURCES OF THE STATISTICAL ANALYSIS USED IN THIS WORK

Two levels of analysis have been favoured:
• the financing of the economy, presented in a table aggregating on the one hand the whole of the sources of financing for the economy, and on the other hand the structure of financial investments by economic agents;
• money in the economy, the key concept being the money stock M2 (residents and non-residents), presented in the form of monthly data from 1910, and its counterparts, presented in quarterly data from the same year.

THE FINANCING OF THE ECONOMY

Definition of the concept employed

Monetary creation is the result of a dual process: the flows of financing which the economy enjoys, and the arbitrages of economic agents between different forms of investment, monetary and non-monetary.

The sources of financing of the economy result from
• the potential excess of the expenditure of the State over its receipts,
• the loans granted by credit institutions (bank and non-bank) to firms, households, local authorities,
• the resources which non-financial firms derive from their direct recourse to the bond market,
• and finally the balance of the transactions between the home country and the rest of the world.

The whole body of the sources of financing, which aggregates essentially the net flow of the indebtedness of the State, firms and households, contributes to the 'irrigation' of the production cycle and the distribution of income; on the completion of this cycle the final beneficiaries of these flows of financing, which have come to them in the form of income from work and from capital, decide whether to hold them in bond investments, savings bank deposits, Treasury bills, fiduciary money or bank money.

The table of the financing of the economy is thus set out theoretically as follows:

TABLE A.1 *The financing of the economy*

Sources of Financing	*Structure of Investments*
Budget deficit Lending by banks and non-bank credit institutions Net issues of bonds by non-financial companies Net miscellaneous uses of funds by credit institutions External	Subscriptions of bonds Deposits in savings banks Treasury bills and similar assets held by the public Sight deposits and quasi-money Notes and coin

Significance and limitations of the concept

The total of the sources of financing can be considered, with the exception of the 'external' item, to represent the standard aggregate 'total domestic credit'.

It will be noted that the issue and take-up of shares are not included in the table of indebtedness which emphasises the notion of *indebtedness* of economic agents.

The item 'miscellaneous uses of funds' is supposed to represent all the balance sheet items of the credit establishments as well as the operations of the Treasury which do not appear in the other lines: physical assets, relations with correspondents, non-distributed profits, operations in securities, amortisations of bond borrowings, payments of coupons, and so on. In fact, particularly during the years before the war, this item should be considered, in the absence of appropriate information, as an 'adjustment' item.

In financial investments, bond subscriptions are the gross subscriptions, the information on net subscriptions being generally poor (amortisations are thus theoretically included in the 'miscellaneous' adjustments). As far as the information is available, they exclude the subscriptions of the Caisse des Dépôts et Consignations which itself managed other assets; the figures for the latter, before the war, are rough estimates.

The 'external' item represents the impact of the overall balance of payments on the liquidity of the economy. This impact results from the balance of current payments and that of the movements of capital by non-financial agents (for example the take-up of foreign negotiable securities or the acquisition by foreigners of shares or bonds issued in France). In the balance sheet of the financial system the impact of the 'external' item has its counterpart in the variation of the net assets in gold and foreign exchange of the Banque de France and in the variation of the debit or credit position of the credit establishments *vis-à-vis* the rest of the world; in the absence of definite information on the latter element, the 'external' item was until 1969 generally represented by the amount of net assets in gold or foreign exchange of the Banque de France. France having lived, during practically the whole of this period, in a regime which was not at all open as regards capital movements, the uncertainty connected with this gap in information was only in fact significant during the years 1920–26, during which, as a result of the floating of the franc, the development of the foreign exchange assets of the Banque de France no doubt reflected less than at other times the overall balance of payments.

The adoption of a presentation in the form of an annual table of the financing of the economy does not express a doctrinal choice favouring the viewpoint of credits rather than that of money; it simply aims to give a picture of the creation of money which we consider more complete. But since this information is only available annually and is frequently in many respects a matter of rough estimates only, a notion of counterparts of the money stock limited to the assets of only those establishments which manage the investments constituting the money stock is without doubt of greater operational value for the decisions of the monetary authorities, as the information is rapidly and frequently available.

The sources of the table of the financing of the economy are as follows:

- the issues of statistics contained in the collections of 'economic movements in France' and the retrospective statistical yearbook of INSEE and, for recent periods, the summary accounts of the Treasury;
- new estimates of the money stock M2 and its counterparts.

THE MONEY STOCK AND ITS COUNTERPARTS

Justification for the aggregate M2

For monetary analysis we have favoured the M2 concept of the money stock, that is, the sum of notes in circulation, coin, and deposits in postal chequing accounts, with the Treasury (since the last war) and in the banks. In fact, although this aggregate has recently been criticised for being too narrow, these criticisms are connected with a recent development in the behaviour of economic agents and the activity of the credit institutions. For the period studied, from the end of the 19th century to the beginning of the 1970s, 'money' was indisputably notes, coin and deposits in the banks and in the CCP. The compartmentalisation of the financial system was a reality and the behaviour of holders of saving bank deposits was not the same as that of the holders of bank deposits; the clienteles were for a long time very specific.

Let us add that until the 1950s M2 was practically the same as M1, for deposits in quasi-money (deposit accounts, bills and pass-books) were quite marginal: in fact they developed only from 1966.

The statistical sources for M2

The problem arises for the period before 1945. Since the war, the Banque de France has prepared complete statistics on a monthly basis, though there are still, however, some relatively small breaks in the series: in 1958–59 with the return of the Saarland to Germany; at the end of 1969 with the beginning of the recording of credits granted by the banks but not financed by them, a reform which was connected with the introduction of new accounting documents which had to be filled in by the banks; and finally in December 1977 with the adoption of an M2 aggregate limited solely to the assets of residents (see below).

Notes in circulation

The amounts of these are taken from the weekly accounts of the Banque de France; figures from the first statement after the end of the month concerned were preferred in the light of the importance of discount operations and end-of-period due dates.

Coin

Two periods must be distinguished.

Up to 1914 it was a question of gold coinage and, more and more marginally, of silver coinage, being used for payments and constituting a very considerable proportion of the means of settlement in circulation (nearly 40 per cent). This item represents without doubt the largest element of uncertainty in our statistics, an uncertainty fortunately limited to the years 1897–1914.

Periodical enquiries were carried out into the total amount of precious metal coins, in 1897, 1903, 1906 and 1913. This very fragmentary information was one of the major reasons for not producing the statistics on a monthly basis before 1910, one of the principal components of the money stock being itself difficult to determine annually. To assess the amount of these coinages *in circulation*, that is to say being held by non-financial agents, the gold and silver holdings of the Banque de France have been deducted from the total amounts in existence, as they were registered in the years mentioned, and as estimated (by simple linear interpolation) for the intervening years.

From 1914 gold and silver underwent a domestic demonetarisation; metal coinage was limited to small change issued by the Treasury and called *monnaie divisionnaire*. Its share in the money stock was always small; it reached a peak during the 1920s but successive withdrawals of certain coins from circulation (notably in 1928 and 1939) brought this share down to 0.8 per cent in 1940. Thus the fact that the information is generally available only annually up to 1945 is a very minor nuisance (the same figure is therefore taken for the whole of the financial year).

Postal chequing accounts (CCP)

Created in 1918 to spread the habit of using chequing accounts, the CCP developed on a moderate scale until the end of the 1920s: they represented 2 per cent of M2 in 1929. Their growth was rather more rapid during the 1930s and in 1940 they represented slightly more than 3 per cent of M2. Monthly data are available from 1931; end-of-month figures previous to this were calculated by linear interpolation between end-of-year figures.

Deposits with the Treasury

Known as individual funds accounts, these deposits became of some importance only from the end of the Second World War; the figures are known precisely, thanks to the monthly statistics drawn up by the Banque de France.

Bank deposits

The figures for deposits with the Banque de France were taken, like those for banknotes, from the monthly statements of the Banque de France.

For deposits with the commercial banks two periods have again to be distinguished:

• Since 1945 the Banque de France has drawn up official monthly monetary statistics based on a survey at the same intervals of the accounts of a number of banks representing about 90 per cent of the operations of the profession.

• Before 1945, not even annual monetary statistics existed. The available materials included first the periodical publications of the totals of deposits and current accounts managed by all the banks which issued a balance sheet. These records refer to the years 1913, 1921, 1926, 1931, 1935, 1936, 1937, and 1938. Secondly there are the monthly statements of the four largest credit establishments up to 1918, the Crédit Lyonnais, the Comptoir National d'Escompte, the Société Générale and the Crédit Industriel, then from that date of five banks, including the Banque Nationale de Crédit (later BNCI by the incorporation of the Crédit Industriel).

The comparison of the regular figures from these establishments with the overall records allowed an outline to be constructed of their share in the total of bank deposits. This share was very considerable in 1913 (over 60 per cent) but declined until 1929 when it went down below 40 per cent: it went up again with the crisis which saw the disappearance of a number of small institutions, and went above 50 per cent in 1936. In 1938 it fell again to 48 per cent; it rose again during the last war to just over 52 per cent in 1944.

These extrapolated coefficients were the bases of the calculations of the monthly data on bank deposits. One might think that the known basis of support for these extrapolations was weak, especially at certain periods (less than 40 per cent in 1929). It must be remembered, however, that in 1939 deposits in the commercial banks still represented only a third of the money stock, the overall monthly movements of which are thus calculated from a certain base of nearly 80 per cent [66 per cent + (33 per cent × 0.4)].[1]

An important connecting point was the year 1938, for which the Banque de France later made an assessment of the money stock. In the same way, surveys relating to the 1930s carried out by the research services of the Banque de France with the statements of a larger number of banks were invaluable benchmarks.

The determination of the money stock M2 up to 1945

The aggregation of banknotes, coin, deposits in the CCP, and deposits in the commercial banks assessed in the way just mentioned gives a 'gross' money stock, since part of the banknotes and deposits were held by the banks themselves and should not be included in constructing the monetary aggregates. It seemed to us difficult not to take this phenomenon into consideration; reading the statistics of the major banks shows in fact that the item 'coin' on the assets side represented a variable and sometimes considerable proportion of the deposits (for example, more than 20 per cent during the 1930s). The same extrapolation coefficients as for deposits were used to estimate from the figures in the statements of the principal banks the overall amount of the reserves in banknotes and deposits which should be deducted to arrive at the money stock M2.

It would have been conceivable to try to go further to assess what might be the share of these reserves held in the form of notes and that held in the form of deposits in the Banque de France and in the other banks. There were no other elements available for this exercise than the respective shares in the money stock of notes, deposits with the Banque de France and deposits with the commercial banks, so that such an assessment seemed to be fraught with danger. The series for banknotes and deposits respectively are thus in gross terms, but the reader has the elements with which to perform the correction if he considers it reliable.

The counterparts of M2

For some years the Banque de France has favoured the notion of the 'residents' money stock (see below). Among the counterparts the 'external' counterpart, the sum of the net position *vis-à-vis* other countries of the Banque de France and of the commercial banks was substituted for the counterpart 'gold and foreign exchange', which was limited to the position of the Banque de France. The series for this new aggregate was extended back to 1970 by the Department of Monetary Research and Statistics of the Banque de France. We would not consider ourselves capable of taking it back beyond this; furthermore, during the postwar years the external relations of the commercial banks began to be important only from 1965, the amount in question remaining in every way limited. We therefore stay with the concept of the money stock M2 (residents and non-residents) for the period 1897–1973 with the counterpart 'net gold and foreign exchange' representing, in the majority of cases, an acceptable approximation of external monetary relationships.

In the new presentation of monetary statistics by the Banque de France, the money stock less the external counterpart is equal to net domestic credit; one can still write that net domestic credit is the sum of claims on the Treasury, claims on the economy (residents) and miscellaneous net uses of funds, less the stable resources of the banks.

We sometimes take up this regrouping, and describe as net domestic credit the money stock less the 'gold and foreign exchange' counterpart. It is obviously a matter of an approximation, but one which can be considered acceptable, at least until the mid-1960s, when account is taken of the minor importance of the banks' position *vis-à-vis* non-residents and of their stable resources.

Gold and foreign exchange

The assessment of this counterpart presents no difficulties since all its elements are covered by the weekly statements of the Banque de France, even though in the 1920s certain reclassifications were necessary, the interventions which preceded the Poincaré stabilisation having then been brought into the accounts under 'adjustments' items.

Claims on the Treasury

Up to 1914 this heading was confined to direct advances from the Banque de France to the State.

From this date onwards, the advances were diversified according to the circumstances: there must also be added

- assets in postal chequing accounts (CCP) of the public and of the Banque de France,
- *monnaies divisionnaires* (coin in circulation and in the Banque de France),

- assets in individual funds accounts at the Treasury,
- Treasury bills held by the banks and the Banque de France,
- Treasury bills discounted to the State by the Banque de France for advances to foreign governments,
- negotiable bills of the Caisse autonome d'amortissement de la dette publique, created in 1928 (with the taxes received from tobacco and matches as the basis of its funding),
- and during the last war advances to the State for payment of occupation charges.

It is appropriate to deduct from this total the assets held in the Banque de France for the Treasury, the Caisse autonome d'amortissement and, during the years 1940–45, the Reichskredit Kassen, the beneficiary of the transfers in respect of the occupation charges.

Only the amount of Treasury bills held by the commercial banks posed an assessment problem, since in the assets sides of the banks' statements they are swamped by the rest of the portfolio. Some points of reference existed, however, with the end-of-year surveys carried out for the following years: 1921, 1922, 1925, 1929, 1930, 1931, 1932, 1935 and 1938.[2]

Credits arranged by the commercial banks

These have been calculated on the basis of the monthly statements of the principal banks used for the calculation of deposits. The extrapolation coefficients follow a similar development but are not identical, those banks for which data were available financing, throughout the period and in varying proportions, more credits than they managed deposits.

The figures worked out are those for credits *financed* – rather than granted – by the banks (this series was substituted for the previous one in the statistics of the Banque de France from 1969).

We have given the series, during the whole of the period under study, the name of 'claims on the economy' which is the nomenclature used at the present time.

THE SPECIFIC NATURE OF THE STATISTICAL PROCEDURE EMPLOYED

This is distinguished from the studies already undertaken in this field[3] as follows:

- by the establishment of data concerning an assessment of the overall financing of the economy and of the structure of the investments of the economic agents,
- by research into the movement of the coefficient of extrapolation of the data from the major banks, whilst in the other studies these coefficients are considered as fixed throughout the period 1914–39,
- by taking into account the banks' reserves of notes and deposits, which leads to a total for the net money stock, often significantly lower than that for the 'gross' money stock,
- by strict respect for the boundaries of the existing aggregates,
- by the calculation of the counterparts of M2,
- and finally by the provision of monthly figures for M2 and quarterly figures for the counterparts, these within-year data being seasonally adjusted by the Census XII method.

1. 1910–45 MONTHLY AND QUARTERLY SERIES

TABLE A.2 *Monthly and quarterly series 1910–45 (FFr billion)*

		unadjusted data						*seasonally adjusted data*				
		notes[1]	*deposits in comm-ercial banks*[1]	*money stock M2*[2]	*gold and foreign exchange*	*claims on the Treasury*	*claims on the economy*	*notes*[1]	*deposits in comm-ercial banks*[1]	*money stock M2*[2]	*claims on the Treasury*	*claims on the economy*
1910	J	5.42	8.07	13.58				5.30	8.10	13.50		
	F	5.29	7.97	13.23				5.28	8.11	13.44		
	M	5.39	8.23	13.55	4.33		10	5.27	8.09	13.60		9.98
	A	5.27	8.25	13.60				5.32	8.09	13.50		
	M	5.18	8.27	13.48				5.34	8.23	13.53		
	J.	5.22	8.53	13.89	4.29		10.26	5.32	8.32	13.73		10.38
	J	5.21	8.72	13.92				5.35	8.53	13.85		
	A	5.11	8.38	13.53				5.22	8.42	13.54		
	S	5.30	8.54	14.88	4.22		10.13	5.24	8.75	14.91	10.27	
	O	5.39	8.80	14.22				5.29	8.86	14.07		
	N	5.30	8.44	13.66				5.28	8.68	13.96		
	D	5.55	8.53	13.94	4.11		10.45	5.34	8.61	13.87	10.19	
1911	J	5.41	8.86	14.17				5.29	8.88	14.07		
	F	5.32	8.48	13.69				5.31	8.62	13.89		
	M	5.34	8.52	13.90	4.08		10.61	5.32	8.38	13.95	10.58	
	A	5.35	9.20	14.42				5.41	9	14.32		
	M	5.20	8.97	14.12				5.37	8.91	14.16		
	J	5.25	9.08	14.31	4.06		11.02	5.36	8.85	14.15		11.15
	J	5.25	8.98	14.21				5.38	8.78	14.16		
	A	5.19	8.73	13.92				5.29	8.78	13.92		
	S	5.53	8.53	13.98	3.92		10.56	5.45	8.76	14.01		10.71
	O	5.49	8.73	13.99				5.38	8.81	13.83		
	N	5.37	8.51	13.43				5.33	8.77	13.72		
	D	5.59	9.17	14.36	3.97		11.66	5.39	9.28	14.29		11.36

1. Including reserves and liquid assets of the banks at the Banque de France.
2. Figures net of the reserves and liquid assets of the banks at the Banque de F

Table A.2 *continued*

(FFr billion)

		unadjusted data						*seasonally adjusted data*				
		notes[1]	*deposits in commercial banks*[1]	*money stock M2*[2]	*gold and foreign exchange*	*claims on the Treasury*	*claims on the economy*	*notes*[1]	*deposits in commercial banks*[1]	*money stock M2*[2]	*claims on the Treasury*	*claims on the economy*
1912	J	5.47	9	14.34				5.35	9.01	14.23		
	F	5.41	9.15	14.36				5.40	9.28	14.55		
	M	5.51	9.75	15.11	4.03		12.24	5.50	9.59	15.19		12.22
	A	5.35	9.48	14.70				5.44	9.27	14.61		
	M	5.30	9.40	14.64				5.48	9.31	14.67		
	J	5.40	9.83	15.07	4.08		11.96	5.52	9.57	14.94		12.11
	J	5.26	9.90	15				5.37	9.67	14.94		
	A	5.26	9.85	15.08				5.33	9.89	15.08		
	S	5.46	9.60	15.08	4.03		12.07	5.35	9.88	15.11		12.24
	O	5.61	9.65	15.51				5.49	9.76	15.33		
	N	5.64	9.60	15.01				5.58	9.89	15.34		
	D	6.01	9.63	15.39	3.87		12.52	5.82	9.76	15.33		12.20
1913	J	5.93	9.28	15.12				5.83	9.32	15		
	F	5.83	9.25	14.91				5.84	9.35	15.09		
	M	5.82	9.31	14.95	3.84		12.13	5.83	9.16	15.04		12.11
	A	5.76	9.31	15.01				5.88	9.11	14.92		
	M	5.66	9.33	15.11				5.86	9.22	15.11		
	J	5.66	9.49	15.08	3.94		12.24	5.78	9.24	14.96		12.40
	J	5.63	9.55	15.94				5.71	9.31	15		
	A	5.66	9.73	15.31				5.69	9.74	15.32		

1. Including reserves and liquid assets of the banks at the Banque de France.
2. Figures net of the reserves and liquid assets of the banks at the Banque de France.

TABLE A.2 *continued* (*FFr billion*)

		unadjusted data						*seasonally adjusted data*				
		notes[1]	*deposits in commercial banks*[1]	*money stock M2*[2]	*gold and foreign exchange*	*claims on the Treasury*	*claims on the economy*	*notes*[1]	*deposits in commercial banks*[1]	*money stock M2*[2]	*claims on the Treasury*	*claims on the economy*
	S	5.84	9.58	15.27	4.09			5.70	9.88	15.32		
	O	5.87	10	15.72				5.74	10.12	15.55		
	N	5.91	10.24	15.96				5.85	10.57	16.31		
	D	6.11	10.02	15.88	4.16			5.98	10.19	15.79		
1914	J	6.03	10.69	16.52				5.97	10.76	16.40		
	F	5.95	10.39	16.10				5.97	10.45	16.27		
	M	6.02	10.66	16.18				6.04	10.52	16.28		
	A	6	10.70	16.47				6.12	10.49	16.39		
	M	6.01	10.17	16.46				6.19	10.02	16.46		
	J	6.14	10.40	15.96				6.25	10.15	15.88		
	J	7.74						7.80				
	A	9.20						9.19				
	S	9.40						9.16				
	O	9.66						9.47				
	N	9.98						9.88				
	D	10.14	6.94	17.74	4.51	3.90	11.37	10.04	7.08	18.09	3.86	11.08
1915	J	10.60	6.90	18.09				10.57	6.97	18.57		
	F	11	6.90	18.46				11.07	6.91	18.67		
	M	11.41	6.91	18.94				11.45	6.87	18.98		
	A	11.72	6.88	19.17				11.90	6.77	19.08		
	M	12.84	7	20.51				12.22	6.89	20.20		
	J	12.24	7.07	19.88				12.38	6.92	19.67		
	J	12.76	7.36	20.62				12.76	7.17	20.32		
	A	13	7.24	20.74				12.93	7.18	20.49		

1. Including reserves and liquid assets of the banks at the Banque de France.

		unadjusted data						seasonally adjusted data				
		notes[1]	deposits in commercial banks[1]	money stock M2[2]	gold and foreign exchange	claims on the Treasury	claims on the economy	notes[1]	deposits in commercial banks[1]	money stock M2[2]	claims on the Treasury	claims on the economy
	S	13.65	7.14	21.29				13.33	7.28	21.13		
	O	14.14	7.36	22				13.91	7.40	21.77		
	N	14.39	7.56	22.55				14.29	7.79	23		
	D	13.51	6.68	20.66	6.42	5.83	10.70	15.53	6.83	21.05	5.78	10.43
1916	J	14.16	6.83	20.83				14.22	6.91	21.39		
	F	14.60	7.12	21.58				14.71	7.12	21.79		
	M	15.13	7.09	22.07				15.16	7.11	22.12		
	A	15.46	7.26	22.57				15.56	7.19	22.45		
	M	15.64	7.33	22.85				18.57	7.21	22.52		
	J	15.99	7.49	23.37				16.06	7.35	23.09		
	J	16.24	7.68	23.82				16.18	7.51	23.45		
	A	16.58	7.90	24.41				16.48	7.81	24.13		
	S	17.05	8.11	25.14				16.76	8.19	24.94		
	O	16.10	7.44	23.44				15.91	7.43	23.19		
	N	16.31	7.74	23.96				16.27	7.94	24.46		
	D	17.06	7.96	25.21	6.09	9.33	11.34	17.22	8.13	25.70	9.23	11.05
1917	J	17.75	8.31	26.03				17.91	8.43	26.74		
	F	18.27	8.61	26.93				18.41	8.58	27.20		
	M	18.85	8.93	27.88				18.82	9.03	27.99		
	A	19.32	9.37	28.98				19.34	9.34	28.83		
	M	19.69	9.78	29.75				19.82	9.64	29.32		
	J	20.17	9.87	30.33				20.13	9.72	29.98		
	J	20.49	10.09	30.95				20.40	9.90	30.47		
	A	20.86	10.44	31.70				20.78	10.32	31.34		

1. Including reserves and liquid assets of the banks at the Banque de France.
2. Figures net of the reserves and liquid assets of the banks at the Banque de France.

TABLE A.2 *continued* (FFr billion)

		unadjusted data						seasonally adjusted data				
		notes[1]	deposits in commercial banks[1]	money stock M2[2]	gold and foreign exchange	claims on the Treasury	claims on the economy	notes[1]	deposits in commercial banks[1]	money stock M2[2]	claims on the Treasury	claims on the economy
	S	21.40	10.63	32.45				21.19	10.63	32.18		
	O	22.23	10.79	33.50				22.04	10.69	33.13		
	N	22.96	10.78	34.28				23.02	11	34.98		
	D	22.93	11.11	34.73	6.37	15.97	13.31	23.24	11.31	35.25	15.80	12.97
1918	J	23.78	10.71	35.29				23.98	10.88	36.39		
	F	24.62	11.82	37.19				24.76	11.77	37.56		
	M	25.99	11.34	38.03				25.87	11.54	38.14		
	A	26.97	11.75	39.40				26.85	11.78	39.15		
	M	27.76	12.26	40.67				27.78	12.09	40.15		
	J	29.04	12.62	42.26				28.92	12.47	41.71		
	J	29.60	13.17	43.22				29.53	13.02	42.58		
	A	29.85	13.40	43.76				29.86	13.31	43.23		
	S	30.47	13.56	44.93				30.37	13.48	44.57		
	O	30.89	14.90	46.30				30.64	14.65	45.88		
	N	28.17	13	41.83				28.29	13.18	42.73		
	D	31.49	13.27	45.22	8.18	20.87	15.47	31.89	13.46	46.32	20.64	15.08
1919	J	32.40	13.96	46.69				32.56	14.19	46.93		
	F	33.13	14.42	48.37				33.24	14.34	48.15		
	M	33.91	14.92	48.89	7.62	27.91	19.37	33.72	15.27	50.31	28.37	19.33
	A	34.37	15.83	51.95				34.19	15.91	52.10		
	M	34.40	16.98	54.01				34.37	16.74	53.58		
	J	34.91	18.34	56.36	7.56	31.06	20.74	34.81	18.15	56.47	31.33	21
	J	35.20	18.75	56.97				35.20	18.64	57.46		
	A	35.71	19.58	57.77				35.84	19.58	58.48		

1. Including reserves and liquid assets of the banks at the Banque de France.
2. Figures net of the reserves and liquid assets of the banks at the Banque de France.

TABLE A.2 *continued* (FFr billion)

		unadjusted data						seasonally adjusted data				
		notes[1]	*deposits in commercial banks*[1]	*money stock M2*[2]	*gold and foreign exchange*	*claims on the Treasury*	*claims on the economy*	*notes*[1]	*deposits in commercial banks*[1]	*money stock M2*[2]	*claims on the Treasury*	*claims on the economy*
	S	36.14	21.16	59.95	7.34	34.36	22.51	36.09	21.01	60.29	33.94	22.83
	O	37.40	22.13	62.34				37.04	21.62	61.23		
	N	37.78	23.82	64.87				37.99	24.06	64.49		
	D	38.04	26.12	66.80	7.20	36.85	26.82	38.48	26.36	66.30	36.46	26.14
1920	J	37.37	26.24	67.72				37.37	26.60	68		
	F	38	28.28	70.32				38.04	28.17	70.04		
	M	38.14	27.38	69.67	6.75	37.85	28	37.93	28.06	70.26	38.41	28.05
	A	37.46	28.51	69.92				37.28	28.68	70.14		
	M	38.01	29.89	72				38	29.47	71.47		
	J	37.93	29.37	71.22	6.72	41.14	26.79	37.98	29.06	71.33	41.47	27.08
	J	37.85	29.95	71.25				37.91	29.89	71.76		
	A	38.02	29.76	70.74				38.24	29.91	71.53		
	S	38.70	31.02	72.78	7.97	45.39	25.23	38.64	30.85	73.13	44.88	25.52
	O	39.37	32.23	74.90				38.89	31.40	73.61		
	N	39.33	32.56	75.40				39.53	32.84	75.13		
	D	37.80	30.48	71.30	6.44	46.74	24.43	38.17	30.58	70.88	46.33	23.84
1921	J	38.83	30.26	72.27				38.70	30.64	72.49		
	F	38.46	30.73	72.53				38.44	30.63	72.29		
	M	38.77	30.29	72.10	6.41	46.76	23.53	38.60	31.02	72.72	47.30	23.67
	A	38.94	31.26	72.95				38.81	31.48	73.14		
	M	38.62	32.02	73.88				38.66	31.61	73.44		
	J	37.67	30.51	71.64	6.48	45.91	21.98	37.84	30.30	71.27	46.24	22.18
	J	36.65	31.01	71.57				36.73	30.96	71.88		
	A	37.41	30.89	71.03				37.62	31.05	71.56		

1. Including reserves and liquid assets of the banks at the Banque de France.
2. Figures net of the reserves and liquid assets of the banks at the Banque de France.

TABLE A.2 *continued* (FFr billion)

		unadjusted data						seasonally adjusted data				
		notes[1]	deposits in commercial banks[1]	money stock M2[2]	gold and foreign exchange	claims on the Treasury	claims on the economy	notes[1]	deposits in commercial banks[1]	money stock M2[2]	claims on the Treasury	claims on the economy
	S	37.75	31.49	71.44	6.43	46.01	23.10	37.65	31.39	71.63	45.58	23.20
	O	37.86	33.06	73.31				37.35	32.19	72.10		
	N	36.79	32.17	72				36.98	32.49	71.98		
	D	37.61	33.25	72.45	6.42	46.11	24.03	37.97	33.25	72.09	45.77	23.53
1922	J	36.94	31.78	70.20				36.73	32.13	70.33		
	F	36.47	32.58	71.3				36.45	32.61	71.28		
	M	35.79	31.64	69.68	6.45	44.13	23.12	37.67	32.33	70.31	44.47	23.37
	A	35.98	32.94	71.19				35.87	33.23	71.40		
	M	35.96	33.41	71.82				36.04	33.02	71.55		
	J	36.04	33.94	72.05	6.43	45.72	25.32	36.29	33.60	72.21	46.07	25.55
	J	36.43	33.36	72.08				36.48	33.21	72.07		
	A	36.30	33.12	71.80				36.46	33.14	72.03		
	S	36.69	33.49	72.48	6.40	46.14	24.64	36.59	33.46	72.56	45.88	24.57
	O	37.19	34.71	73.71				36.72	33.89	72.67		
	N	36.40	33.38	71.67				36.56	33.78	72		
	D	36.22	34.50	72.64	6.40	46.13	25.82	36.55	33.46	72.43	45.79	25.39
1923	J	37.17	35.04	74.09				36.92	36.38	74.03		
	F	37.18	33.78	72.98				37.18	33.89	73.04		
	M	37.44	34.20	73.24	6.44	46.77	24.84	37.36	34.88	73.90	46.94	25.22
	A	37.12	34.09	73.54				37	34.50	73.78		
	M	36.74	34.91	73.94				36.85	34.59	73.84		
	J	36.75	35.48	74.41	6.41	46.35	26.85	37.03	35.08	74.56	46.72	27.02
	J	37.31	35.11	74.99				37.29	34.69	74.59		
	A	37.30	36.69	76.24				37.40	36.49	76.18		

1. Including reserves and liquid assets of the banks at the Banque de France.
2. Figures net of the reserves and liquid assets of the banks at the Banque de France.

TABLE A.2 *continued* (FFr billion)

		unadjusted data						*seasonally adjusted data*				
		notes[1]	*deposits in commercial banks*[1]	*money stock M2*[2]	*gold and foreign exchange*	*claims on the Treasury*	*claims on the economy*	*notes*[1]	*deposits in commercial banks*[1]	*money stock M2*[2]	*claims on the Treasury*	*claims on the economy*
	S	37.73	37.89	78.05	6.42	47.08	29.41	37.64	37.96	78.04	47.04	29.23
	O	38.19	36.42	76.61				37.77	35.65	75.67		
	N	37.16	35.69	75.55				37.30	36.24	76.24		
	D	37.76	37.46	77.32	6.42	47.12	30.28	38.09	37.52	72.25	46.66	29.82
1924	J	38.85	37.95	79.69				38.57	38.23	79.39		
	F	39.09	38.92	80.58				39.14	39.08	80.78		
	M	40.01	38.64	81.69	6.42	47.72	31	39.95	39.32	82.38	47.69	31.44
	A	40.03	38.43	81.37				39.89	38.99	81.71		
	M	39.73	38.12	80.39				39.87	37.85	80.49		
	J	39.82	39.12	80.88	6.41	47.82	32.10	40.13	38.54	81.03	48.28	32.39
	J	40.18	39.99	82.52				40.08	39.18	81.72		
	A	40.31	41.09	83.43				40.36	40.69	83.12		
	S	40.32	39.40	82.09	6.42	47.07	32.77	40.28	39.62	82.14	47.37	32.59
	O	40.55	39.64	81.89				40.18	38.94	80.98		
	N	40.68	40.53	82.84				40.79	41.30	83.84		
	D	40.60	38.06	81.03	6.43	47.47	32.27	40.92	38.26	81.05	46.83	31.71
1925	J	40.73	38.34	81.33				40.42	38.54	80.77		
	F	40.80	38.55	80.99				40.88	38.81	81.22		
	M	40.88	39.24	81.85	6.43	48.08	33.41	40.85	39.93	82.49	47.77	33.7
	A	42.52	39.83	83.98				42.38	40.47	84.48		
	M	42.96	42.23	86.25				43.11	41.97	86.50		
	J	43.27	43.91	88.05	6.44	49.81	35.43	43.62	43.12	88.18	50.19	36.02
	J	44.31	45.84	91.94				44.16	44.56	90.81		
	A	44.93	46.55	92.93				44.97	46.06	92.51		

1. Including reserves and liquid assets of the banks at the Banque de France.
2. Figures net of the reserves and liquid assets of the banks at the Banque de France.

TABLE A.2 *continued* (FFr billion)

		unadjusted data						seasonally adjusted data				
		notes[1]	deposits in commercial banks[1]	money stock M2[2]	gold and foreign exchange	claims on the Treasury	claims on the economy	notes[1]	deposits in commercial banks[1]	money stock M2[2]	claims on the Treasury	claims on the economy
	S	45.58	49.26	96.94	6.44	54.89	38.40	45.58	50.47	97.18	56.03	38.34
	O	46.74	50.29	98.08				46.37	49.50	96.28		
	N	47.93	50.83	98.57				48	51.97	99.85		
	D	49.87	52.35	103.21	6.43	60.90	41	50.23	52.79	103.25	59.90	40.05
1926	J	51.19	53.96	106.37				50.74	54.16	105.12		
	F	51.13	54.57	106.41				51.27	54.88	106.70		
	M	51.80	54.03	106.79	6.45	61.56	42.20	51.77	54.95	107.58	60.61	42.22
	A	52.33	54.99	108.79				52.13	55.78	109.58		
	M	52.80	57.95	112.64				52.96	57.54	112		
	J	53.21	61	114.91	6.47	62.42	49	53.67	59.76	115.03	62,48	50.37
	J	54.94	63.69	119.68				54.77	61.69	118.17		
	A	56.08	62.29	120.04				56.18	61.83	119.64		
	S	55.05	59.63	115.89	8.64	61.92	47.08	55.11	60.52	116.58	64.39	47.21
	O	55.25	63.27	119.34				54.88	62.37	117.90		
	N	54.47	59.92	115.71				54.53	61.27	117.12		
	D	52.86	61.58	116.80	10.05	61.63	47.78	53.18	62.15	116.85	60.82	46.28
1927	J	53.20	61.50	118.22				52.64	61.67	116.95		
	F	52.28	64.92	118.15				52.38	65.09	118.33		
	M	52.36	69.84	117.65	16.56	54.88	43.12	52.32	71.09	118.53	53.43	42.98
	A	52.75	66.52	116.47				52.56	67.31	117.43		
	M	52.47	66.51	114.06				52.61	65.95	114.37		
	J	52.48	67.31	114.97	28.28	50.06	34.86	52.94	65.82	114.88	49.34	36.06
	J	53.33	69.36	119.42				53.21	69.13	117.97		
	A	53.14	65.50	121.38				53.34	65.36	121.25		

1. Including reserves and liquid assets of the banks at the Banque de France.
2. Figures net of the reserves and liquid assets of the banks at the Banque de France.

		unadjusted data						seasonally adjusted data				
		notes[1]	deposits in commercial banks[1]	money stock M2[2]	gold and foreign exchange	claims on the Treasury	claims on the economy	notes[1]	deposits in commercial banks[1]	money stock M2[2]	claims on the Treasury	claims on the economy
	S	53.84	66.08	121.26	29.59	47.65	38.22	53.94	67.37	122.22	50.45	38.56
	O	55.25	68.83	127.97				54.96	67.93	126.14		
	N	55.54	67.82	126.84				55.97	69.22	128.08		
	D	35.97	70.76	131.55	32.67	47.14	46.79	56.22	71.36	131.50	46.88	44.95
1928	J	57.88	72.92	137.35				57.20	73.13	135.90		
	F	57.92	72.42	135.79				57.93	72.47	135.98		
	M	58.75	76	139.92	31.72	46.28	53.17	58.62	77.26	141.03	44.65	52.94
	A	59.36	78.34	143.96				59.13	78.97	145.27		
	M	59.68	91.87	156.21				59.85	90.27	156.62		
	J	59.18	90.64	154.46	65.59	23.15	57.26	59.69	88.65	154.17	22.40	59.47
	J	60.19	92.92	156				60.16	90.43	154.34		
	A	61.07	91.87	153.79				61.47	91.87	153.93		
	S	61.64	89.73	154.55	64.27	15.61	72.24	61.83	91.64	156.08	16.91	72.98
	O	61.85	91.10	155.06				61.60	90.12	152.64		
	N	61.96	91.63	157.65				62.04	93.05	158.93		
	D	62.27	95.15	161.17	63.65	14.24	86.12	62.41	95.78	161.24	14.30	82.49
1929	J	63.87	93.96	161.49				63.05	94.28	159.64		
	F	63.02	94.13	160.72				62.90	94.07	160.84		
	M	63.29	90.74	158.53	63.12	13.35	85.42	63.01	92.13	159.76	12.78	85.24
	A	63.67	89.71	157.68				63.43	90.28	159.12		
	M	63.12	89.54	157.32				63.30	88.64	157.76		
	J	63.48	88.66	157.38	62.39	12.63	87.28	63.97	86.84	157.02	12.06	90.48
	J	64.61	86.67	155.60				64.74	84.87	154.09		
	A	64.78	86.51	155.73				65.39	86.58	156		

1. Including reserves and liquid assets of the banks at the Banque de France.
2. Figures net of the reserves and liquid assets of the banks at the Banque de France.

TABLE A.2 *continued* *(FFr billion)*

		unadjusted data						*seasonally adjusted data*				
		notes[1]	*deposits in commercial banks*[1]	*money stock M2*[2]	*gold and foreign exchange*	*claims on the Treasury*	*claims on the economy*	*notes*[1]	*deposits in commercial banks*[1]	*money stock M2*[2]	*claims on the Treasury*	*claims on the economy*
	S	65.76	87.57	157.10	65.10	10.72	78.84	66.05	89.32	158.39	11.73	79.51
	O	66.80	91.47	163.36				66.66	90.73	163.54		
	N	66.87	90.64	162.98				66.97	91.36	161.88		
	D	67.38	90.62	161.53	68.45	12.50	99.60	67.31	91	160.94	12.62	95.72
1930	J	69.05	91.76	161.48				68.17	92.22	163.53		
	F	69.43	93.29	167.08				69.21	93.35	166.19		
	M	70.26	91.46	164.33	68.01	16.98	87.70	69.78	92.69	163.94	16.25	87.73
	A	71.06	92.42	165.57				70.79	93.01	165.74		
	M	71.51	94.80	165.56				71.69	93.95	166.25		
	J	72.27	95.21	170.50	69.38	18.83	86.34	72.74	93.53	169.69	17.93	89.05
	J	72.62	94.48	170.63				72.96	93.02	170.87		
	A	72.07	93.55	170.74				72.89	93.67	173.35		
	S	72.97	90.76	166.92	74.69	13.73	85.85	73.38	92.11	168.03	14.95	86.18
	O	73.66	91.86	169.62				73.63	91.26	169.73		
	N	74.86	91.76	170.32				74.96	91.76	169.09		
	D	76.74	89.53	170.21	80.30	12.47	92.94	76.41	89.76	169.56	12.61	90.13
1931	J	77.77	87.88	169.99				76.86	88.31	169.03		
	F	78.33	87.11	170.21				78.03	87.44	169.48		
	M	79.47	86.88	170.23	82.41	12.32	90.28	78.78	88.03	169.73	11.83	90.42
	A	78.97	87.16	170.21				78.74	87.86	170.42		
	M	77.80	87.50	171.21				77.95	86.95	172.21		
	J	78.51	86.57	168.07	72.66	15	85.13	78.89	85.35	167.52	14.41	87.14
	J	79.86	82.40	162.53				80.36	80.33	162.58		
	A	78.93	80.77	161.56				79.89	80.77	160.10		

1. Including reserves and liquid assets of the banks at the Banque de France.

TABLE A.2 continued (FFr billion)

		unadjusted data						seasonally adjusted data				
		notes[1]	deposits in commercial banks[1]	money stock M2[2]	gold and foreign exchange	claims on the Treasury	claims on the economy	notes[1]	deposits in commercial banks[1]	money stock M2[2]	claims on the Treasury	claims on the economy
	S	81.51	77.30	163.26	85.49	14.51	84.51	82	78.04	163.77	15.55	84.64
	O	82.80	77.70	164.84				82.90	77.13	164.73		
	N	83.02	76.54	165.96				83.09	76.21	164.97		
	D	84.90	75.15	164.70	90.80	18.92	75.17	84.30	75.25	163.83	19.02	73.56
1932	J	84.44	74.88	163.90				83.66	75.17	163.17		
	F	82.58	75.39	160.86				82.26	75.99	160.41		
	M	83.44	74.66	163.38	90.37	21.84	65	82.67	75.57	162.86	21.20	65.05
	A	82.38	74.31	160.22				82.18	74.95	160.48		
	M	82.40	74.13	161.18				82.56	73.87	162.56		
	J	82.71	75.25	161.45	90.07	21.07	67.48	83.01	74.51	161.33	20.54	68.76
	J	81.60	74.58	161.37				82.15	73.73	161.46		
	A	81.18	74.81	158.20				82.13	74.87	160.10		
	S	82	75.31	160.70	89.14	25.38	63.79	82.42	75.65	160.63	26.61	63.62
	O	83.02	74.94	160.86				83.17	74.21	160.45		
	N	83.20	76.17	163.88				83.17	75.76	163.33		
	D	84.41	75.60	163.76	88.71	28.27	65.24	83.70	75.65	162.85	28.23	64.40
1933	J	84.62	71.69	163.31				84.15	71.77	162.61		
	F	85.54	69.77	163.85				85.32	70.43	163.48		
	M	85.38	69.16	163.73	87.02	28.46	66.43	84.67	69.96	163.10	27.83	66.36
	A	84.75	68.18	162.14				84.56	68.73	162.32		
	M	84.62	69.24	161.40				84.73	69.17	163.12		
	J	83.86	69.55	160.85	86.54	27.84	61.25	84.03	69.08	161.21	27.74	62.20
	J	82.88	70.35	160.43				83.40	69.75	160.72		
	A	82.90	67.82	158.69				83.78	68.08	160.44		

1. Including reserves and liquid assets of the banks at the Banque de France.
2. Figures net of the reserves and liquid assets of the banks at the Banque de France.

TABLE A.2 *continued* (FFr billion)

		unadjusted data						seasonally adjusted data				
		notes[1]	deposits in commercial banks[1]	money stock M2[2]	gold and foreign exchange	claims on the Treasury	claims on the economy	notes[1]	deposits in commercial banks[1]	money stock M2[2]	claims on the Treasury	claims on the economy
	S	82.64	67.39	158.89	86.08	27.12	60.18	82.91	67.63	159.55	27.79	60
	O	82.20	66.51	156.58				82.35	65.62	157.40		
	N	82.13	65.08	153.36				82.02	64.77	153.56		
	D	82.31	64.45	152.13	79.65	27.25	57.30	81.56	64.40	153.32	26.98	56.70
1934	J	81.11	64.92	152.09				80.97	64.73	152.72		
	F	82.64	60.76	149.91				82.57	61.19	150.29		
	M	82.28	60.18	149.32	77.41	27.64	57.88	81.78	60.76	149.88	27.32	57.87
	A	81.66	60.73	150.18				81.48	61.23	150.05		
	M	81.60	60.66	149.78				81.72	60.68	147.94		
	J	81.87	60.72	151.96	82.31	26.44	54.34	81.96	60.50	150.89	26.70	55.04
	J	81.77	63.19	153.91				82.18	62.84	153.24		
	A	81	61.93	154.63				81.67	62.51	152.98		
	S	81.34	64.56	154.35	84.89	26.63	53.80	81.38	64.89	155.37	26.85	53.62
	O	81.12	64.11	152.69				81.20	62.98	154.18		
	N	81.30	60.56	151.49				81.10	60.39	151.53		
	D	83.61	61.57	152.67	84.39	27.71	53.31	82.87	61.44	154.27	27.39	52.84
1935	J	83.32	61.52	153.41				83.55	61.12	154.06		
	F	83.84	61.07	153.74				84.01	61.17	154.17		
	M	83.28	63.32	155.39	84.25	27.44	49.69	82.98	63.90	155.90	27.25	49.75
	A	83.30	60.37	153.02				83.13	60.88	152.89		
	M	82.08	60.25	150.49				82.20	60.21	148.49		
	J	82.23	59.19	150.53	73.67	30.96	48.39	82.24	59	148.89	31.50	48.88
	J	82.20	57.89	148.64				82.52	57.61	145.60		
	A	82.02	57.59	149.57				82.49	58.46	147.79		

1. Including reserves and liquid assets of the banks at the Banque de France.
2. Figures net of the reserves and liquid assets of the banks at the Banque de France.

TABLE A.2 continued (FFr billion)

		unadjusted data						seasonally adjusted data				
		notes[1]	deposits in commercial banks[1]	money stock M2[2]	gold and foreign exchange	claims on the Treasury	claims on the economy	notes[1]	deposits in commercial banks[1]	money stock M2[2]	claims on the Treasury	claims on the economy
	S	83.25	57.84	149.28	74.55	31.34	46.35	83	58.45	148.08	31.29	46.28
	O	82.61	58.07	149				82.57	57	147.08		
	N	82.73	56.67	145.92				82.46	56.75	145.93		
	D	82.25	55.60	145.71	68.79	30.54	44.86	81.54	55.37	143.71	30.17	44.46
1936	J	80.62	55.92	143.07				81.17	55.44	142.39		
	F	81.04	56.28	143.77				81.41	56.03	143.24		
	M	82.56	55.79	143.85	66.85	29.55	44.19	82.42	56.22	143.31	29.55	44.41
	A	84.11	56.46	146.32				83.99	58.87	146.46		
	M	84.86	56.36	148.05				85.12	56.12	150.11		
	J	86.52	56.41	149.40	57.04	44.36	44.03	86.56	56.15	151.70	31.01	45
	J	84.90	53.45	145.04				85.20	53.13	146.41		
	A	84.60	53.05	144.78				84.83	54.08	146.74		
	S	86.03	53.67	147.67	61.02	41.52	49.32	85.32	54.62	146.38	41.49	49.31
	O	86.69	59.27	156.47				86.40	58.41	153.86		
	N	87.26	60.19	156.99				86.87	60.60	156.62		
	D	88.42	61.64	164.54	63.32	47.60	57.80	86.74	61.18	161.61	46.92	57.22
1937	J	86.91	64.64	167.52				87.72	64.10	166.90		
	F	87.01	64.65	168.02				87.70	64.15	167.54		
	M	86.88	67.21	163.21	59.78	47.56	55.68	86.90	67.59	162.66	47.54	56.05
	A	86.90	61.24	161.91				86.93	61.46	162.26		
	M	87.04	60.44	162.11				87.48	59.91	161.31		
	J	88.72	60.77	162.44	51.12	51.35	58.82	88.76	60.27	165.49	52.20	58.92
	J	89.63	62.87	167.89				89.99	62.34	169.79		
	A	90.02	62.67	168.27				90.02	64.02	170.94		

1. Including reserves and liquid assets of the banks at the Banque de France.
2. Figures net of the reserves and liquid assets of the banks at the Banque de France.

		unadjusted data						seasonally adjusted data				
		notes[1]	deposits in commercial banks[1]	money stock M2[2]	gold and foreign exchange	claims on the Treasury	claims on the economy	notes[1]	deposits in commercial banks[1]	money stock M2[2]	claims on the Treasury	claims on the economy
	S	90.88	64.68	172.58	56.79	50.33	61.54	89.73	66.31	171.04	50.39	61.69
	O	90.90	67.71	177.19				90.28	67.23	174.29		
	N	91.86	65.11	173.61				91.39	65.81	172.87		
	D	93.43	65.58	175.54	60.58	56.72	60.35	92.81	64.96	172.09	55.58	59.63
1938	J	92.62	62.84	174.24				93.53	62.38	173.62		
	F	94.18	63.88	175.10				95.06	63.35	174.56		
	M	98.06	62.01	179.69	56.66	64.90	59.46	98.23	62.13	179.11	65.09	60
	A	99.91	63.19	179.36				100.23	63.22	179.87		
	M	101.03	73.88	180.83				101.79	73	183.19		
	J	101.52	69.68	179.16	66.60	66.67	59.94	101.66	68.87	182.80	67.64	59.89
	J	101.40	71.38	184.79				101.86	70.66	187.05		
	A	101.77	69.96	186.09				101.52	71.36	189.34		
	S	118.28	58	194.35	55.81	76.31	61.99	116.42	59.59	192.70	76.87	62.22
	O	108.71	65.55	195.63				107.67	65.57	191.96		
	N	109.51	65.06	203.20				108.87	65.98	202.22		
	D	111.50	70	202.83	87.26	53.02	65.48	110.83	69.28	198.42	51.67	64.76
1939	J	111.86	71.52	213.30				112.85	71.10	209.83		
	F	114.15	73.08	207.52				115.25	72.74	208.15		
	M	120.30	74.20	207.77	88.02	57.49	68.30	120.68	74.23	208.83	57.72	68.88
	A	125.36	77.61	218.24				126.08	77.46	218.81		
	M	122.90	81.39	215.50				124	80.26	216		
	J	123.48	77.26	215.46	92.99	59.82	70.53	123.77	76.15	218.09	60.61	70.44
	J	122.45	78.23	222.80				125.13	77.33	225.54		
	A	146.15	71.02	229.07				145.67	72.12	229.35		

1. Including reserves and liquid assets of the banks at the Banque de France.
2. Figures net of the reserves and liquid assets of the banks at the Banque de France.

		unadjusted data						seasonally adjusted data				
		notes[1]	deposits in commercial banks[1]	money stock M2[2]	gold and foreign exchange	claims on the Treasury	claims on the economy	notes[1]	deposits in commercial banks[1]	money stock M2[2]	claims on the Treasury	claims on the economy
	S	145.72	74.02	233.41	97.33	72.27	61.52	143.28	75.87	230.88	73.07	61.78
	O	146.89	77.50	234.38				145.33	77.85	232.47		
	N	149.50	81.63	241.90				148.60	83.05	242.20		
	D	151.30	90.39	255.44	97.38	93.68	67.08	150.34	89.65	254.18	91.08	66.49
1940	J	154.41	92.14	263.62				155.43	91.66	259.39		
	F	156.14	93.64	256.26				157.26	93.68	266.14		
	M	157.89	100.20	274.11	84.72	110.77	67.24	158.46	100.20	275.59	111.21	67.78
	A	158.94	102.89	287.80				160.11	102.45	288.42		
	M	173.34	105.58	283.80				175.12	104.04	284.89		
	J	185	108.27	284.04		N.D.	N.D.	185.72	106.62	287.07		
	J	198.57	110.96	303.98	84.65	154.55	86.41	199.77	109.94	307.35	N.S.	N.S.
	A	201.25	113.64	326				200.85	144.77	326.49		
	S	208.66	116.33	350.28	84.69	177.51	79.66	205.28	118.49	346.63	179.48	79.96
	O	213.43	121.80	358.23				211.20	122.35	355.21		
	N	216.35	126.06	366.30				215.09	128.46	366.79		
	D	220.90	126.70	370.66	84.66	205.54	75.03	219.27	125.95	369.04	199.74	74.28
1941	J	223.30	127.38	373.66				224.02	126.78	368.66		
	F	228.08	132.64	328.02				229.10	133.50	389.34		
	M	231.20	137.63	395.93	84.66	217.46	84.89	232.12	137.85	398.11	218.33	85.57
	A	232.48	139.07	402.50				234.33	138.34	403.36		
	M	236.53	142.64	414.71				238.98	140.69	415.91		
	J	238.99	147.72	418.10	84.64	242.09	83.68	240.13	145.55	421.53	245.27	83.59
	J	241.98	144.49	416.07				243.63	143.57	419.92		
	A	246.20	147.54	420.24				246.23	148.35	421.10		

1. Including reserves and liquid assets of the banks at the Banque de France.
2. Figures net of the reserves and liquid assets of the banks at the Banque de France.

TABLE A.2 *continued* (FFr billion)

		unadjusted data						seasonally adjusted data				
		notes[1]	deposits in commercial banks[1]	money stock M2[2]	gold and foreign exchange	claims on the Treasury	claims on the economy	notes[1]	deposits in commercial banks[1]	money stock M2[2]	claims on the Treasury	claims on the economy
	S	252.27	149.03	426.90	84.64	251.72	86.22	248.71	150.64	422.35	254.52	86.56
	O	256.67	149.97	430.90				254.34	150.20	427.22		
	N	262.51	147.88	433.20				261.50	150.57	433.55		
	D	271.24	151.80	447.40	84.64	278.38	81.18	269.01	151.54	446.12	270.53	80.37
1942	J	274.78	158.80	461.50				274.71	158	456.83		
	F	281.74	154.50	463				281.96	156.04	464.82		
	M	286.49	154.52	468.80	84.64	303.60	79.53	287.34	155.10	471.76	304.81	80.17
	A	294.39	158.77	483.20				296.66	158.10	484.39		
	M	300.47	163.99	495.80				303.40	162.11	496.46		
	J	308.99	167.19	507.20	84.64	340.86	79.06	310.74	164.96	509.77	345.35	78.98
	J	318.07	170.05	523.60				320.35	169.46	527.14		
	A	328.24	173.11	537.20				328.90	173.47	538.72		
	S	339.79	174.87	550.50	84.64	385.34	75.28	335.63	175.17	544.90	389.63	75.58
	O	352.11	178.19	571.30				348.95	177.47	566.51		
	N	370.30	172.04	578.40				369.34	174.92	579.03		
	D	382.90	175.33	589.30	84.64	442.66	63.30	378.81	175.24	588.13	430.19	62.67
1943	J	390.42	176.41	605.90				389.78	175.72	601.47		
	F	401.91	165.09	608				401.69	167.25	610.77		
	M	409.81	167.66	618.20	84.64	479.58	62.36	410.86	169.08	622.40	481.51	62.86
	A	416.41	181.44	639.20				419.44	181.24	640.95		
	M	424.40	186.47	649.90				428.27	184.67	650.11		
	J	433.84	184.83	658.90	84.64	511.71	66.12	436.61	182.65	660.74	518.45	66.05
	J	443.42	182.46	667.90				447.02	181.81	670.95		
	A	453.84	183.76	676.40				455.37	183.78	678.66		

1. Including reserves and liquid assets of the banks at the Banque de France.

TABLE A.2 continued (FFr billion)

		unadjusted data						seasonally adjusted data				
		notes[1]	deposits in commercial banks[1]	money stock M2[2]	gold and foreign exchange	claims on the Treasury	claims on the economy	notes[1]	deposits in commercial banks[1]	money stock M2[2]	claims on the Treasury	claims on the economy
	S	471.55	187.19	699.82	84.64	560.17	63.24	466.38	186.26	692.89	566.41	63.65
	O	479.94	192.09	715.11				475.98	190.73	709.43		
	N	481.78	179.76	720.74				481.42	193.01	721.71		
	D	502.42	198.49	741.58	84.64	598.37	69.13	496.62	198.62	741.35	581.51	68.45
1944	J	510.83	195.56	751.53				509.60	194.75	746.48		
	F	520.87	201.45	771.71				519.89	204.30	774.98		
	M	535.15	205.60	788.50	84.64	644.12	66.74	535.92	208.08	794.47	646.70	67.28
	A	543.93	212	803.42				547.33	212.04	805.31		
	M	558.20	216.75	825.40				562.99	214.73	824.92		
	J	580.93	221.55	847.57	84.64	702.11	67.84	584.97	219.14	849.21	711.35	67.77
	J	592.41	229.62	870.52				597.62	228.65	873.11		
	A	621.68	228.30	887.38				624.57	228.14	890.71		
	S	632.29	233.27	902.64	84.64	740.73	77.97	625.68	231.58	894.82	748.97	78.28
	O	622.56	227.10	892.37				617.83	225.23	885.94		
	N	597.14	236.30	879.70				597.27	240.81	881.83		
	D	574.90	231	847.03	75.19	673.97	95.48	568.24	231.15	847.32	654.98	94.53
1945	J	569.90	207	836				568.51	203.10	831.01		
	F	574.30	218.47	840.95				573.26	221.57	844.33		
	M	583.52	227.36	850.66	105.59	711		584.39	230.10	857.53	713.85	
	A	587.81	233.40	870.91				591.47	233.05	872.65		
	M	473.10*	283.92*	865.40				477.15	281.27	864.54		
	J	*	351.19*	*				*	347.37	*		
	J	444.48*	344.74*	844.10	105.36	716.48		448.38	343.30	845.79	725.18	
	A	479.31	333.31	870.58				481.52	333.08	874.08		

1. Including reserves and liquid assets of the banks at the Banque de France.
2. Figures net of the reserves and liquid assets of the banks at the Banque de France.
* Exchange of banknotes with temporary freeze on FFr5000 notes.

TABLE A.2 *continued* (FFr billion)

		unadjusted data						seasonally adjusted data				
		notes[1]	deposits in commercial banks[1]	money stock M2[2]	gold and foreign exchange	claims on the Treasury	claims on the economy	notes[1]	deposits in commercial banks[1]	money stock M2[2]	claims on the Treasury	claims on the economy
1945	S	509.31	331.9	904.32	75.61	725.26		504	329.49	897.14	733.33	
	O	534.81	333.11	933.89				530.78	328.45	927.40		
	N	555.76	335.6	959.31				555.87	342	962.20		
	D	577	367	997	128	780	123	570.33	367	998	758	121.78

1. Including reserves and liquid assets of the banks at the Banque de France.
2. Figures net of the reserves and liquid assets of the banks at the Banque de France.

2. SERIES FROM 1945

From 1945 monetary statistics were drawn up by the Banque de France and published under the imprint of the Conseil National du Crédit.

The appendices to the reports of the CNC contain collections of detailed retrospective series, to which the reader can refer.

Wc reproduce below the most important of these series.

TABLE A.3 *Monthly series 1946–69*

1946–69

(a) Money stock M2, unadjusted, 1946–58

(FFr billion)

Year	*Jan*	*Feb*	*Mar*	*Apl*	*May*	*Jun*	*Jul*	*Aug*	*Sep*	*Oct*	*Nov*	*Dec*
1946			1113			1177			1235			1363
1947	1358	1383	1419	1435	1465	1517	1532	1567	1594	1617	1641	1694
1948	1740	1617	1661	1682	1724	1783	1910	1927	1993	2090	2076	2191
1949	2192	2214	2195	2319	2282	2340	2511	2500	2593	2733	2626	2750
1950	2726	2751	2744	2790	2827	2887	2938	2959	3001	3036	3035	3189
1951	3193	3221	3263	3299	3291	3404	3459	3495	3576	3673	3618	3775
1952	3766	3787	3871	3876	3909	3958	4017	4088	4079	4117	4134	4287
1953	4306	4297	4352	4363	4366	4437	4544	4624	4552	4594	4645	4794
1954	4791	4788	4839	4860	4892	4937	5026	5036	5100	5182	5229	5465
1955	5444	5466	5507	5550	5611	5638	5744	5745	5852	5921	5980	6169
1956	6152	6165	6281	6335	6352	6451	6590	6586	6591	6531	6572	6817
1957	6703	6690	6828	6901	6931	7056	7208	7224	7244	7305	7301	7535
1958	7426	7402	7441	7460	7508	7585	7621	7579	7556	7624	7685	7927

TABLE A.3 *continued* — *(b) Money stock M2, seasonally adjusted, 1946–58* — *(FFr billion)*

Year	*Jan*	*Feb*	*Mar*	*Apl*	*May*	*Jun*	*Jul*	*Aug*	*Sep*	*Oct*	*Nov*	*Dec*
1946			1136			1189			1223			1320
1947	1349	1390	1443	1469	1505	1536	1512	1563	1575	1586	1643	1641
1948	1729	1624	1688	1719	1769	1803	1887	1922	1971	2052	2081	2128
1949	2178	2222	2227	2363	2336	2363	2484	2493	2568	2687	2637	2681
1950	2711	2761	2775	2831	2887	2910	2913	2953	2980	2996	3056	3118
1951	3174	3229	3288	3333	3346	3426	3439	3488	3562	3640	3650	3699
1952	3742	3795	3886	3903	3962	3979	4002	4081	4074	4097	4170	4206
1953	4278	4306	4359	4385	4411	4460	4529	4615	4555	4586	4683	4705
1954	4763	4801	4842	4879	4936	4962	5003	5026	5107	5181	5267	5364
1955	5419	5486	5512	5570	5653	5664	5708	5731	5862	5930	6023	6057
1956	6132	6192	6290	6356	6395	6475	6538	6566	6598	6538	6613	6689
1957	6699	6732	6847	6927	6976	7077	7142	7197	7252	7315	7347	7395
1958	7428	7453	7464	7488	7558	7604	7546	7549	7566	7638	7738	7786

TABLE A.3 *continued* *(c) Gold and foreign exchange, unadjusted, 1946–58* *(FFr billion)*

Year	*Jan*	*Feb*	*Mar*	*Apl*	*May*	*Jun*	*Jul*	*Aug*	*Sep*	*Oct*	*Nov*	*Dec*
1946			130			95			95			95
1947	95	95	83	83	83	65	65	65	53	53	65	65
1948	61	61	61	61	61	61	61	61	61	61	61	61
1949	53	53	53	53	53	61	88	108	120	128	135	151
1950	154	155	163	183	203	214	214	358	414	428	431	443
1951	460	478	491	472	480	465	477	454	436	348	282	245
1952	214	148	143	156	172	186	234	250	251	238	234	214
1953	193	178	183	144	146	114	120	156	173	201	213	204
1954	226	237	244	256	281	266	275	276	296	317	333	380
1955	401	444	468	503	546	548	607	637	663	672	687	680
1956	656	647	629	615	607	566	525	510	506	483	415	373
1957	334	308	259	208	173	143	66	74	80	29	–26	–31
1958	–33	–21	–21	–40	–100	–30	48	66	81	88	74	–7

TABLE A.3 *continued*

(d) Claims on the Treasury, unadjusted, 1946–58 *(FFr billion)*

Year	Jan	Feb	Mar	Apl	May	Jun	Jul	Aug	Sep	Oct	Nov	Dec
1946			828			884			889			940
1947	923	948	988	1004	1020	1057	1070	1080	1108	1100	1093	1116
1948	1116	1157	1159	1139	1131	1128	1183	1230	1248	1250	1251	1283
1949	1273	1296	1286	1306	1298	1329	1372	1380	1404	1415	1383	1407
1950	1425	1415	1414	1416	1414	1428	1451	1389	1387	1380	1343	1386
1951	1388	1398	1427	1378	1379	1412	1426	1505	1529	1510	1494	1570
1952	1624	1639	1704	1718	1730	1741	1761	1773	1761	1775	1786	1795
1953	1876	1874	1974	1955	1957	2010	2094	2095	2008	1983	1972	2055
1954	2077	2059	2117	2074	2013	2107	2133	2122	2099	2086	2119	2222
1955	2154	2147	2131	2107	2120	2165	2193	2209	2203	2169	2150	2228
1956	2250	2299	2317	2316	2288	2344	2396	2465	2435	2344	2367	2414
1957	2451	2453	2468	2458	2487	2670	2806	2911	2909	2936	2951	3013
1958	3115	3054	3110	3111	3076	3150	3111	3116	3086	3081	3024	3075

TABLE A.3 *continued*

(e) Claims on the Treasury, seasonally adjusted, 1946–58 *(FFr billion)*

Year	*Jan*	*Feb*	*Mar*	*Apl*	*May*	*Jun*	*Jul*	*Aug*	*Sep*	*Oct*	*Nov*	*Dec*
1946												931
1947	929	944	987	1014	1041	1060	1062	1068	1091	1092	1107	1106
1948	1122	1152	1157	1150	1153	1130	1173	1216	1230	1244	1270	1276
1949	1277	1291	1281	1317	1320	1331	1358	1362	1388	1411	1407	1405
1950	1427	1413	1404	1425	1435	1429	1433	1369	1377	1383	1372	1387
1951	1385	1399	1411	1382	1396	1410	1404	1482	1527	1522	1530	1572
1952	1617	1643	1679	1722	1751	1736	1730	1744	1763	1797	1830	1797
1953	1866	1878	1943	1959	1983	2002	2057	2057	2011	2015	2017	2055
1954	2066	2061	2088	2084	2045	2099	2094	2078	2098	2120	2163	2221
1955	2141	2146	2113	2123	2161	2156	2153	2160	2195	2201	2190	2229
1956	2234	2293	2309	2342	2337	2333	2354	2404	2415	2372	2407	2416
1957	2435	2447	2471	2492	2543	2658	2760	2835	2876	2966	2998	3019
1958	3096	3046	3120	3157	3147	3137	3061	3031	3047	3111	3074	3085

TABLE A.3 *continued* — *(f) Claims on the economy, unadjusted, 1946–58* *(FFr billion)*

Year	*Jan*	*Feb*	*Mar*	*Apl*	*May*	*Jun*	*Jul*	*Aug*	*Sep*	*Oct*	*Nov*	*Dec*
1946												312
1947	314	318	330	329	338	342	377	400	408	437	464	491
1948	525	585	588	618	647	675	760	715	742	831	802	851
1949	874	895	902	1004	941	977	1075	1001	1084	1214	1119	1189
1950	1181	1196	1192	1216	1228	1267	1279	1254	1254	1269	1285	1356
1951	1363	1379	1383	1464	1468	1517	1548	1542	1609	1767	1791	1906
1952	1916	1972	2003	1977	2023	2026	2012	2057	2095	2115	2121	2272
1953	2214	2208	2184	2240	2240	2274	2281	2305	2329	2377	2430	2519
1954	2447	2453	2462	2521	2555	2547	2600	2609	2681	2745	2781	2860
1955	2862	2853	2927	2948	2958	2930	2953	2922	2999	3059	3134	3299
1956	3248	3214	3346	3357	3426	3524	3617	3595	3662	3692	3801	4024
1957	3953	3945	4105	4194	4249	4254	4280	4268	4291	4378	4443	4577
1958	4420	4445	4436	4412	4549	4540	4532	4498	4468	4570	4723	4809

TABLE A.3 *continued* — *(g) Claims on the economy, seasonally adjusted, 1946–58* — *(FFr billion)*

Year	*Jan*	*Feb*	*Mar*	*Apl*	*May*	*Jun*	*Jul*	*Aug*	*Sep*	*Oct*	*Nov*	*Dec*
1946												307
1947	311	314	329	328	341	347	372	410	415	424	468	483
1948	520	579	587	617	654	684	752	734	755	807	809	835
1949	865	885	904	1001	950	986	1066	1028	1104	1182	1129	1164
1950	1169	1184	1199	1209	1239	1276	1274	1287	1277	1242	1295	1320
1951	1348	1366	1395	1455	1479	1525	1549	1580	1636	1742	1801	1848
1952	1894	1959	2021	1963	2033	2037	2021	2104	2127	2099	2124	2196
1953	2191	2200	2199	2227	2246	2289	2295	2354	2359	2371	2428	2430
1954	2424	2457	2472	2509	2557	2564	2615	2660	2711	2748	2773	2756
1955	2841	2873	2932	2940	2955	2945	2964	2973	3032	3070	3124	3181
1956	3230	3251	3345	3350	3417	3532	3623	3653	3706	3707	3783	3879
1957	3941	4005	4101	4192	4235	4253	4279	4334	4347	4400	4423	4414
1958	4408	4519	4430	4411	4534	4532	4528	4565	4531	4598	4704	4641

TABLE A.3 *continued* *(h) Money stock M2, unadjusted, 1959–69* (*FFr billion*)

Year	*Jan*	*Feb*	*Mar*	*Apl*	*May*	*Jun*	*Jul*	*Aug*	*Sep*	*Oct*	*Nov*	*Dec*
1959	78.50	78.81	80.12	80.37	80.95	83.56	85.13	85.23	85.32	86.48	86.77	90.66
1960	89.43	88.44	90.57	91.92	92.31	94.80	97.06	97.85	99.51	100.07	101.01	105.81
1961	105.96	106.52	108.93	110.16	110.44	113.42	115.83	116.16	116.89	118.11	119.39	124.04
1962	123.81	124.42	126.70	127.92	129.03	133.52	136.60	137.36	139.28	140.00	141.44	147.19
1963	146.76	148.30	150.35	151.42	151.99	155.48	159.47	159.45	161.00	161.54	161.15	167.68
1964	166.36	166.09	168.35	168.60	169.30	172.44	177.31	176.02	176.61	177.50	176.67	184.33
1965	182.49	181.63	183.98	186.35	187.13	190.84	195.82	195.22	196.51	197.87	196.77	204.44
1966	202.96	202.86	205.76	207.87	208.47	213.29	218.39	216.71	218.20	218.54	217.24	226.05
1967	224.18	223.14	226.50	231.02	229.14	234.79	240.80	240.25	244.78	246.15	244.15	255.62
1968	252.98	252.89	256.78	259.13	271.31	273.54	276.84	275.53	279.11	281.02	279.85	287.9
1969	282.93	284.82	289.24	293.57	290.41	295.74	300.96	300.77	301.91	300.53	299.03	305.46

TABLE A.3 *continued*

(i) Money stock M2, seasonally adjusted, 1959–69 (FFr billion)

Year	Jan	Feb	Mar	Apl	May	Jun	Jul	Aug	Sep	Oct	Nov	Dec
1959	78.32	79.37	80.27	80.80	82.00	83.35	84.14	84.97	85.04	86.89	87.62	89.11
1960	89.19	89.03	90.71	92.39	93.49	94.57	95.91	97.54	99.18	100.54	102.02	104.00
1961	105.68	107.25	109.10	110.73	111.82	113.21	114.39	115.73	116.46	118.56	120.56	121.81
1962	123.61	125.42	126.98	128.63	130.64	133.36	134.78	136.81	138.81	140.48	142.98	144.63
1963	146.50	149.53	150.71	152.24	153.80	155.33	157.14	158.74	160.46	161.96	163.05	164.80
1964	166.15	167.60	168.86	169.50	171.27	172.25	174.50	175.22	176.06	177.81	179.00	181.30
1965	182.24	183.34	184.64	187.30	189.23	190.55	192.50	194.25	195.80	197.92	199.40	200.94
1966	202.91	205.07	206.76	208.96	210.82	212.90	214.54	215.63	217.41	218.46	220.26	222.25
1967	224.14	225.65	227.70	232.20	231.70	234.30	236.50	239.10	243.96	246.11	247.69	251.50
1968	254.41	256.65	258.68	259.11	274.33	272.86	272.36	274.71	277.24	280.06	282.14	282.92
1969	284.96	289.35	291.15	293.72	293.59	294.86	296.21	300.24	300.42	299.62	301.31	299.60

(j) Gold and foreign exchange, unadjusted, 1959–69 (FFr billion)

Year	Jan	Feb	Mar	Apl	May	Jun	Jul	Aug	Sep	Oct	Nov	Dec
1959	.77	1.74	2.66	3.33	4.38	5.16	5.98	6.49	6.46	6.73	7.16	7.16
1960	7.19	7.47	7.85	8.23	8.93	8.79	9.32	9.87	10.11	10.26	10.53	10.48
1961	10.91	11.34	12.17	12.59	13.18	13.98	14.93	13.99	14.06	14.25	14.62	15.27
1962	15.63	15.97	16.89	17.42	19.38	19.69	18.72	19.14	19.64	20.06	20.64	20.06
1963	20.67	21.39	21.97	22.17	22.91	23.24	22.99	23.46	23.50	23.71	24.06	24.22
1964	24.36	24.44	24.64	24.90	25.64	26.07	26.45	26.46	26.60	26.90	27.30	28.02
1965	28.64	29.07	29.41	29.74	30.03	30.38	30.44	30.67	30.84	30.92	31.20	31.35
1966	31.41	31.55	31.89	32.49	32.85	33.32	34.09	34.30	33.97	33.80	33.51	33.18
1967	33.17	33.23	33.16	33.27	32.64	32.97	33.20	33.24	33.34	33.44	34.90	34.36
1969	34.24	34.14	34.05	32.61	25.38	23.55	21.47	19.93	19.90	17.56	18.64	

TABLE A.3 *continued*

(k) Claims on the Treasury, unadjusted, 1959–69 (*FFr billion*)

Year	*Jan*	*Feb*	*Mar*	*Apl*	*May*	*Jun*	*Jul*	*Aug*	*Sep*	*Oct*	*Nov*	*Dec*
1959	33.16	33.38	33.77	33.76	33.29	34.64	35.23	36.12	34.48	33.97	33.35	33.40
1960	33.70	32.84	32.87	32.37	32.36	34.28	34.86	35.66	35.42	34.45	33.84	36.03
1961	36.02	35.59	35.75	34.38	34.13	35.97	36.38	37.94	39.08	37.57	37.18	38.29
1962	37.97	37.29	37.68	37.57	36.75	39.76	41.55	42.69	42.32	40.29	41.10	42.29
1963	44.18	44.55	45.08	43.73	43.62	45.63	47.75	49.24	49.45	47.60	47.34	47.22
1964	48.36	49.26	48.73	45.99	47.92	48.34	49.47	51.24	48.74	46.07	45.80	47.79
1965	50.00	48.39	47.71	48.70	47.46	48.59	50.45	53.47	51.93	48.76	47.58	49.82
1966	50.73	50.79	50.98	52.45	51.67	53.50	54.79	53.40	53.17	51.91	48.82	51.37
1967	52.82	51.95	52.65	52.85	50.05	52.40	54.48	54.25	56.41	55.19	53.87	56.63
1968	54.16	53.72	53.9	53.47	50.36	58.03	59.7	61.21	62.74	60.72	59.22	59.89
1969	60.38	59.84	61.55	60.92	59.82	64.54	65.68	67.03	66.96	65.06	62.76	63.4

(l) Claims on the Treasury, seasonally adjusted, 1959–69 (*FFr billion*)

Year	*Jan*	*Feb*	*Mar*	*Apl*	*May*	*Jun*	*Jul*	*Aug*	*Sep*	*Oct*	*Nov*	*Dec*
1959	32.84	33.82	34.16	34.88	34.87	34.53	34.37	34.53	33.36	34.04	33.93	33.31
1960	33.36	33.22	33.21	33.43	33.91	34.19	33.98	34.07	34.26	34.58	34.45	36.04
1961	35.68	35.90	36.05	35.49	35.75	35.90	35.42	36.19	37.77	37.84	37.94	38.39
1962	37.67	37.48	37.94	38.69	38.43	39.78	40.44	40.61	40.88	40.76	42.14	42.56
1963	43.92	44.65	45.39	44.76	45.42	45.66	46.40	46.64	47.83	48.39	48.93	47.70
1964	48.13	49.31	49.03	46.69	49.69	48.40	48.06	48.38	47.23	46.91	47.71	48.47
1965	49.83	48.45	48.02	49.04	48.99	48.58	48.97	50.36	50.47	49.64	49.93	50.56
1966	50.59	50.92	51.33	52.52	53.25	53.47	53.20	50.26	51.73	52.80	51.50	52.13
1967	52.69	52.15	53.06	52.74	51.52	52.33	52.89	51.04	54.93	56.16	57.02	57.47
1968	54.35	54.70	54.36	54.51	53.05	58.51	57.93	58.27	60.02	59.78	60.14	60.13
1969	60.93	61.27	61.91	62.66	63.34	65.21	63.63	63.77	63.90	63.65	63.00	63.74

TABLE A.3 *continued*

(m) Claims on the economy, unadjusted, 1959–69 *(FFr billion)*

Year	Jan	Feb	Mar	Apl	May	Jun	Jul	Aug	Sep	Oct	Nov	Dec
1959	48.64	48.34	47.89	47.35	47.92	48.32	48.88	47.56	49.28	51.07	51	55.29
1960	54.09	53.62	54.88	56.37	55.53	56.86	58.39	57.6	59.43	60.77	61.22	64.23
1961	64.19	64.54	65.38	67.21	66.53	68.44	69.94	69.7	70.37	71.41	72.4	76.22
1962	75.03	75.67	76.98	77.63	77.54	79.23	82.27	81.94	83.47	86	85.92	91.26
1963	88.65	89.55	89.49	91.91	92.42	93.94	95.2	93.72	95.75	97.72	97.14	103.27
1964	100.92	98.43	101.4	104.32	102.02	102.9	107.53	105.45	106.88	111.46	111.3	115.76
1965	111.8	111.64	113.22	113.96	115.56	117.92	121.62	117.57	119.88	124.67	125.3	130.17
1966	127	125.63	127.47	127.98	128.16	131.78	135.49	135.53	138.04	140.69	142.54	148.95
1967	146.15	145.02	148.16	151.77	152.14	155.89	161.61	161.19	163.93	167.38	167.5	174.93
1968	171.73	172.76	176.98	178.66	186.38	191.44	194.41	196.33	198.73	205.38	207.14	212.22
1969	209.83	212.75	216.42	221.17	221.67	224.8	228.5	229.26	231.2	234.91	232.77	236.07

(n) Claims on the economy, seasonally adjusted, 1959–69 *(FFr billion)*

Year	Jan	Feb	Mar	Apl	May	Jun	Jul	Aug	Sep	Oct	Nov	Dec
1959	48.84	48.88	48.18	47.30	47.92	47.79	48.49	47.98	49.62	50.87	50.85	54.31
1960	54.34	54.22	55.27	56.32	55.53	56.24	57.93	58.14	59.84	60.52	61.04	63.09
1961	64.45	65.26	65.84	67.14	66.50	67.70	69.38	70.25	70.87	71.13	72.18	74.87
1962	75.33	76.51	77.52	77.55	77.44	78.37	81.62	82.59	84.06	85.70	85.69	89.65
1963	89.00	90.55	90.12	91.82	92.12	92.92	94.37	94.48	96.43	97.34	97.88	101.44
1964	101.33	99.52	102.11	104.22	101.82	101.78	106.68	106.41	107.63	111.05	110.94	113.71
1965	112.24	112.88	114.02	113.85	115.26	116.64	120.65	118.64	120.73	124.20	124.86	127.87
1966	127.51	127.03	128.37	127.85	127.66	130.35	134.41	136.76	139.01	140.04	142.13	146.32
1967	146.74	146.63	149.20	151.62	151.54	154.19	160.33	162.65	165.09	166.52	167.01	171.84
1968	172.42	174.68	178.23	178.48	185.61	189.36	192.86	198.11	200.13	204.49	206.53	208.47
1969	210.67	215.12	217.95	220.95	220.83	222.35	226.69	231.34	232.82	233.97	232.07	231.90

3. 1970–84. RESIDENT AGGREGATES

An important methodological reform was introduced in 1984: it consisted in the limitation of the contents of the monetary aggregates to the assets of residents only.

This reform also involved the recasting of the counterparts. The series were retrospectively amended back to 1970.

In the following pages, after a methodological exposition on the new aggregates reproduced from official documents of the Banque de France, series are presented relating to the aggregate M3 (total of liquid assets) as well as M2 and its counterparts.

M3 is defined as M2 plus investments in savings banks, Treasury bills *sur formules*, post office (PTT) certificates, and bills of the Caisse Nationale de l'Energie.

In effect, from the 1970s the differences, as much in clientele as in usage, between savings bank deposits and pass-book deposits in the banks became much smaller. The monetary authorities progressively integrated the M3 aggregate, in parallel with M2, into their statistical monitoring.

The reform of the monetary aggregates carried out in 1986, which favoured a new concept described as M3, the content of which was very close to that of the old M3, constituted the logical conclusion of this development.

METHODOLOGICAL NOTE ON THE 1984 MODIFICATIONS TO THE PRESENTATION OF THE MONETARY STATISTICS

The new presentation of the monetary statistics which came into force in January 1984 limited the coverage of the various monetary aggregates to those assets held by *resident* non-financial agents only. Money narrowly defined, the money stock and the total of liquid assets have since been designated respectively by the initials M1R, M2R and M3R.

The new totals thus bring together the whole of the means of payment destined to be used within the national territory. Since they are more homogeneous they also give a better indication of the impact of external operations on the creation of money.

The specific nature of residents' assets

The monetary assets of resident non-financial agents are destined by their nature to be used on the market for goods and services, which is not the case in principle with the deposits of non-residents.

The foreign exchange assets of non-residents constitute, for their holders, an investment in a Euromarket; there is thus no call whatever for them to be converted into francs. As for the francs registered in the accounts of foreign customers, if they can be used for direct settlements of transactions (commercial or financial) within the national territory, they comprise, in fact, either transactions balances characterised by a certain inertia, or investments which betoken the taking of a position in francs.

The counterparts of the money stock (M2R)

External relationships and the domestic sources of monetary growth are henceforward sharply differentiated (Table A.4 states precisely the correspondence between the old and the new counterparts):

- the 'external' counterpart shows the balance of all the claims and liabilities of the Banque de France (in gold and foreign currency) and of the other banks (as opposed to non-bank financial institutions), in francs and in foreign currency, towards the rest of the world;
- the different kinds of monetary financing of domestic origin (to the economy and to the State) are grouped together in the concept of 'net domestic credit', equal by construction to M2R less the 'external' counterpart.

Net domestic credit is disaggregated into:

- *claims on the Treasury*: this counterpart, unchanged from that of the previous presentation, records the monetary indebtedness of the State;
- *claims on the economy*: this new series comprises the major part of the credits granted by banks to non-financial resident agents, other than the State. It is distinguished from the old 'bank-type lending to the economy' granted to residents, insofar as it does not include operations which do not possess well-established economic significance and the variations of which are erratic (net encashments, miscellaneous debit and credit items, and so on), which hencefor-

ward are reclassified among the 'net miscellaneous' items (see below). Claims on the economy thus comprise:

- on the one hand, *credits* corresponding to the old series of bank-type credits to the economy (exclusive of credits to non-residents) to which are added participatory loans, fixed assets leased on hire-purchase and immediate-credit instruments;
- on the other hand, *investment securities* of residents held by banks.

Stable resources (to be deducted)

This item takes in borrowings by bonds issued by banks on the French market, participatory borrowings and own capital[4] net of fixed assets and participatory securities.

Miscellaneous net items

This item includes henceforth encashment operations (net, less immediate-credit instruments), net obligations to non-bank financial institutions and the net values of reconciliation and result accounts.

NOTES TO STATISTICAL APPENDIX

1. Extrapolations based on a restricted number of institutions, however, run the risk of amplifying the effect of the aberrant developments which can, in some months, affect a bank's figures. When such exceptional variations have been identified in a bank's balance sheet this institution has been withdrawn from the sample and its data added to the extrapolation made on a reduced basis. Thus, let us suppose four banks A, B, C and D, where D's figures seem aberrant. We calculate the total of bank deposits, less the figures from D, by extrapolating the share of A + B + C in this partial total, and then add in D's data to the result thus obtained.
2. We have also used the estimates contained in the excellent work of Teneul (1961). It has also been possible to calculate some invaluable checks thanks to the studies already quoted of the Research Department of the Banque de France.
3. The following are the main works already in existence: estimates by INSEE; calculations by Saint-Marc (1983); and very recently the study by Jeanneney (1985).
4. Including participatory securities.

TABLE A.4 *New and old presentations of the money stock and its counterparts*

New presentation	*Old presentation*
External – Balance of claims and liabilities of the Banque de France – – Balance of claims and liabilities of other banks: * Credits to non-residents (FFr and other) * Deposits of non-residents (FFr and other) * Net liabilities of French banks to foreign correspondents (FFr and other) * Net position in securities (Non-resident securities held by French banks (FFr and other) minus French bank bonds held by non-residents) * Net miscellaneous items (including claims of banks on the Fonds de Stabilisation des Changes)	Gold and foreign exchange
Net domestic credit Claims on the Treasury – Claims on the economy * Credits (FFr and other) (Including * participatory loans * fixed assets leased out * immediate-credit instruments in course of clearance) * Investment securities (of residents) (including participation in SCI)	Claims on the Treasury Bank-type lending to the economy – Bank-type credits to the economy: * to residents (FFr and other) * to non-residents (FFr and other) – Other bank-type lending to the economy. * Leasing: fixed assets hired out fixed assets not hired out * Participatory loans * Clearing operations (net) (including immediate-credit instruments) * French agencies and branches (net) * Net position in securities * Miscellaneous debtors and creditors * Investment securities: – residents – non-residents * Participations in SCI
Less: stable resources: – Bond borrowings (other than CODEVI) – Participatory loans and securities – Own capital net	*Less*: Non-monetary resources – Net liabilities to non-bank financial institutions – Bond borrowings (other than CODEVI) * residents * non-residents (FFr and other) – Participatory loans – Surplus of own capital over fixed assets – Other (FDES grants)
Net miscellaneous items: – Clearing operations (net) other than immediate-credit instruments – Net position *vis-à-vis* non-bank financial institutions – Fixed assets not leased out – French agencies and branches (net) – Net position in securities – Miscellaneous debtors and creditors – Other non-monetary resources – Net cash position – Surplus of revenues over costs – Reconciliation and adjustment accounts	Miscellaneous: – Net liabilities to foreign correspondents (FFr and other) – Claims of banks on Fonds de Stabilisation des Changes – Net cash position – Surplus of revenues over costs – Reconciliation and adjustment accounts
Money stock residents M2R (FFr and other)	Money stock M2 M2R (FFr and other) Deposits of non-residents (FFr and other)

SOURCE Banque de France

TABLE A.5 *Monthly series December 1969–84 (FFr billion)*
(a) Money stock, residents, M2R, unadjusted

Year	*Jan*	*Feb*	*Mar*	*Apl*	*May*	*Jun*	*Jul*	*Aug*	*Sep*	*Oct*	*Nov*	*Dec*
1969												300.00
1970	296.09	295.15	300.60	305.46	204.57	310.27	317.31	316.73	319.47	326.98	330.23	345.91
1971	342.13	343.74	352.81	356.43	360.29	369.71	379.08	376.98	381.34	388.91	389.12	408.08
1972	400.37	402.41	416.69	420.66	424.69	442.44	453.49	451.39	459.20	462.80	467.82	484.65
1973	469.37	468.21	478.50	491.74	495.07	503.69	513.51	512.77	519.47	524.59	523.64	555.66
1974	543.43	542.70	558.88	563.40	562.96	576.13	591.54	586.15	593.90	606.58	616.24	642.59
1975	633.15	632.32	646.57	648.27	650.09	671.77	686.18	685.59	700.23	714.95	723.34	758.81
1976	746.45	748.78	764.60	778.18	779.88	795.57	809.45	802.10	809.01	821.80	821.06	852.23
1977	841.95	840.87	858.48	867.80	870.96	878.85	905.19	900.41	913.25	926.83	926.76	973.47
1978	953.44	958.21	972.58	986.75	981.13	1004.88	1024.82	1021.09	1022.49	1043.35	1050.09	1092.39
1979	1073.56	1076.96	1104.24	1112.54	1118.43	1137.43	1150.22	1150.25	1165.76	1181.94	1180.91	1245.09
1980	1212.99	1213.31	1238.74	1244.03	1242.54	1259.64	1271.00	1274.59	1284.98	1295.07	1296.65	1350.17
1981	1333.49	1341.07	1357.25	1381.43	1390.03	1409.09	1434.57	1442.59	1436.82	1451.95	1440.06	1490.44
1982	1488.89	1494.54	1517.22	1542.20	1555.97	1567.98	1597.10	1592.40	1599.04	1633.93	1611.34	1651.50
1983	1653.39	1650.77	1666.85	1680.94	1695.59	1706.90	1732.38	1721.10	1719.58	1755.73	1762.45	1836.75
1984	1802.51	1791.84	1821.05	1838.43	1834.72	1873.60	1865.78	1862.38	1887.31	1889.94	1872.56	1989.79

(b) Money stock residents M2R, seasonally adjusted

(*FFr billion*)

Year	*Jan*	*Feb*	*Mar*	*Apl*	*May*	*Jun*	*Jul*	*Aug*	*Sep*	*Oct*	*Nov*	*Dec*
1969												293.00
1970	297.67	300.79	301.72	306.51	307.37	308.35	312.12	317.49	320.07	326.45	332.32	337.57
1971	343.80	350.13	353.86	357.36	363.43	367.57	373.32	378.11	382.22	388.49	391.50	397.96
1972	402.15	409.63	417.48	421.61	428.38	440.18	447.04	452.89	460.06	462.35	470.24	472.24
1973	471.47	476.61	479.23	492.90	499.81	501.40	506.69	515.08	520.85	524.60	526.43	540.79
1974	544.96	551.45	559.34	564.36	568.42	574.18	584.43	589.18	595.70	606.86	619.55	625.13
1975	634.20	641.24	646.95	648.78	656.73	670.23	678.50	689.78	702.68	715.28	727.21	737.57
1976	747.24	758.59	764.85	778.57	788.24	794.17	801.24	807.37	811.92	822.13	825.39	829.92
1977	842.67	850.57	858.28	867.77	879.85	877.90	897.00	905.76	916.48	927.31	931.42	949.19
1978	954.71	968.51	972.13	986.19	989.71	1003.85	1016.73	1026.16	1036.65	1044.08	1056.08	1067.06
1979	1075.68	1087.79	1104.02	1111.31	1126.45	1135.73	1141.71	1154.94	1169.38	1183.01	1188.92	1218.81
1980	1215.21	1223.97	1238.58	1242.04	1248.68	1257.67	1262.31	1278.83	1289.66	1296.52	1307.67	1323.96
1981	1335.46	1352.11	1357.64	1378.54	1394.17	1406.67	1424.92	1446.88	1442.98	1453.76	1455.25	1461.46
1982	1489.97	1506.15	1518.68	1538.38	1558.36	1564.81	1585.80	1597.11	1606.69	1634.77	1629.44	1618.26
1983	1655.23	1664.16	1670.57	1676.86	1697.31	1703.58	1719.59	1726.48	1728.66	1756.89	1783.59	1798.75
1984	1803.86	1805.78	1825.80	1833.81	1835.57	1870.31	1851.96	1868.10	1898.69	1892.18	1896.37	1947.72

(c) External

(*FFr billion*)

Year	*Jan*	*Feb*	*Mar*	*Apl*	*May*	*Jun*	*Jul*	*Aug*	*Sep*	*Oct*	*Nov*	*Dec*
1969												21.87
1970	22.77	23.02	23.05	23.20	25.16	26.09	27.25	28.59	27.72	27.94	28.98	30.62
1971	31.78	32.14	32.55	32.93	33.34	33.50	38.61	42.35	40.54	40.35	41.56	44.70
1972	44.53	44.87	44.85	44.83	44.88	49.55	50.72	50.89	51.18	51.17	51.15	51.11
1973	51.21	51.48	54.33	55.24	55.85	54.01	54.15	53.60	52.80	47.35	42.58	44.19
1974	37.30	37.11	37.19	37.12	37.20	37.59	38.32	39.36	39.72	41.45	41.59	42.80
1975	98.95	99.56	100.43	101.54	103.59	98.79	95.03	96.34	97.23	101.62	103.93	99.93
1976	101.91	97.82	93.60	90.44	90.32	87.51	87.99	87.58	87.90	89.00	88.92	92.76
1977	94.83	94.92	94.92	95.51	95.80	105.76	104.28	104.63	104.56	104.86	104.49	110.17
1978	109.24	107.84	108.36	110.37	113.21	118.44	121.20	122.70	122.80	123.23	124.28	135.71
1979	135.99	137.16	164.62	165.10	164.76	187.00	191.34	191.44	191.04	193.73	194.59	253.93
1980	259.29	261.54	265.34	282.91	283.90	345.27	352.85	354.08	354.49	362.97	366.83	420.01
1981	433.41	439.55	436.41	430.69	426.54	422.66	418.07	410.55	400.91	396.61	396.94	376.78
1982	369.06	370.04	361.90	348.23	339.41	320.01	324.04	313.79	307.40	306.26	300.92	397.14
1983	408.47	405.81	407.31	422.91	424.53	449.69	453.25	448.95	451.43	457.30	458.34	459.99
1984	458.58	457.14	465.67	470.00	473.35	475.03	479.19	481.30	482.22	481.73	482.62	487.71

(d) Net claims on the Treasury, unadjusted

(FFr billion)

Year	*Jan*	*Feb*	*Mar*	*Apl*	*May*	*Jun*	*Jul*	*Aug*	*Sep*	*Oct*	*Nov*	*Dec*
1969												65.11
1970	61.30	60.06	61.90	59.31	56.76	58.88	62.07	63.78	62.83	62.03	62.44	63.98
1971	65.52	65.51	66.83	65.30	64.81	66.36	70.61	71.10	70.96	71.17	68.33	67.13
1972	63.92	62.51	65.36	61.12	60.75	64.65	66.61	68.09	66.40	63.73	64.66	64.89
1973	55.27	53.47	61.56	58.39	57.61	61.25	62.61	65.13	66.87	62.33	56.16	56.10
1974	59.88	52.27	55.60	54.92	52.32	56.44	59.80	60.93	66.00	68.31	70.98	67.61
1975	70.80	68.60	71.06	68.12	67.64	81.32	88.12	93.77	103.17	105.36	103.82	104.08
1976	101.08	101.70	110.29	111.53	106.65	111.45	116.06	117.69	124.58	125.53	123.17	120.28
1977	106.46	106.40	119.79	116.51	114.19	114.78	119.43	125.59	135.34	128.54	126.89	121.31
1978	126.90	126.10	134.09	135.85	131.21	139.74	148.32	150.94	159.13	154.31	150.79	124.77
1979	146.12	145.47	162.68	159.37	155.55	157.75	163.69	164.80	162.51	163.22	153.75	136.96
1980	145.05	143.17	158.48	153.38	152.39	145.58	152.00	162.54	159.52	148.47	145.51	130.78
1981	136.23	134.82	146.21	151.39	156.12	165.96	165.38	180.18	180.26	189.89	181.54	165.03
1982	177.97	185.79	200.61	208.75	216.71	217.22	220.75	236.77	239.57	240.17	238.43	197.52
1983	240.63	242.46	247.16	259.21	277.41	283.82	298.47	308.93	305.58	307.60	299.49	254.78
1984	294.87	288.29	296.51	311.51	312.58	330.20	326.63	342.81	347.87	328.45	307.95	273.49

(e) Net claims on the Treasury, seasonally adjusted

(FFr billion)

Year	Jan	Feb	Mar	Apl	May	Jun	Jul	Aug	Sep	Oct	Nov	Dec
1969												65.00
1970	62.97	62.64	62.03	62.07	60.42	59.88	60.25	60.34	59.74	60.13	61.19	63.91
1971	67.28	68.49	66.95	68.29	69.13	67.46	68.59	67.37	67.21	68.72	66.72	67.33
1972	65.53	65.61	65.66	63.94	64.98	65.70	64.83	64.70	62.41	61.03	62.76	65.40
1973	56.75	56.46	62.05	60.98	61.87	62.25	61.10	62.19	62.43	59.22	54.14	56.85
1974	61.52	55.55	56.13	57.16	56.20	57.45	58.62	58.42	61.05	64.46	68.30	68.96
1975	72.95	73.32	71.72	70.34	72.52	82.90	86.50	90.25	94.92	99.16	100.01	107.31
1976	104.34	109.00	111.12	114.20	113.47	113.66	113.84	113.29	114.39	118.09	119.52	125.69
1977	110.44	114.09	120.27	118.19	120.07	116.84	116.77	120.54	124.56	121.16	124.04	128.95
1978	132.44	135.43	134.07	136.83	135.82	141.63	144.76	143.82	147.06	145.71	148.81	134.98
1979	153.45	156.17	162.59	159.52	158.53	158.86	159.49	155.96	151.05	154.33	152.61	150.77
1980	152.77	153.39	159.11	153.23	153.04	145.49	148.02	152.78	149.34	140.34	144.89	146.20
1981	143.50	143.88	147.97	151.17	155.11	164.50	161.17	168.64	169.54	179.76	180.87	186.65
1982	186.96	197.73	204.50	208.71	213.79	213.67	215.42	220.78	225.89	227.63	237.26	225.00
1983	252.21	257.52	253.67	259.48	273.12	277.46	291.50	287.66	288.05	292.52	297.85	291.46
1984	308.54	305.68	305.12	312.08	307.50	321.82	318.93	319.08	328.21	312.99	306.09	313.96

(f) Claims on the economy, unadjusted

(FFr billion)

Year	*Jan*	*Feb*	*Mar*	*Apl*	*May*	*Jun*	*Jul*	*Aug*	*Sep*	*Oct*	*Nov*	*Dec*
1969												264.74
1970	265.98	266.69	266.77	269.00	270.71	273.66	276.96	277.79	280.40	289.26	299.86	313.24
1971	313.51	315.42	320.53	326.46	331.06	335.69	343.31	340.00	346.15	351.68	357.00	374.45
1972	373.22	375.66	385.67	393.25	396.07	413.58	422.23	419.92	431.10	437.79	446.62	464.89
1973	460.60	459.62	464.40	478.26	483.57	493.63	503.39	502.13	509.97	517.59	526.14	544.03
1974	541.02	539.54	553.44	573.10	571.76	575.74	584.91	588.63	593.74	601.79	607.31	625.17
1975	625.81	627.08	635.29	640.38	643.98	650.05	656.50	656.38	660.91	673.85	682.23	704.25
1976	699.64	700.23	713.16	722.44	724.42	735.28	756.29	751.75	757.91	769.59	774.97	797.48
1977	802.28	804.77	808.26	816.17	824.30	829.05	839.05	839.00	847.72	853.37	859.79	886.86
1978	887.85	892.93	892.10	899.03	896.13	908.81	921.38	916.25	925.30	934.08	944.71	979.17
1979	968.18	971.82	987.08	1001.17	1002.52	1022.08	1036.81	1035.70	1048.70	1059.55	1072.73	1108.00
1980	1110.05	1110.40	1126.82	1134.95	1139.69	1164.70	1177.70	1180.61	1194.53	1211.62	1223.60	1290.77
1981	1294.50	1304.05	1307.90	1321.18	1328.16	1344.16	1360.18	1365.65	1371.14	1384.60	1397.00	1449.41
1982	1461.03	1466.74	1478.08	1495.42	1507.13	1535.58	1565.06	1567.06	1577.59	1594.61	1615.24	1676.31
1983	1679.33	1682.87	1696.91	1706.34	1709.01	1732.58	1760.07	1768.17	1780.50	1800.09	1810.40	1875.94
1984	1861.40	1861.13	1885.30	1891.99	1895.99	1936.83	1939.32	1944.71	1968.38	1979.46	2000.04	2068.28

(g) Claims on the economy, seasonally adjusted

(*FFr billion*)

Year	*Jan*	*Feb*	*Mar*	*Apl*	*May*	*Jun*	*Jul*	*Aug*	*Sep*	*Oct*	*Nov*	*Dec*
1969												258.14
1970	264.14	268.33	267.18	268.83	270.99	273.69	275.11	281.63	282.68	291.55	300.67	305.38
1971	311.36	317.29	321.03	326.13	331.34	335.73	341.06	344.46	348.85	354.27	357.95	365.32
1972	370.99	377.91	386.36	392.81	396.39	413.56	419.45	424.77	434.12	440.21	447.45	454.51
1973	458.62	462.62	465.34	477.72	484.11	493.73	500.37	507.33	513.63	520.07	527.43	532.49
1974	538.64	542.73	554.27	572.29	572.72	575.95	581.86	593.81	598.01	604.16	609.03	612.96
1975	622.76	630.26	635.91	639.30	645.58	650.55	653.68	661.47	665.65	676.41	684.46	691.47
1976	695.34	702.99	713.42	721.11	727.00	735.93	753.57	757.23	763.44	772.81	777.91	783.48
1977	796.35	807.11	807.92	814.62	828.29	829.80	836.11	845.17	853.99	857.70	863.56	871.41
1978	879.99	894.67	891.31	897.45	901.39	909.31	918.26	922.96	932.24	939.91	949.49	962.00
1979	958.51	972.50	986.09	999.69	1009.02	1022.48	1033.27	1043.09	1056.87	1067.31	1078.89	1088.32
1980	1098.00	1109.77	1125.60	1133.82	1147.44	1165.24	1173.94	1188.35	1204.23	1221.16	1231.37	1267.17
1981	1280.17	1302.10	1306.11	1320.76	1337.62	1345.21	1356.04	1373.81	1382.95	1396.05	1406.95	1422.93
1982	1444.08	1463.09	1475.45	1495.63	1517.91	1537.44	1560.65	1574.73	1590.35	1606.38	1626.11	1643.72
1983	1661.61	1679.41	1694.79	1708.27	1721.98	1735.44	1755.20	1776.03	1794.62	1812.86	1822.65	1839.20
1984	1841.96	1857.12	1883.13	1894.59	1910.65	1940.55	1934.01	1953.32	1984.21	1993.77	2014.38	2028.64

(h) Net domestic credit, unadjusted

(*FFr billion*)

Year	*Jan*	*Feb*	*Mar*	*Apl*	*May*	*Jun*	*Jul*	*Aug*	*Sep*	*Oct*	*Nov*	*Dec*
1969												294.15
1970	288.47	287.53	292.53	295.72	293.27	298.73	305.22	303.70	306.63	314.51	316.85	332.09
1971	328.04	330.05	339.17	342.36	344.49	354.21	360.42	353.52	361.70	368.99	367.46	382.89
1972	376.01	378.09	393.30	398.01	402.90	417.38	427.00	424.36	432.15	436.48	442.21	457.81
1973	443.53	443.03	450.82	462.25	463.90	474.69	482.55	479.02	491.02	497.10	495.72	525.78
1974	519.61	518.15	534.20	539.55	541.38	554.65	570.74	563.99	572.61	582.90	592.20	615.85
1975	604.30	602.95	614.54	614.65	613.23	630.82	647.39	644.90	655.27	667.19	671.45	704.40
1976	690.15	693.24	714.51	726.14	727.06	741.61	753.67	746.96	754.23	765.89	763.26	794.04
1977	784.34	786.13	803.35	809.91	805.81	815.08	834.69	833.77	845.30	852.47	848.33	892.33
1978	870.41	875.26	891.31	900.24	891.07	908.82	922.97	916.71	926.30	936.40	936.07	974.27
1979	954.80	960.13	983.92	990.89	994.40	1009.55	1017.50	1017.74	1035.42	1044.99	1048.48	1106.11
1980	1074.96	1078.55	1098.70	1108.49	1108.85	1117.68	1127.08	1133.49	1144.42	1152.34	1152.77	1196.22
1981	1171.91	1179.76	1207.87	1231.77	1248.91	1274.02	1292.17	1307.95	1310.76	1331.01	1329.22	1367.99
1982	1379.96	1375.60	1414.94	1428.16	1475.57	1486.80	1513.34	1509.72	1520.44	1561.53	1539.57	1580.85
1983	1616.02	1603.04	1641.13	1655.80	1667.65	1668.19	1702.17	1697.24	1692.50	1734.18	1733.17	1796.48
1984	1786.00	1758.30	1793.94	1818.84	1812.65	1836.45	1821.53	1809.48	1835.33	1847.78	1838.56	1949.38

(i) Net domestic credit, seasonally adjusted

(*FFr billion*)

Year	*Jan*	*Feb*	*Mar*	*Apl*	*May*	*Jun*	*Jul*	*Aug*	*Sep*	*Oct*	*Nov*	*Dec*
1969												287.50
1970	290.66	292.37	292.39	295.61	295.53	296.72	300.93	306.00	307.72	313.99	318.83	324.19
1971	330.35	335.50	338.89	342.19	347.16	351.99	355.37	356.24	363.05	368.44	369.80	373.28
1972	378.47	384.25	392.85	398.09	406.20	415.00	420.99	427.59	433.48	435.67	444.70	446.13
1973	446.42	450.30	450.29	462.64	468.00	472.54	476.01	482.75	492.77	496.65	498.90	511.51
1974	522.29	525.96	533.27	539.88	546.39	552.85	563.61	568.22	574.66	582.62	596.46	598.85
1975	606.89	611.14	613.30	614.40	618.99	629.73	640.05	649.40	657.82	667.10	676.80	685.21
1976	692.73	701.42	712.79	725.19	733.57	740.94	746.40	751.91	756.87	765.90	769.91	773.13
1977	787.45	794.54	801.23	808.07	812.02	814.47	828.12	838.75	847.68	852.71	856.65	870.00
1978	874.56	884.30	889.15	897.60	896.27	907.59	917.31	921.16	928.18	936.94	945.02	951.26
1979	959.87	970.51	982.23	987.60	997.86	1007.44	1011.87	1021.53	1037.52	1045.81	1059.31	1081.76
1980	1080.20	1091.02	1097.52	1104.99	1110.11	1114.75	1120.71	1136.67	1147.44	1153.58	1165.71	1171.63
1981	1175.81	1194.67	1207.39	1227.55	1247.80	1270.32	1284.38	1311.40	1315.50	1333.36	1346.38	1341.61
1982	1381.42	1393.58	1414.52	1422.38	1472.07	1482.30	1503.37	1513.35	1526.51	1564.14	1560.25	1549.47
1983	1616.31	1626.09	1641.93	1648.83	1662.91	1663.34	1690.23	1702.19	1700.03	1737.76	1758.34	1760.44
1984	1784.47	1783.96	1794.60	1810.88	1806.85	1831.30	1808.15	1815.83	1844.50	1852.36	1866.86	1911.01

(j) Total liquid assets of residents M3R, unadjusted

(FFr billion)

Year	*Jan*	*Feb*	*Mar*	*Apl*	*May*	*Jun*	*Jul*	*Aug*	*Sep*	*Oct*	*Nov*	*Dec*
1969												430.46
1970	429.54	429.35	434.44	440.17	439.89	444.93	453.74	454.69	457.92	467.41	471.47	492.55
1971	491.69	494.48	503.49	509.98	514.38	524.47	535.51	534.47	539.87	549.00	550.42	576.07
1972	571.20	573.75	588.51	593.49	597.75	616.86	629.49	628.84	637.67	642.95	650.03	674.28
1973	661.49	661.21	672.90	686.89	690.78	700.74	712.21	713.44	720.96	727.99	728.03	769.07
1974	759.82	760.46	777.46	782.96	782.71	797.50	815.70	812.54	821.79	835.73	845.93	885.01
1975	880.32	881.60	898.15	903.19	906.70	931.07	949.85	952.67	970.50	990.11	1001.61	1055.60
1976	1049.94	1055.71	1074.85	1092.05	1095.47	1113.92	1132.51	1129.38	1139.11	1155.59	1156.69	1206.78
1977	1201.10	1202.24	1222.78	1235.50	1239.06	1249.47	1279.34	1277.99	1293.18	1310.18	1313.24	1385.46
1978	1371.56	1379.09	1396.86	1414.65	1410.31	1436.71	1460.80	1461.85	1479.32	1494.32	1504.09	1573.09
1979	1562.14	1569.35	1601.39	1613.35	1620.33	1642.28	1659.29	1664.01	1681.69	1701.08	1701.49	1796.04
1980	1767.68	1769.15	1796.06	1803.89	1802.31	1820.92	1837.57	1845.95	1859.05	1871.97	1876.76	1966.70
1981	1956.33	1966.43	1986.07	2013.45	2022.22	2041.18	2068.72	2080.10	2076.31	2099.33	2089.61	2183.86
1982	2188.11	2195.51	2221.49	2249.50	2261.87	2276.26	2311.16	2312.47	2321.42	2359.03	2336.84	2429.07
1983	2435.07	2432.73	2450.32	2470.72	2484.71	2496.44	2526.01	2518.84	2517.39	2555.73	2562.04	2691.56
1984	2659.85	2647.31	2677.46	2695.03	2688.40	2730.69	2729.49	2729.73	2754.04	2756.51	2736.93	2907.07

(k) Total liquid assets of residents M3R, seasonally adjusted

(FFr billion)

Year	*Jan*	*Feb*	*Mar*	*Apl*	*May*	*Jun*	*Jul*	*Aug*	*Sep*	*Oct*	*Nov*	*Dec*
1969												421.76
1970	428.46	432.88	434.38	440.37	442.83	443.74	449.47	456.63	460.47	468.89	476.01	482.18
1971	490.32	498.46	503.13	509.93	517.68	523.19	530.80	536.93	542.99	550.91	555.68	563.54
1972	569.50	578.26	587.61	593.33	601.62	615.55	624.14	631.79	641.00	645.09	655.71	659.16
1973	659.76	666.64	671.69	686.79	695.75	699.57	706.64	717.46	725.26	731.16	734.84	750.82
1974	756.87	765.77	775.54	782.36	788.40	796.84	810.03	817.60	827.02	839.76	854.12	863.42
1975	876.12	886.45	895.63	901.72	913.57	931.10	943.98	959.38	977.17	995.19	1011.77	1028.95
1976	1044.11	1060.39	1071.33	1089.76	1104.03	1114.51	1126.71	1137.94	1147.34	1161.98	1169.00	1177.53
1977	1193.77	1205.74	1217.96	1232.14	1248.11	1250.93	1274.20	1287.34	1302.64	1317.94	1327.42	1352.56
1978	1363.31	1382.07	1390.83	1410.08	1418.98	1438.52	1456.57	1471.83	1489.93	1503.96	1521.56	1537.02
1979	1552.92	1571.46	1594.46	1607.37	1628.42	1643.99	1655.59	1674.60	1694.06	1712.83	1722.94	1756.72
1980	1756.75	1769.89	1788.28	1796.55	1808.46	1822.82	1834.43	1856.91	1873.73	1885.76	1903.06	1925.01
1981	1943.16	1966.21	1977.86	2004.58	2026.40	2043.24	2065.39	2092.03	2093.96	2115.60	2122.49	2136.92
1982	2171.54	2194.25	2213.14	2238.90	2264.25	2278.11	2306.97	2325.69	2341.99	2375.96	2374.46	2374.19
1983	2417.53	2432.31	2443.61	2459.52	2486.74	2498.83	2521.12	2533.64	2540.85	2574.84	2604.93	2629.25
1984	2639.79	2646.17	2670.80	2682.74	2689.70	2733.60	2724.33	2745.79	2781.34	2778.56	2784.71	2839.08

Bibliography

The bibliography for a century of the French economy is enormous. Only those works which we have actually used in writing this book are included here.

Aftalion, A. (1948). *Monnaie, prix et change*, 3rd edition, Paris: Sirey.

Allinne, J. P. (1983). *Banquiers et bâtisseurs, Un siècle de Crédit Foncier, 1852–1940*, Paris: Centre National de Recherche Scientifique.

Anonymous (1937). *L'expérience Blum, un an de Front Populaire*, Paris: Editions du Sagittaire.

Barrère, A. (1947). *Les crises de reconversion*, Paris: Rivière.

Belin, A. (n.d.). *Problèmes monétaires*, Lecture course at the Institut d'Etudes Politiques de Paris.

Bernard, P. (1975). *La fin d'un monde 1914–26*, Paris: Le Seuil (Nouvelle histoire de la France contemporaine no. 12).

Bettelheim, C. (1947). *Bilan de l'économie française, 1919–1946*, Paris: PUF.

Bloch-Lainé, F. and P. de Vogüé (1960). *Le Trésor Public*, Paris: PUF.

Bouvier, J. (1984). 'The French Banks, Inflation and the Economic Crisis, 1919–1939', *Journal of European Economic History*, vol. XIII, no. 2, pp. 29–80.

Braudel, F. and E. Labrousse (eds) (1970–82). *Histoire économique et sociale de la France*, 7 vols, Paris: PUF.

Bredin, J. D. (1980). *Joseph Caillaux*, Paris: Hachette.

Carré, J. J., Dubois, P. and E. Malinvaud (1972). *La croissance française*, Paris: Le Seuil.

Catinat, M. (1981). 'La production industrielle sous la IVe République', *Economie et Statistique*, janvier.

Crédit Lyonnais (1963). *Un siècle d'économie française, 1863–1963*, Paris.

Crouzet, F. (1970). 'Un indice de la production industrielle française au XIXe siècle', *Annales*, pp. 56 ff.

Dauphin-Meunier, A. (1936). *La Banque de France*, 5th edn, Paris: Gallimard.

De Gaulle, C. (1954–59). *Mémoires de Guerre*, Paris: Plon.

Delanney, L. (no date). *Le marché des valeurs mobilières en France de 1900 à 1927*, Paris: PUF.

Dubief, H. (1976). *Le déclin de la IIIe Republique, 1929–38*, Paris: Le Seuil (Nouvelle histoire de la France contemporaine no. 13).

Faure, E. (1982). *Avoir toujours raison, c'est un grand tort*, volume I: Memoires, Paris: Plon.

Fontaine, C. (1966). *Les mouvements de prix et leur dispersion (1892–1963)*, Paris: A. Colin.

Germain-Martin (1936). *Le problème financier*, Paris: Domat-Montchrestien.

Gignoux, C. J. (no date). *L'économie française, 1919–39*, Paris: Société d'Editions Economiques et Sociales.

Guébhard, P. (1923). 'Le marché monétaire', *Revue d'Economie Politique*.

Homer, S. (1963). *A History of Interest Rates*, New Brunswick: Rutgers University Press.

INSEE (1966). *Annuaire Statistique de la France, 1966, Résumé rétrospectif*.

Jeanneney, J. M. and E. (1985). *Les économies occidentales*, Paris: Presses de la FNSP.

Jeanneney, J. N. (1982). *La faillite du Cartel 1924–26*, new edn, Paris: Le Seuil.

Jèze, G. (1934). *Cours de Science des finances*, 6th edn, Paris: Girard.

Koch, H. (1983). *Histoire de la Banque de France et de la monnaie sous la IVe République*, Paris: Dunod.

Laroque, G. (1981). '1946–1949: la fin des restrictions', *Economie et Statistique*, janvier.

Lescure, J. (1932). *Des crises générales et périodiques de surproduction*, Paris: Domat-Montchrestien.

Lindert, P. (1969). *Key Currency and Gold, 1900–1913*, Princeton Studies in International Finance.

Lutfalla, G. (1964). *La situation actuelle du crédit à court terme et du crédit à moyen terme*, report to the Conseil Economique et Social, Paris: J. O.

Lysis (no date). *Contre l'Oligarchie financière de la France*, 11th edition, Paris: A. Michel.

Marjolin, R. (1941). *Prix, monnaie et production*, Paris: Alcan, PUF.

Marjolin, R., Sadrin, J. and O. Wormser. (1968). *Rapport sur le marché monétaire et les conditions du crédit*, Paris: La Documentation française.

Meynial, P. (1925). 'La balance des comptes de la France', *Revue d'Economie Politique*, pp. 5 ff.

Michalet, C. A. (1968). *Les placements des épargnants français*, Paris: PUF.

Miquel, P. (1984). *Poincaré*, new edn, Paris: Fayard.

Moliexe, F. (1942). *Le système monétaire français, son évolution depuis 1936*, Paris: Jouve.

Moreau, F. (1954). *Souvenirs d'un Gouverneur de la Banque de France, Histoire de la stabilisation du franc, 1926–28*, Paris: Génin.

Neymarck, A. (1913). *Que doit-on faire de son argent?* Paris: Marchal & Godde.

Ramon, G. (1929). *Histoire de la Banque de France*, Paris: Grasset.

Rébérioux, M. (1975). La République radicale 1898–1914, Paris: Le Seuil (Nouvelle histoire de la France contemporaine no. 11).

Revue d'Economie Politique, 'Annuaire' (Annual Report), from 1923. The introductions are by G. Pirou and then W. Oualid, and finally, for the whole of the 1930s, by C. Rist.

Rist, C. (1914). 'La circulation monétaire française de 1878 à 1910', *Revue d'Economie Politique*.

Rist, C. (1926). 'Elements de la situation financière de 1920 à 1925', *Revue d'Economie Politique*.

Rivoire, J. (1985). *Histoire de la monnaie*, Paris: PUF.

Saint-Etienne, C. (1983). 'L'offre et la demande de monnaie dans la France de l'entre-deux-guerres (1920–39)', *Revue Economique*, mars.

Saint-Etienne, C. (1985). *L'Etat français face aux crises économiques du XXe siècle*, Paris: Economica.

Saint-Marc, M. (1983). *Histoire monétaire de la France 1800–1980*, Paris: PUF.

Sauvy, A. (1978). *La vie économique des Français de 1939 à 1945*, Paris: Flammarion.

Sauvy, A. (1984). *Histoire économique de la France entre les deux guerres*, 2nd edn, 3 vols, Paris: Economica.

Sédillot, R. (1971). *Histoire du franc*, Paris: Sirey.

Singer-Kerel, J. (1961). *Le coût de la vie à Paris, de 1840 à 1954*, Paris: A. Colin.

Statistique Générale de la France (1932). *Indices généraux du mouvement économique en France de 1901 à 1931*, Paris: Imprimerie Nationale.

Teneul, G. F. (1961). *Le financement des entreprises en France depuis la fin du XIXe siècle à nos jours*, Paris: R. Pichon et R. Durand, Auzias.

Théry, A. (1921). *Les grands établissements de crédit français avant, pendant et après la guerre*, Paris: Sagot.

Théry, E. (1922). *Conséquences économiques de la guerre en France*, Paris: Belin.

White, H. D. (1933). *The French International Accounts*, Cambridge, Massachussetts: Harvard University Press.

Index

Note: square brackets contain brief explanations or, in inverted commas, translations of index entries.